The Road to Ndawo

Book 4 of the series

Songs of Warriors, Chants of Freedom

Mac Nicolson

ISBN 978-989-53286-7-3

Cover photo by : Ashish Singh

Introduction

I spent a morning inside Vasishta's Cave one day a few years back, and the following morning, words began to flow onto my computer. I honestly never knew I was about to write a book.

But the stories contained within, when I reflect back on it, had their origins in a series of visions and lucid dreams over a longer period of time, all of which translated into remarkable experiences and surprising memories.

The Road to Ndawo is the fourth and last of the series. The first three are each a tale of three warriors, and their quests for spiritual and physical freedom fought on behalf of their people against seemingly insurmountable odds – and their love of a woman.

The Road to Ndawo is about a quest for the very essence of freedom, freedom from existence itself.

Each story has a connection of sorts to that great Indian epic, The Mahabharata, which is where the first tale begins, and each tale terminates with its own part in the story of a Jaguar – the watcher who represents the fearless aloneness of our own nature.

May all of humanity be free of tyranny, of the tyranny of others and above all, the tyranny of our own minds.

Contents

In dissolution
of all of his beginnings
he remembers her name
love calling from a distant shore
love calling him by his name

There is fire in the wind
and desolation
from her lips and their sacred curse
a holy incineration
from his last rasping breath
until his naked first

For all the things that bind us
and that
which in the end must find us
are but the stories that recall
love's holy incineration
of all that he became

THE YOGI OF THE KUMOAN – Part 1

Chapter 1

Kavita's Love

Kavita spooned the steaming kitcheree into the brass container, sprinkling a small handful of cashew nuts on top.

"You spoil him," grumbled her mother who now began washing the pots in the alcove outside of their wood and white washed mud and stone house. The house sat perched above terraced fields in a small settlement in the to the north and west of Rishikesh. A stream ran down this valley and spilled recklessly into the Ganga through narrow valleys and wild forest as it made its way to join the mother of all rivers.

Kavita would walk up in the other direction before taking a path up the steep slope that climbed the south side of the valley. This path wound up through dense forest for more than a kilometer and a half following a rivulet fed by a spring that had its source alongside a large cave and inside this cave lived the Yogi for whom her food was lovingly prepared.

The forest was not a safe place for a single girl, complained her mother, and though Kavita had once been surprised by a tiger and by numerous leopards her main fear were the elephants. They were less predictable and only a tiger that had been injured or wounded by hunters would turn rogue and begin to stalk humans as prey. Otherwise, they would leave you alone, preferring the flesh of chital deer and wild boar.

Although there had once been a man-eating tiger roaming the district in her childhood and the villagers had lived in terror for months, losing three children and a grown man before the tiger was hunted and killed. But it had passed a long time ago.

That was shortly after the young and handsome sadhu had arrived in the valley and began living in the cave. At first, he had shared the cave with an old yogi from whom he had learnt his yoga and meditation practices before the old Yogi became too frail and had moved down to the small ashram at the bottom of the valley to live out his days.

If truth be told, Kavita was desperately in love with the younger Yogi but it was a hopeless love that could only be sated by her turning brahmacharini and becoming his devotee. The Yogi, however, had taken a firm vow to never come within fifty steps of a woman so Kavita would walk up the hill with her food each day and place the container fifty steps from the front of the cave.

She would then make her way over to a little hut she had erected with sticks and grass that sheltered her from the sun but allowed her a view of the cave entrance and sitting there she would begin to chant devotional songs to Devi Durga, the mother,

⁓ ⌣ ⌣ ⌒

Ya *devi sarva bhutesu, shanti rupena sansitha*
Ya devi sarva bhutesu, shakti rupena sansthita
Ya devi sarva bhutesu, matra rupena sansthita
Namastasyai, namastasyai, namastasyai, namo namaha!
The goddess who is omnipresent as the personification of universal
mother
The goddess who is omnipresent as the embodiment of power
The goddess who is omnipresent as the symbol of peace
I bow to her, I bow to her, I bow to her again & again.
The Yogi saw Kavita place the food above the rock platform that had

been built up in front of the cave by its numerous inhabitants as they had lived, practiced yoga and meditation and died, one after the other over centuries. He studied the girl for a moment and could not help but notice the gracefulness of her movements as she knelt and even from fifty feet, note the fineness of her long fingers as she hung his pot of food on a rusted metal hook. The hook had been impaled into a neem tree that rose up from the forest floor to generously shade that part of the platform.

This was his sternest test of each day. To have to watch the young devotee place his food there and to have to experience the longing the sight of her induced.

Soon the feeling would pass. He would return to his meditations and raise the snake to its holier place in the higher realms of his consciousness but right now he would eat and enjoy his food and while he would eat, he would listen to her chant to the mother and her voice would fill his heart and sooth his longing.

Finishing his food, he walked to the spring where a pool had been fashioned with stones and here, he washed the pot and his hands and mouth before drinking some water and placing the pot back in its place. He stole a glance at the girl who was now sitting quietly in meditation but as his glance wandered to her, she opened her eyes and their eyes met for a just a moment. The Yogi nodded to her, abruptly turned around and retreated to within his cave.

For a half hour he would lie down and sleep and then, knowing that the girl would be gone he would go outside to relieve himself and bathe for the second time of his day before entering the cave again to meditate on the frayed leopard skin.

Entering the full lotus, he chanted his mantra to Durga in the form of the goddess Chamonda.

Aum Aing Hring Kleeng Chamundaye Vichohey Aum
Aum Aing Hring Kleeng Chamundaye Vichohey Aum

As the Yogi sat within, facing his shrine of the mother, his mind became absorbed in the vibration of the mantra as it rolled now involuntarily in a barely discernible hum from within the back of his throat.

A clan of Langur monkeys bounded by the cave entrance. A single monkey propped on his long grey tail and stared his black and curious face within, took some steps inside and sat for a few moments before instinct urged to him rejoin his clan.

Chapter 2

The Woman in the Dream

The Yogi had wakened from his sleep troubled by his dreams. He slept only a few hours a night and again for half an hour after eating. His daily ritual was clocklike and had been the same for most of the twenty-five years he had lived in that cave. He rarely left it other than to take his morning walk in the forest which came after his two hours of asanas and pranayama and he would be back to his cave before Kavita would arrive with his food so as not to risk a chance encounter on the path.

The only thing that had changed was that now, after eating, he would entertain a small group of disciples outside of the cave and sometimes groups of pilgrims that would seek him out for his darshan, his blessings. His reputation had spread as his power had grown, his presence commanding a stillness that silenced the minds of the people sitting in reverence at his feet.

His disciples included two more women who had to sit at a distance in the now expanded bamboo and thatch hut with Kavita. One of them was the younger sister he had left behind when he abruptly disappeared from home and who had finally discovered him after two years of searching and having being surprised to find that he had only travelled such a short distance from home.

Such was his stoicism and seclusion for so many years, he had remained undiscovered and almost forgotten except by his sister. She was almost twenty years younger than he but she had worshipped him

5

and adored him in the absence of their father who died in an accident when she was only two years old. She lost her brother eight years later when he had suddenly and without notice, disappeared, and then, as soon as her mother had left her body and Deveshi had seen the last embers die within her funeral pyre, the girl had gone in search of her him.

Adopting the white garb of a brahmacharini she travelled the countryside convinced she would find her last remaining family.

Deveshi now lived in a small ashram and walked the five kilometers each day to sit the afternoons with her brother. He would not talk to her, however, and as with Kavita, she would have to pass written notes to him and await his reply and his instruction.

After they left, he would sit absorbed in meditation from late afternoon until well into the night, his mantra humming from his throat,

Aum Aing Hring Kleeng Chamundaye Vichohey Aum
Aum Aing Hring Kleeng Chamundaye Vichohey Aum

But this morning his dreams had troubled him. He dreamed of a girl unknown to him and it was not Kavita, another one, and younger. The dream had been erotic and at the last moment he had pushed her away and run in to the forest but had stumbled upon a dead man and seeing the dead man had known he was the killer.

He would resolve to redouble his efforts to purify himself. He was not to blame for the man's death, he told himself not for the first time, but yet, he had run away in shame, in disgust with himself and in disgust of the world.

The Yogi was severe on himself and liked to show to his disciples and indirectly to the other holy men that none could surpass him in the discipline of his meditations. He felt he must elevate others by his example and attained lengthy states of samadhi in which he would remain absorbed for hours. This is what brought him peace, both the samadhi itself and also the attainment of it, so if his consciousness slipped into the lower realms of lust and violence, he would become disturbed and plunge even more stoically and relentlessly into his meditation and yoga.

Aum Aing Hring Kleeng Chamundaya Vichohey Aum
Aum Aing Hring Kleeng Chamundaya Vichohey Aum

But as the Yogi chanted, he saw something large partially block the light from the cave entrance. At first, he though it to be Deveshi or Kavita returning for something they had forgotten but opening the half-closed slits of his eyes wider and beginning to feel irritated by the uninvited presence he saw it was neither.

Entering the cave was a large leopard and while the sight of the occasional tiger was not uncommon, they usually slunk away from him if he encountered them. The leopard, instead walked right into his cave and lay down, observing him with its keen feline eyes. He missed perhaps one or two beats in his chanting but then continued, now pleased and less apprehensive about the cat's presence. He was chanting for Durga, the mother, the woman upon whom he showered his love now and the Goddess who rode lions and tigers. He decided that the leopard was drawn to the mother's name and it was welcome.

Aum Aing Hring Kleeng Chamundaya Vichohey Aum
Aum Aing Hring Kleeng Chamundaya Vichohey Aum

Chapter 3

The Passage

In his eighties now, the old Yogi lay dying. Kavita had passed on the year before and now he relied on his sister, Deveshi, to attend to his needs. He had finally allowed Kavita to enter his cave after she had insisted that she would breathe her last in his presence and in her dying breath had promised him she would search for him in her next life just as she had done in this one. Her promise had slightly unnerved him and created a lingering doubt within his mind that his goal of complete liberation had been attained. He had renewed his efforts but his body was fast failing him.

Deveshi was harsher with him than Kavita and now, allowed to attend him in person and not have to sit away from him, she mothered him and at times even scolded him when he was unable to complete a menial task properly. He never answered her back.

They spoke rarely, if at all and for the forty years she had been his disciple he had only ever given her teachings in hand written notes and that never changed.

She loved him as both her teacher and brother but now in her older age she became angry sometimes to think. that after he left, she would have no-one.

⌣⌣

Deveshi had aged gracefully and handsomely and was devoted and religious, always attending to her long grey hair and meticulously placing the tilak and turmeric paste on her forehead with the help of a small mirror. She recited her mantras and sang her bhajans daily and always on perfect time and the disciples that still devotedly made their way to the cave some days had made it their habit of touching her feet in reverence as they arrived. And she enjoyed it, secreting away increasing amounts of rupees and unknown to the Yogi, encouraging more and more gifts.

"Help me sit up Deveshi."

Deveshi moved over to him and took his frail shoulders in her hands. His skin had taken on a silky feel, slightly moist. Her nostrils picked up the sweet smell of impending death.

Her heart sunk with dread.

This would be his last night, so Deveshi made sure he was comfortable on his cushion and before moving over to the front of the cave to sit and sing, she placed her head on his feet and allowed a few tears to trickle down her face.

Ya devi sarva bhutesu, shanti rupena sansitha
Ya devi sarva bhutesu, shakti rupena sansthita
Ya devi sarva bhutesu, matra rupena sansthita
Namastasyai, namastasyai, namastasyai, namo namaha!

The Yogi had no need to recite his mantra. It had fixed itself in the back of his throat as a permanent vibration that hummed constantly, almost imperceptibly to the ear. He sat now in full lotus and felt the kundalini life force keep his body erect where his muscles and spine would have failed him.

He didn't know when his body stopped breathing or his heart beat its last.

He passed through a field of pure light and found himself emerging from the light in ecstasy - as an ethereal body flying through the air above the mountains.

Two black ravens flew to either side of him and began dismembering his body and as each body part fell away his feeling of bliss increased. His arms left him, his head left him and then his torso and legs. Bliss, eternal bliss was his.

But when the ravens reached his genitals a rush of energy shot to that forbidden and neglected part and images of a naked beautiful woman wrapped herself around him while insatiable lust overpowered his every sense.

He found himself crashing, free falling to the earth with a roaring sound deafening his ears as he fell.

Now he was making love and his desire was ferocious .

"Where are you? Where have you been?" he called.

But she disappeared again.

After some time, he could hear his heart beating. But it was not his. There were two hearts beating in unison. He moved his hands to his face and they felt tiny. He slept deeply, dreamlessly as his memories slowly sank beneath an ocean of milk.

DIARIES FROM GONDWANA - *Part 2*

Chapter 1

Messages from the unknown

Marcus could never quite be sure of when he had had that dream, but it was certainly the first he could remember. And then, it may not have been a dream at all but an actual memory. He couldn't be sure but one thing was very clear – it was that inflamed sexual desire that had brought him falling to the earth after his flight into ecstasy with the two ravens at either side of him.

Anyway, he decided it best to tell it as if it were a rebirthing experience because having sexually explicit dreams as a small child had long since become politically incorrect.

~⁓~

The Tasmanian Midlands is a place of cold and windy winters with frost laden grass in the early mornings and of warm dry days in the summer. Famous for its fine wool, the low rolling hills and river flats are a maze of fences and old and finely built farmhouses and paddocks dotted with sheep and where scattered thickets of eucalypts and invasive gorse provide a form of relief to the all-pervading yellow-green.

This was Marcus' birthplace and where his idyllic early years of fishing and family picnics and play with siblings and cousins were later interlaced by long stints at the boarding school in the city – a place he hated but a place where he learned to survive things that a young boy should by rights have never had to.

He was only five when he realized he was going to die. And from that moment the specter of death and the questions that followed consumed his life and he would sometimes imagine and sometimes fear the descent into sleep at night, knowing it to be a form of, well, death.

At eight years old he saw, in a lucid moment while walking with his mother in the city street, during one of those brief visits that brought him fleeting relief from the hated school, that he, and indeed all of humanity, were living in either the past or the future and that no-one, no one he could see, was truly present.

A moment when the previously alive figures sharing the street with him were no more than dead people walking, an instant in a twilight world that was neither real nor unreal.

He looked to his beautiful mother with her winning smile and began to speak but then hesitated to ask the question, the one he knew she couldn't answer.

A short time after, the mantra started vibrating from his throat but he didn't know it was a mantra then. For Marcus it was an unwanted intrusion, an uninvited and involuntary sound from somewhere within.

But years later in India, when describing the sound vibration to an old Swami, he was told that it was a Durga mantra – Durga, the goddess who rode the tiger, the mother, the shakti power of the universe and Durga was already calling him home.

Om Aim Hreem Kleim
Chamundaye Vichche Namah
Om Aim Hreem Kleim
Chamundaye Vichche Namah

Chapter 2

The River, Saranath and the Train to Agra

Marcus was barely nineteen when he arrived in Banaras as it was then called. In times long past it was known as Khasi and more recently the name had changed to Varanasi but in truth it was all three, depending on which part of the city you were in.

And it wasn't that easy for him to leave the Ganga after discovering it, or rather, after the river's enchantment had discovered him.

Staring into the waters as they slid past from his vantage point at the edge of the little temple off to the side of the main ghat, his attention would only be fleetingly interrupted by the next wave of pilgrims ecstatically throwing themselves into the green grey waters.

Days passed before he managed to drag himself away from the mesmerizing currents loaded with marigolds that called to him from another time. Away from the smells and colours that adorned the banks of the river and the meandering back alleys that zig zagged parallel to it with their enticing surprises of temples, tiny hole in the wall shops, sweet curds, sweets and bang houses.

Marcus finally discovered a bus heading to Saranath after that holiest of rivers had stimulated within him a naked restlessness that yearned for more, but what that was remained a mystery to him.

Saranath was everything that the city was not – green with crumbling brown stupas and temples set amidst parklands of flowers and bougainvillea and abundant Ficus Religiosa, the holy figs of India, one of which was famously the tree beneath whose branches the Buddha was enlightened.

Sitting quietly upon the soft grass between the crumbling stupas, Marcus was overcome all of a sudden by an overwhelming desire to free himself from everything, to throw his worldly possessions away, except he had little. Just an old army kitbag into which he had hastily thrown a few clothes after having slept in late before his flight to Sydney - and his passport and traveller's cheques.

He would encounter that feeling many times on his journeys throughout that land, stumbling upon and seeking out the holy places, while every cave opening seemed to call to him to enter and stay forever and every shamanic pipal tree smeared with red and yellow paste and adorned with strips of coloured cloth within every village would beckon him to its shade and to share its stories. It had been like that from the moment Marcus had stepped out on to the Delhi streets and caught his first breath of Bharat.

Two days later and a somewhat directionless Marcus hopped on a train to Agra if for no other reason than the Taj Mahal was where people went, even though it was barely of interest to him being no more than an outlandish demonstration of Mughal passion that had near bankrupted the Kingdom.

Anyway, he never made it, for in his cabin he met a well to do Indian family who started with the customary chat, "from where are you coming? to which country do you belong? what is your purpose?" but more saliently "why do you foreigners all go to the Taj Mahal and not visit our wonderful state of Madhya Pradesh? we have also the temple of Khajuraho you know – and beautiful nature also."

"And tigers?" asked Marcus, his interest piqued all of a sudden.

"And tigers also – yes of course – why not?"

"Ok, where do you leave the train?"

"We alight the train at Satna, good sir."

Marcus' mood brightened. He had been wondering why he had not lingered longer in Varanasi, explored more of the back lanes behind the ghats where he loved to sit – and watch.

But he knew why, he was young, innocent and lonely in an immense and strange land but a land both welcoming, familiar and exciting to his every sense.

He decided he would also 'alight' the train at Satna which is exactly what he did and in doing so, chose well. That same night as his train pulled into Agra without him aboard, the military airport and the train station had bombs rained down upon them from the Pakistani Airforce in the opening salvo of the Indo-Pakistan war over Bangladesh - and Marcus' train had been left a burned-out crematorium of charred corpses.

The moment Marcus' new found friend set foot on the Satna platform, Marcus realised he had met a very important man. A bevy of officials accompanied by an obviously high-ranking police officer immediately sprang forward to greet him, palms together in the customary namaste greeting. As if feeling necessary to explain himself, the man turned to Marcus, saying,

"I am the District Forest Commissioner – I command all the vast forests in Madhya Pradesh and if you will excuse me, I must now attend a very important meeting."

"So, I should wait with your family?" asked Marcus

"No, no - just wait one moment if you please."

The Commissioner immediately summoned the Police chief to his side, spoke to the smaller man and motioned to Marcus. The next minute Marcus found himself in a police jeep with four, armed policeman heading out of town to a place of which he had no idea, bouncing along pot holed roads and passing through forests that were chiefly home to wild animals and bandits and accompanied by a troop of moustachioed officers who spoke almost zero English, their eyes darting left and right with old 303 rifles loaded and cocked as they passed nervously through the forest.

Two hours later the jeep pulled up at the front of a dilapidated old palace that stood alone in a forest clearing – a crumbling monument to some distant past when silken clothed Rajas had housed themselves here with their hunting guests.

Still, the policemen didn't speak, and with rifles in hand, two of them motioned to Marcus to follow them to the entrance steps where a single poorly dressed man had emerged from inside the walls.

"You come, follow," beckoned the man to Marcus.

"Where are we going? what is this place?" pleaded a slightly nervous Marcus.

"You come," was the only response.

The party of four entered the massive opening where once a grand pair of gates would have stood, immediately turned right through a stone doorway and began descending hundreds of well-worn steps. Down they went until Marcus saw the first door – a massive heavy wooden structure with an opening at the top and set with heavy iron bars.

"Oh fuck…it is the palace dungeon," he realised. But before that thought gave itself enough time to realise a second more paranoid one, a massive head had thrown itself violently against the bars in a fury of fur and frighteningly large teeth – and roared less than a meter away from Marcus' ear. His hair stood on end, literally stood on end – he had come face to face with the tiger of his dreams.

The Indians laughed, their joke complete, but they had yet another surprise. Aside from proudly informing him he was the first foreigner to visit the palace, the breeding centre of the white tigers that would soon begin to populate zoos, the world over, the bigger surprise was when they led him to the deep courtyard which must have been where prisoners in ancient times were either exercised or executed – or both.

The 'jailer' unlocked a metal cage door and motioned Marcus to enter, only for him to turn around and see the others standing on the other side and laughing hilariously at Marcus locked within.

He turned back to see two full sized leopards emerge from the shadows within the building. The big cats turned out to be completely tame and playful and Marcus was left there to frolic with them to their feline hearts content, rolling in the dust in the most memorable play fight of his life.

India! is not to be resisted but embraced. India will tell you where to go in its own way, in its own time – if you listen to her, she will.

And who
is calling
And who by the fire
is writing my story
in its ashes

And who
is this dancing
And singing my song
within the longing
of its lyrics

Chapter 3

Tat Walla Baba

It was a fair climb from his own low slung waterside cave to that of the Yogi and a climb he was happy to make in the company of the friend who had first invited him to his new home. During the night a tiger's roar had awoken him more than once from close by, but it was the elephants, his friend had advised, that posed the greater danger.

Marcus could barely believe that he now lived alongside the Jim Corbett national park. The fabled, hunter and environmentalist's books about his encounters with man-eating tigers had been both a source of fascination and terror for Marcus as a child as he had devoured all he could find about India.

Marcus labored somewhat as they ascended the stony path where savage thorns periodically grabbed at the flesh of their lower legs. Just ten days ago he had escaped the local hospital and a near-death bout of hepatitis and had survived only through the grace of a tough girl from Leeds who had found him dreamily entering unconsciousness on a rotting mattress with a well-used drip sticking out of his arm and surrounded by the painful cries and death throes of the overcrowded room where he had lain.

Sitting before the Yogi within the leafy bamboo mandapam that sat on a broad ledge outside a somewhat grand cave, he had been too culturally shy to touch the Yogi's feet as Graeme had done.

He sat there taking in the magnificence of the being who sat in apparent blissful trance upon a well but crudely cushioned stone seat. The Yogi was a big man and his brown skin shone with a certain luster as he gazed into nothingness. But it was his matted locks which were the stand out of his physical features, knotted as they were into a massive bun on top of his head. Graeme had told him that the Yogi's hair, when unleashed, reached all the way to the ground from his more than six-foot stance.

Marcus was too timid to ask such a being a question and anyway, he really didn't know what to ask. All he knew about meditation was that it had something to do with being here now so he crossed his legs just like he had seen that Californian hippie in the magazine do a few years back and focused on a small glimpse of the Ganga that he could see through the trees in front of the cave where the holy river first meandered and then cascaded in a violent rush - past the lesser caves he now called home far below where the Goddess became somewhat impatient and angry in her rush to bring abundance to the plains of Bharat.

⌒◡◡◠

Marcus had taken to visiting the Yogi on a regular basis, finding the courage to go alone and sometimes the mandapam would be crowded with pilgrims, at other times with more serious devotees and as each one arrived, they would touch the Yogi's feet and make a small offering, be it fruits or flowers or even a few crumpled and soiled rupees, but as he entered, Marcus would simply bow and sit at the far end of the mandapam from the Yogi and fix his eyes on the narrow glimpses of the distant Ganga below. From time to time, the Yogi would give short and sharp answers, at other times surprisingly long-winded discourses but for the most part he was silently staring into the abyss.

But there came a day when Marcus was sitting alone with the Yogi for some time when two well to do elderly gentlemen arrived, promptly touched the Yogi's feet and placed a generous portion of fruits, flowers and money before their object of reverence and salvation. They sat down at right angles to Marcus and in that particular Indian way, began asking of him the usual questions in their educated English until changing course to lightly chastise Marcus for choosing the life of a Sadaka at such a young age, imparting all of their traditional knowledge to him of how things should and should not be done within the great traditions of their country.

Marcus had never heard the Yogi speak a word of English and when questioned by foreigners in his presence the Yogi had always turned to his devotee and translator who was at that moment inside the cave preparing the meal. All of a sudden, as if understanding the entire conversation perfectly, the Yogi began shouting and gesticulating at the two men in rapid Hindi until each of them got up shaking in fear, prostrated before the Yogi, picked up all of their offerings they had previously placed at his feet, placed the entirety at the feet of Marcus and prostrated before him. They then rose, bowing once more to both Marcus and the Yogi in turn and left. Marcus rose to his feet, picked up the offerings anew, placed them before the Yogi and prostrated before him, resting his outstretched hands upon the Yogi's feet.

⌒‿‿⌒

Descending the hill from the Yogi's cave, Marcus came across a host of Rajasthani pilgrims, the men adorned in their outlandishly large and brightly colored turbans, the women in their beautifully and colorfully embroidered tops and skirts flashing tiny sunbeams from the multiple small mirrors woven into the cloth. They were making their way up the path to receive darshan from the Yogi and as Marcus stepped to one side to allow them to pass, each one stopped to touch his feet before palming their hands to his heart.

A tiger's roar
awakens the sleeper
drawn
to Nataraja's dance
did he
in his innocence forget
his careless joy?

Chapter 4

The Story of Renuka

The walk back to the village ran from the town and along the southern side of the sacred lake for about one and a half kilometers before entering the forest. Night was closing in and for that reason Marcus already felt a little apprehensive as he passed beneath the canopy and began walking the path through the dense trees and undergrowth. Barely a minute had passed before the low and unmistakable growl of a Leopard issued from beneath the shrubs and vines that strangled and covered a gully running parallel to the path.

Marcus' heart raced but he told himself not to run.

"Meditate walking, keep calm, do not run," he thought to himself, but he knew the predator would feel the fear and this primordial fear harked back to ancient times.

"If he wanted to kill me, he would not have growled," he assured himself, "keep walking, do not run - nothing excites a predator more than its prey running away from it," he reasoned, rather hoping he would be right.

Most days when he returned through the forest after his once-a-week provisions shop in the town for such basics as rice, chapati flour and crude molasses sugar - or from a simple swim on the lake - it would have been earlier in the afternoon and Marcus would hear the girls from the village singing and calling out to each other as they cut tree leaves as fodder for the cows. But at this late twilight hour all was still and getting darker and the girls with whom he would normally call back to had already departed for the village.

Ten minutes down the path and another growl from the gully sent his heart racing faster.

"The cat is following me - do not run, keep walking."

Marcus had encountered leopards before of course - the pair he had been introduced to within the crumbling Maharaja's palace in central India that had been as tame and playful as kittens, but on this darkening evening his shadow was a wild leopard, all too real and possibly hungry.

Ten more minutes passed and he made it to the first fields of the village and began to feel more at ease. The house of Tulsi Ram and his family beckoned a short way ahead and reaching the house, Marcus tried to explain in his very limited Pahari dialect that he had been followed by a leopard, but they half smiled, not quite trusting that Marcus had heard right.

Tulsi Ram's wife was sitting on her haunches making chapatis while simultaneously breast feeding a baby and smoking an enormous hookah and laughing at her jokes not particularly concerned if Marcus understood or not.

Still, he knew for sure that the girls who called to each other constantly while cutting leaves in the forest did so because of the Himalayan Black bears that sauntered down into the valley's during the colder months.

"Why not a leopard?" he thought, a thought that melted and surrendered to the pleasure of relaxing on the porch with his favorite family as they went about their chores with each one taking the time to sit down beside him, to speak without expecting to be understood, to play with his hair or a baby crawl into his lap while the aromas of the cooking fire became increasingly inviting.

After the usual tea and banter conducted through a mix of words, smiles and gestures he left their house and continued along the path through the valley to his own little hut.

Which was when he heard the roaring - the big cat had killed a cow on the edge of the village.

Now Marcus' hut had been used for storing cow fodder and had no door to speak of so he slept that night listening to the occasional roar of the leopard in addition to the scuttling sounds of cobras pursuing rats across the cracked earthen floor of which he was already half accustomed to during his fitful sleeps.

"I would be misleading myself if I said that I do not feel afraid," he thought as he lay there on his mat feeling vulnerable to the wild.

This village was where Marcus was forced to face many of his fears from childhood.

Lying only upon a straw mat he taught himself to sleep without moving, until after one morning waking up with a crushed scorpion under his back he had decided to plaster over the cracks and rat holes with a coating of fresh cow dung.

The villagers had shown him how it was done, as did the two eldest and beautiful daughters of Tulsi Ram better his cooking skills on their regular visits to his humble hut, laughingly taking from his hands whatever it was that he was doing in the moment, whether it be cooking, sowing or cleaning.

They were the warmest moments, moments when he could easily have accepted a different fate to marry one or both of them and live out his life in imagined serenity within those welcoming hills. Marriage to the daughters was, after all, their plan for him, or so he finally concluded later on when wiser to the realities of an Indian family burdened by multiple daughters.

But as Marcus lay there listening to the roars of the predator, he had another fear to face - one that must have been deep rooted because he had dreamt frequently of being face to face with a tiger, when, in his dream before the big cat would attack him, he would launch himself at it snarling.

Fear, he knew, was to be faced and somehow, in the strangest of ways, he knew this leopard had been drawn to him through his dreams, but fear was not the only feeling that challenged him during those days.

Loneliness too was a sometime unwelcome companion while learning to live without anyone from his own culture, his own kind. But the tiger, the leopard and the jaguar of that other continent he was destined to reach were solitary animals, magnificent and content in their aloneness.

Marcus had been summoned to find this lake because that was what the I Ching had told him, "Go to the Joyous Lake," it had said.

Marcus had shortly before celebrated his twentieth birthday in front of his cave on the Ganga but events had taken place there that had led him to the lake and the village that became Marcus' home for five months, and this lake had a story.

The village sat in the valley beneath the high hill upon which the Rishi Jamadagni had meditated and practiced austerities in ancient times.

At the foot of the western ridge that led down from the hill was the lake named after his wife, the goddess Renuka, and the clear green lake where Marcus often swam, if you looked down from above, was in the shape of a woman with a severed head with 'the head' resting at the feet of the goddess in the form of a large pond, and at the point of the lady's breast a crafted stone nipple of the Goddess from where, in ancient times it was said, flowed abundant milk.

And this is that story;

One day Renuka went to the river to fill the water jars whereupon she saw reflected in the waters the erotic play of heavenly spirits and became aroused. Upon her return to the hermitage her husband, the all-seeing Rishi, ordered her sons to cut off her head, and standing before them accused of infidelity, the first two sons refused their fathers order but the third, Parasurama, obeyed his father and dutifully cut off his mother's head.

Pleased with his son, the Rishi offered him a boon, whereupon Parasurama immediately and successfully implored his father to restore Renuka's head to its rightful place.

It was told that Kartavirya, a powerful king, once went to Jamadagni's home, and after having been served a sumptuous meal full of delightful sweet meats and curds, stole the Rishi's fabled cow — a cow by the name of Kamadhenu that was renowned for giving endless quantities of milk. An enraged Jamadagni pursued and slew the king and brought Kamadhenu back to his hermitage.

Upon hearing of this, the son of the king subsequently returned and killed Jamadagni - sending the slain Rishi's son, the immortal Parasurama, on his eternal war against all evil Kshatriya kings and never again would Parusurama think of entertaining a Kshatriya.

<hr>

Parusurama emerges much later in the times of the Kuru kings as the teacher of Drona and, after Drona refuses Karna because of his apparent lowly caste, Parusurama becomes the teacher of Karna.

The young warrior had come to him disguised as a brahmin and Parasurama's curse on Karna for deceiving his teacher by dressing as a brahmin led to Karna's death, of course, on the battlefield of Kurukshetra — a story that had its beginnings upon the hill at whose feet Marcus dwelt and a story that was a constant throughout his life.

Swimming in blue waters
of the Goddess' milk
He dived to their depths on a whim
of darkness and light
of hope and hope's sin
and the flickering fires
fanned by a lie
to surface again
and again

Chapter 5

Juliana

Marcus was woken up by the bell at four in the morning. His head hurt and his mouth felt seedy from the night before when he and a few friends had hit the chang in Saranath, the field of ancient Buddhist shrines that lay on the outskirts of Varanasi. Chang was a milky Tibetan beer usually made from barley and one of those drinks that creeps up on you somewhat harshly.

So, the first day of the ten-day meditation retreat didn't get off to the perfect start and the first session was a case of more minutes passed nodding than of being conscious of the breath.

After breakfast he felt a bit better but what happened next made him feel amazingly better.

He was entering the hall when something made him turn around and doing so, he caught the eye of the most beautiful woman he had ever seen.

She was standing about twenty meters away to his left with one arm wrapped around her midriff and the other with the hand held lightly holding her chin. She wore an almost full-length dress that showed up her curves and her thick dark golden hair fell curling loosely past her shoulders. Olive skinned and with almond shaped green eyes and full lips she looked, to Marcus' adoring eyes, a goddess incarnate.

Marcus, at twenty years of age was shy with women and quickly turned away from the eye contact but he couldn't resist another look before entering the meditation hall and was startled to see that she was still staring straight at him. As their eyes met again, instead of turning away, she stood there in all of her wonder and smiled a beautiful smile. This time Marcus managed a smile back before walking inside but any chance of his mind becoming concentrated on his breath had long gone.

After lunch he saw her again standing by herself soaking up the winter sun and tentatively approaching her, she gave him that smile again. Shyly he sidled up to her trying to manifest as much courage as possible.

"Hullo"

"Hullo"

He noticed an exotic accent.

She was smiling at him, her eyes thoroughly checking him over, slightly down and then up to his face again.

"My name is Juliana."

"Hi…I am Marcus."

"Where are you from, Juliana?"

"From Brazil"

"And you?"

"From Tasmania"

They were not meant to talk really, it being a "silent" retreat but they were not the only ones transgressing the rules and well, for Marcus and Juliana, they didn't even give it a thought.

Juliana laughed and her eyes twinkled in mirth.

"Tasmania? Where is Tasmania?"

"At the bottom of the world."

Marcus gave her a shy grin.

"OK, it is an island, part of Australia."

"Ahh, yes, the Tasmanian devil."

Marcus winced.

"How long you been in India Marcus?"

"Oh, a bit over a year."

"What you being doing in India all this time?"

"Oh, I spent some time living in a cave and most of the last half of the year in a village in the mountains."

Juliana turned to face him forcing Marcus to look directly at her and as she did so Marcus felt her eyes penetrating his, completely unravelling his soul in the process and he felt equally terrified and beautified at the same time.

He could not surmise her age. She had a child-like demeanor and innocence on the one hand and her features were near perfect yet the edges around her eyes were just very slightly wrinkled from squinting in the sun and the eyes themselves were deep, green pools of ancient history.

"Really, a cave? you were alone there?"

"No, there were a few westerners and a few sadhus."

"And the village, you were alone there?"

"I was the only westerner there, yes."

"How was that for you?"

Marcus looked down at his feet and kicking away a stone replied,

"I was too lonely in the end."

Juliana was smiling broadly by this stage while subtly nodding and her face in the hot morning sun shone back at him in delight.

Marcus, having survived a month retreat in the mountains through the previous October, had intended to do the whole month once again but on the tenth day Juliana turned to him and asked him if he wished to travel to Bodh Gaya, the birth place of the Buddha,

"Yes, sure, let's," he could barely conceal his joy.

***

Marcus and Juliana were climbing into the rickshaw outside the gate when Anita, a feisty red headed Dutch woman who Marcus knew from the previous Himalayan retreat rushed out to wish them well. Laughing, she thrust her hand into the hand of Juliana.

"Hey beautiful couple, have fun - here take these - pure Californian Sunshine, the very best."

The two women laughed together and embraced and before long Marcus and Juliana were clattering over the uneven streets of Varanasi heading to the railway station. Passing by a sweet vendor they looked at each other and in silent agreement Marcus bade the rickshaw wallah stop - Kier kadams are the best of the best amongst the Indian sweetmeats and a treat to be shared on any journey, and they chatted some more, and more still on the train to Gaya when he learned that Juliana was thirty-two years old and had two children back in Brazil. An artist, she had divorced her wealthy industrialist husband four years ago and had arrived in India on an overland "freak" bus from London.

Finding a room in the Burmese Vihara the two of them soon wandered off in the direction of the main temple that stood alongside the famous Bodhi Tree, the tree under which the Buddha had sat two and a half thousand years before and where he had attained enlightenment.

The sun was beginning to set over the fields as they walked in silence, Surya's colors splashing off the waters of the rice paddies and silhouetting date palms that reached longingly into the pink sky with black, leafy fingers while in the distance a farmer drove his oxen home along the narrow path between the fields.

A place of peace and serenity, of temples and monks from Buddhist countries from all parts of Asia but the majority of monks in Bodh Gaya at that time were the Tibetans who were encountered almost always smiling, always friendly.

Marcus, who had never taken acid before, had come to India lured in part by the abundance of hashish and had really liked the opium he had consumed in Goa but had left it all behind from the moment he began to live in the caves in Rishikesh and embarked upon the path of meditation.

"Have you taken acid before?" asked Marcus as they strolled along the fields.

Juliana smiled at him and asked him to stop.

"Open your mouth, Marcus."

She deftly slipped one of the tabs onto his tongue at the same moment feeding herself the other.

"This will make the gods very happy," she assured him, "yes, Marcus, acid is part of my diet - it reveals truths to us that lie hidden - now we will be silent again," she softly commanded.

They continued walking until they reached the fabled tree and climbed the stone platform upon which candles had been placed by the monks. The tree sat at a short distance from the main temple with just a few small gardens intersected by pathways separating them. The temple at this hour was coming to life with the fall of night, the flickering candles sending shadows dancing along its sculptured outer walls while Tibetan monks occasionally passed by reciting prayers while moving the beads of their malas lovingly through their fingers.

It took a little while amidst the magic of his surroundings before Marcus realized his perception was changing, and the lights he was seeing were far more exaggerated than the lights of the candles. It was when he looked up at Juliana however, that his world, the world and the limitations he had placed around himself up until that moment, the fears and uncertainties that had imprisoned him, simply exploded.

She was looking at him with a virtual torrent of love pouring from her eyes and heart and never had he seen such beauty in his life, never felt so loved, never dreamed that such a divine moment, such a gift could come true. He was totally, irrevocably consumed.

"You are so beautiful," she smiled.

A smile that sent waves of ecstasy coursing through his being.

"You are the most beautiful person I have ever met," he answered.

And they began to giggle in mirth and joy.

A Tibetan monk came up to the tree and placed some more candles on the platform where they sat. He paused to look at both of them for a moment before breaking out into a huge smile, walking away chuckling.

They looked up into the branches of the ancient tree and saw the lights of devas dancing in the branches, and whatever celestial beings were playing in the high branches of the sacred tree he did not know but Marcus turned away and looked to Juliana and then back again and they both looked up to see the same.

Meanwhile more and more people were arriving at the temple to pray, to prostrate and chant. Bells were ringing and voices talking.

"Let's move on and find some quiet nature," said Juliana, her eyes starry and her face golden in the candlelight.

They got up and started to walk but Juliana turned to Marcus and said,

"I don't know the way, you lead me."

Marcus was seeing multiple realities simultaneously and real life and time was only one of them but he knew he now had to be the man leading this star woman through the maze of an Indian night so they slowly made their way along the street of the village past children begging, past little cafes and shops and people brushing past. He held her hand while he used all of his will in the face of his altered perceptions to recognize and follow the real places and time.

An ox cart came rumbling past jingling with bells amidst the cries of the driver who maneuvered his beasts through the milling street. Marcus' eyes met those of the ox and he became aware of the animal's innermost being, of its pain and its surrender in that lucid moment. His eyes met the eyes of a mother begging in the street surrounded by her children in rags and he reached out to take the hand of a child in his. Juliana smiled.

They reached a woodland on the outskirts of the village and now alone again Marcus began to dance and he danced out his life before Juliana, danced his fears and his dreams and left nothing behind. All the while she sat wrapped in her shawl watching, smiling and telling him he was crazy and loving him with those shining eyes.

They didn't make love that night. Nor the next, nor on their journey south, but the first night in Goa on Christmas Eve with the church bells ringing in the distance and the sound of the waves lapping on the beach they did.

⁓

Marcus arrived in Rio in the middle of Carnaval and was dancing in the street with Juliana and her children within two hours of the plane touching down. She had brought with her to the airport, satin clothes for him in hues of pink and green, the colors of her favorite Samba school, Mangueira, which in Portuguese translates as 'Mango Tree'.

If India was a journey into the inner world, then Brazil during Carnaval was a riotous homage to the senses. Glistening with sweat in the heat of the summer, spectacular bodies adorned with feathers and glitter cavorted and writhed and sambaed in perfect rhythm to the drumming and trumpets. All to the back-drop of mountainous hills covered in tropical forest and skirted by the famous beaches of Copacabana, Leblon and Ipanema.

Dotted along the tops of the hills were the favelas that gave birth to both the adrenalin and the fear of the city, but lording over all, the massive Christ the redeemer stretched out his arms in supplication to the city of Catholicism, Candomblé and shameless sin.

The children were dancing with them, Bia and Carlinhos. Bia was a skinny and very pretty girl of eight with long dark wavy hair, much like her mother. Carlinhos was eleven and a beautiful looking boy a little more reserved in nature but regularly showered with kisses from an adoring Juliana.

Their house was in truth the house of the husband, but he had moved out years ago and left it for them, a large two-story house perched half way up one of the tropical hills with a view to the ocean.

Juliana had opened the house after her divorce to all manner of artists, musicians, screen writers and lost beautiful boys where they almost came and went as they pleased - dropping acid, smoking weed, playing music and painting.

That was until Juliana had been interrupted during a ten-day brown rice and acid fast.

It had disturbed her mother to the brink of desperation upon one of those hot summer days when finding her daughter on acid staring at her tropical fish tank for two hours without saying hullo. Her mother had had her dragged away screaming by men in white coats carrying large needles.

For a year this was Marcus' home and there they painted and listened to music, meditated and made love. Juliana was an extraordinary teacher for him. He had never had a real lover before and had little experience - mostly because of his difficulty to be intimate with women since his interrupted adolescence, but Juliana broke down the barriers quickly,

"Marcus I haven't had sex for years and have said no to many, many mens – I have been chased by musicians, actors, artists and beautiful boys – but I hadn't needed it when I had been taking acid during those years of painting and psychedelia," so she explained to Marcus, "the sun had been my lover – I felt it when lying in the lagoon at Arambepe one day on acid – my belly receiving the gift of the sun-god - I was feeling so well loved by the sun that I felt I don't need no-one else - but, now, in you, Marcus, I feel like I have found the gift of the sun god," she had told him with her beautiful smile.

Juliana was making up for lost time - they both were. They were willing explorers of every sensual bodily part and every imaginable position. She with her beautiful curves, her olive skin, her full lips, Madonna breasts and sweet smell and he with his twenty-year old torso, his pleasing size for her, his long blond hair and his smile and their love making was as insatiable as the luxurious tropical growth that steamily enveloped the hills of Rio.

Sensuality and wild perversity and slow tantric lovemaking became the punctuation marks of their dreamy existence.

Until they quarreled and that happened pretty much once a month.

Marcus could be emotional and fearful of losing her. She could be merciless with his faults and fearful of losing him. He would react. She would tell him to leave. He would storm out with not her but Fabiana, the mulatta maid, begging him at the door to stay. He would be back before night mostly.

They would make up and make love and then Fabiana would throw her arms around him when he came into the kitchen alone, herself teary.

There was a time when Marcus didn't come home the same night but that was the second year of their time together and by then they had moved out of Rio to a sitio in the hills.

⌒⌒⌒

Marcus had become too claustrophobic in the city and there in the country he did what he loved to do, to dig the earth and make a garden and ride a horse and by now Bia with her persistent chatter had helped him learn enough Portuguese to communicate with her and it was Bia who was his constant companion in the garden after school hours. Flittering around him, hitching a ride on his back, chatting, never stopping.

Juliana, sometimes over conscious of their age difference, more than one time looked at them and remarked,

"You two should get married when I get too old for you."

In fact, the age difference between Marcus and Bia and between Juliana and Marcus was the same, twelve years, but Marcus would look at her and say,

"Juliana, look at you, you are still the most beautiful woman in the world - I will never tire of you."

"Oh yes you will."

In the mornings the two children would climb into bed with them. Carlinhos to his mother's side and Bia to Marcus', and often her little hand would reach out to caress his chest and neck.

⌒⌒⌒

But still the pattern of the lovers continued. Life was fun and it was passionate and full of lust and then they would fight and it didn't take much for Marcus to upset Juliana and when it happened it was explosive because he wouldn't allow himself to be intimidated by anyone.

He had learnt at boarding school that to survive the violence and sexual predation of the teachers and the bullying of older students he had to fight back and had even vowed before the gods as a young adolescent that he would never allow anyone ever again to make him feel afraid.

But the irony was that he himself in his reaction could be scary to confront. At over a hundred and ninety centimeters of toned muscle Marcus in all of his fury was a sight to behold but Juliana when enraged was a wildcat. Though he never struck her he would throw her back on to the bed as she tried to tear at his hair.

In later years, Bia would tell Marcus that she always felt sorry for him and that she had blamed her mother for those fights.

It was right in the middle of an eclipse of the moon when they fought again but this time, with only the clothes on his back, Marcus walked out onto the highway that passed along the side of the valley, hitched a ride and was gone.

～～～

Marcus felt drawn by India's call once more, unfinished with his spiritual search he had many times begged Juliana to come with him to live in India. But she couldn't take the children away from their father and wouldn't think to part from them for too long anyway. In his mind he was heading back to his calling, but with no money and not even a change of clothes, he had formed an idea in his head that he would hitch a ride to the northeast of Brazil where he had heard from someone that fishing boats sometimes ventured to Africa and from Africa, he thought, he would a find a way to India.

By the second day he had sold his shoes for oranges and was sleeping under a bridge on the highway. Rides were hard to come by in the interior of Brazil in the seventies where bandits and thieves were plenty and where police death squads still did their dirty work for the military dictatorship.

So, Marcus walked until he came across a parked refrigerated meat truck and surprised the life out of the driver as the tall, long haired and barefoot Gringo rapped on his window.

"Can I get a ride with you north," he asked in his limited Portuguese.

The truck driver, a black man around thirty years of age, with kind eyes, Marcus noticed, hesitated, suspicious.

But the driver, Paulo was his name, eventually relented and the two unlikely companions headed north and Paulo, it turned out, happened to be hauling meat to where Marcus wanted to go - a week on the road to the North-East.

Within hours they were friends and after half a day they stopped at a border town that was, in those days, nothing more than truck stops, dingy little cafes and whore houses where men roamed the streets with barely concealed guns and hard-ons looking for accommodation. After buying Marcus a meal in the cafe where a matronly patroa ruled with a benevolent but stern hand, Paulo gave Marcus a blanket to sleep with under the truck while he commandeered the cabin with a voluptuous girl of about sixteen at best.

"You good down there, Marcus? you need a girl?

"Thanks, Paulo, but I got no money, remember," he answered as the girl started to giggle and soon after, to pant and gasp.

They travelled for another two days and while Marcus never asked for food, Paulo would never eat without offering him some. Paulo was raised in the favelas, had struggled all his life to survive since a hungry childhood but he had a great sense of humor a love for life and a natural charm and was generous with all he had.

Marcus was lucky - no money, no shoes, maybe no future even, but he felt lucky anyway.

After a few days travelling together and while approaching a desolate town, Marcus suddenly asked him to stop. It was the northern interior of Bahia where the country was dry and covered with low lying drought resistant trees and shrubs, a region better known as the Caatinga.

"Paulo I'm going back."

"What you mean you going back? you going back to your woman? hey there are millions of women out there Marcus - the sea is full of fish – 'Cara', that woman treated you bad - get another one, maybe two or three?"

Paulo was genuinely disappointed.

"No, something suddenly changed - just a minute ago - I got a message that I had to go back - thanks Paulo, you have been a good friend."

Paulo grinned, "E voce é louco, muito louco."

And shaking his head at Marcus,

"Tchau amigo"

He gunned the truck and it pulled out on to the highway climbing through the gears and years later Marcus would wish he could meet him again to see if he could repay him somehow, but he never did.

Marcus made his way into the town that lay just off the highway and asked for the police station. He was directed to the top of the hill on the edge of town.

He had heard that the police would sometimes give poor people money for a bus fare just to get them out of town. It was worth a try although at other times they might just kill someone and dump them out of town instead.

He walked into the police station and realized he had walked into a movie set from the wild west - except it was real. There was basically one large room with peeling whitewashed walls flecked with suspicious splashes of brown that were probably dried blood. To one side of the room there was the counter, behind which lazed a couple of police in tattered chairs. Another policeman was half slouching across the counter staring at Marcus as the gringo came into the room. To his front and to his right were floor to ceiling cell bars and crowded to overflowing with prisoners, all of them black, some still bleeding. They were sullen, almost silent, but every eye was on Marcus. They had probably never seen a gringo before let alone one like Marcus - tall, young, long blond hair. Even being a man, he probably looked better to them than anything they had raped in recent times.

"What you want gringo?"

"I heard you might be able to give me a bus ticket - I have no money."

A malicious smirk crossed the policeman's mouth

"Where you want to go?"

"To near Rio."

"That's a long way."

"So, can I get a ticket?"

"No"

He motioned Marcus to the door and standing beside him pointed to the highway stretching out below as it snaked through the Caatinga.

"You need to go that way."

Marcus turned to him about to ask something else,

"Now."

When he reached the highway again, barefoot, no food, no water, Marcus thought he should stay around the edge of town to hitch but he wanted to get far away from that hell hole so he walked and kept on walking in the heat of the sun until the town was lost from sight. After walking several kilometers there came into view a small group of people huddled by the side of the road in the distance, with the sun beating down on the asphalt creating a visible shimmer of heat above and around them.

Arriving closer he could see that most of them were young, seven in all, two men maybe not much older than himself and two very young mothers holding tiny babies and a teenage girl about fourteen years old. They looked lost and without hope and the anxiety written across the face of one of the young mothers was palpable. She could not have been more than fifteen herself noted Marcus.

They all silently stared at him in bewilderment and he realized that to them he must have looked like Jesus appearing out of the wilderness. He introduced himself in his bad Portuguese.

They were refugees from the drought stricken north-east trying to make their way to São Paulo and a better life, they told him.

"Do you have any food or water?" the young man with the beard asked and gesturing to the young mother, said, "she is losing her milk and the baby is crying from thirst."

"No, I don't - I am very sorry, nothing at all."

Marcus slumped to the ground next to them and wondered if they were all going to die there together and then he saw, placed on the red dust amongst their scant bundles of belongings trussed up in old strips of bed sheets, a figurine of Iemanjá the Orixá, the goddess of the sea, standing next to a picture of Christ.

He remembered something he had with him and he fumbled in his pocket and drew out a picture card from India of Krishna recounting to Arjuna in his golden chariot the teaching that later became famous as the Bhagavad Gita. He had been using it to copy a drawing he was doing of that scene just before his fight with Juliana. He placed the picture delicately in the dust alongside Iemanjá and the Christ.

"Tell us, is this an Orixá?" asked the mother with the baby.

"Kind of," said Marcus, before pausing to construct what he wanted to say in his limited Portuguese.

"It's a story about this God, Krishna, who tells this great warrior he must fight and not be afraid - he tells him that everything that will happen is already done because it is God's will and so the warrior has no need to feel sad about who he will kill."

"Like Oxala and Ogum?" asked the girl.

"Yes, maybe," answered Marcus.

"So now," pondered Marcus aloud and half to himself, "all we have left seems to be faith so I will add my faith in the will of God to yours and we will wait," he said, feeling partly holy and partly wretched, and looking up to the cloudless blue sky and the scorching sun he motioned to the small pieces of shade that the thorny Caatinga offered.

"I think we should all just take a siesta out of the sun because no cars are passing anymore - I think all we have now are our Gods," he added.

Each of them shared their names and who was whose brother and whose sister, wife, husband, uncle, aunt, and smilingly, the young mothers handed him their frail little babies to hold for a minute before all lay down scattered around the scrub hugging to the miserly patches of shade - and waited for a miracle.

Funnily enough Marcus really expected a miracle and it happened sooner than he thought.

He must have drifted into sleep for a while for when he woke-up, he opened his eyes to heavy grey clouds and the clap of thunder where shortly before only clear blue sky had been as far as the eyes could see. The rain came bucketing down and without standing up he lay there with cupped hands and let the water pour through his parched lips.

The family, meanwhile, had scrambled for a couple of battered tin cooking pots from amongst their things and were collecting water. Drenched by the downpour their clothes wet and clinging to their visibly brown skin the girls stared over at Marcus who had by now, walked over to the road where he stood watching an old pick-up truck making its way along the highway towards them up the steady gradient to the top of the rise.

As the truck approached, he heard the engine cough, give a couple of splutters and then die as it slowly rolled to a halt right in front of him.

Laden with bananas and pineapples it must have been returning from the market in the town.

An old farmer and his wife emerged from the vehicle looking despondent and upon seeing Marcus and showing their obligatory surprise asked him if he could help them push the vehicle to the top of the rise. That was when their eyes strayed to the family and babies emerging from the scrub, wet bedraggled and starving. Without a word the old couple broke off hands of ripe bananas and passed them around, and there they stood, soaked to the skin silently eating bananas in the middle of the empty highway.

The old man again asked Marcus if they could all help him push his truck, apologizing that he couldn't offer them a ride because he wasn't going very far and they didn't have a lot of gasoline.

"That's no problem," replied Marcus, 'we will find a way - and you won't need our help to push the car, it will start now."

Marcus wondered how he was so sure it would - but he was.

The teenage girl stood on the road next to him and stared at Marcus with mouth open. The farmer's wife hesitated at the door of the truck and she too stared at him with tears in her eyes before getting back in the vehicle.

The old man slid creakily into the driver's seat and turned on the ignition. The engine roared into life and they chugged over the hill and left.

The brown skinned girl with the wet and now see-through shirt crossed herself.

Marcus turned to his new friends, smiling, and said,

"I think it best if we part now because with so many it will only make it harder for you to get a lift so I will keep walking - I have been very happy to meet you and I wish you luck and the best life in São Paulo."

He felt sure they would make it. After all, miracles don't happen for no reason.

And with his parting words hanging amidst the steam vaporing off the quickly heating asphalt and with the hot sun reasserting its flaming wroth upon the Caatinga, he left them to their fate and walked on over the rise and along the highway and the land dried out in no time at all and the sky was blue and cloudless once again.

The odd car and truck that thundered past at high speed gave no suggestion that he might get a ride. Only once since he left the house had anyone stopped for him and a hint of despair started entering his mind again so he stopped, lay down on his back on the edge of the highway looked up to the gods and thought,

"Fuck it then, I leave it up to you again."

He had lain there all of five minutes when a small white car drove past and seeing him prostrate by the road, screeched to a stop.

The driver was short and skinny while an older woman seated in the passenger seat was almost twice his size. The younger man pushed their luggage in the back seat to one side so Marcus could get in while both eyed him nervously.

"We stopped because we thought you might be injured."

"Thank you."

"We can only take you as far as the next town."

"Thank you."

Marcus told them his story. They didn't believe a word of it and they couldn't hide their nervousness. Marcus could see they were wondering why they had stopped for him, the skinny man casting suspicious glances in Marcus' direction through the rear vision mirror while the fat woman turned occasionally to make conversation.

She was returning to Sao Paulo from her sister's funeral in the Northeast in the state of Pernambuco and her nephew had offered to drive her as she couldn't afford the bus fare. As they talked, Marcus was aware that she was trying to reassure herself that he wasn't about to murder them.

"Both a savior and a roadside killer all in the one day," he laughed somewhat dryly to himself while he began to hum to himself one of his favorite tunes;

Riders on the storm
Riders on the storm
Into this house, we're born
Into this world, we're thrown
Like a dog without a bone
An actor out on loan
Riders on the storm
There's a killer on the road...........

It took a full twenty-four hours for them to feel somewhat safe with him.

In the end they drove him all the way back to where the highway passed the turn off to Rio. Each night the driver would sleep in a cheap motel, his aunt in the car and Marcus, well Marcus just slept anywhere.

Through one night he had slept on the pavement of the same town where he had lain under Paulo's truck.

Cowboys galloped drunk along the street firing guns and whores and music spilled out of the bars all night long - too cold and uncomfortable to sleep anymore he had been joined by two drunken teenage prostitutes sitting alongside him.

"Why are you sleeping here?"

"I have no money."

"No money to pay me for a nice favor?"

"No sorry," he smiled tiredly.

"You have a nice smile - maybe I can give you a favor for free," she kindly offered.

"Oh no, it's OK."

"Why, I am not pretty enough for you?"

"Your beautiful - and sweet - hey just come here and lay down with me and let's keep each other warm," he finally asked - he was cold.

So, they kept each other warm and from that day on there were two innocent whores in a border town in the interior of Brazil that could tell their clients all about Australia and its exotic animals - including the deadly drop bear.

Marcus was walking the last twenty kilometers until, within a short distance of Juliana's house, her driver pulled up beside him.

"Senhor Marcus"

"Hi, Sebastião, how you doing?"

Getting out of the car the driver motioned Marcus in the direction of the enormous swimming pool that lay about a hundred meters from Juliana's house in the expansive and manicured gardens of the neighboring Count's estate.

Barefoot and dusty he made his way through his own garden before passing through a break in the trees into the gardens surrounding the clear blue pool. Bia was the first to see him and came running into his arms with Juliana following close behind.

"Don't ever leave me again," she whispered as she hung her arms around his neck, laying her head on his breast.

Juliana had spent the first two days driving up and down the highway searching for him, another two days crying and on the sabbath she had visited a Mae da Santa - a woman with the sight.

The Mae da Santa had told Juliana that Marcus was safe - that he was traveling with a black man who had a good heart and at that moment, the moment she was speaking to Juliana, Marcus would turn back - that he would return finally on foot and that she, Juliana, need not worry as Marcus had the strongest protection she had yet seen.

"His protector? she comes from across the seas, from the East," she had answered Juliana.

This was the world that Juliana lived in. The real world was not easy for her and she depended on her ex-husband to take care of that side greatly and she depended on Marcus for the rest, but she dwelt for the most part in the realms of the spirit and of magic.

A wonderful story-teller, Marcus could sit fascinated by her tales for hours on end as she talked and painted, as she recounted them in bed after making love.

Bia would tell Marcus years later that her mother had made up some of those stories, but Marcus just laughed and said he didn't mind, because all of life was just a story in a way - none of it was real and Juliana's stories were the best.

One of his favorite's he was certain was actually true, and anyway, even if it wasn't it had a great teaching of sorts, and this is that story;

Juliana had been spending the summer in Salvador where she had left Bia and Carlinhos with their father at the grand-parents grand estate overlooking the bay. The old colonial two story house had been in the children's grandmother's family for generations and was surrounded by five acres of gardens and over fifty different species of mangos - the largest mango trees to be found in all of Bahia that spread their heavily laden boughs across sweeping lawns and tropical greenery. Below in the bay, colorful fishing boats bobbed in the clear green waters. It was here that Bia and Carlinhos would pass many happy summers with their cousins – enough of them to form a tribe.

Directly below the family estate stood the Yacht Club where Salvador's elite would gather to discuss business and politics and the success stories and failures of family and acquaintances while being served and waited on by the sons and daughters of the slaves, shipped into that very harbor centuries before while cramped in stinking and filthy rat infested holds below decks.

Around the point was the beach of Barra. a popular beach of the people where black coconut oiled flesh ruled with the smell of frying acarajé and the cries of the beach hawkers.

Onto this beach the shipwrecked Portuguese sailor, Diogo Alvares had dragged himself out of the sea five hundred and seventy years ago to be adopted by the local Tupinambá tribe and given the name, Caramuru.

Caramuru had then proceeded to marry the chief's daughter followed by so many wives that half of the population of the entire city claimed him as their ancestor, Carlinhos and Bia's family included. His was the ancestral link that bonded the elite with the children of the slaves by blood and history if not by status.

For Juliana it was a time to stay with friends at Arembepe beach to the north of the city where travelers rented fishermen's huts and passed the days playing music, lazing on the beach, smoking maconha and dreaming of the coming golden age. One of those friends, Silvana, told Juliana about a powerful magician whom she had visited.

"He is just so amazing Juliana - you have to see him - I swear he changed my luck."

Naturally, Juliana was curious enough to seek him out.

~⌣⌣~

The Bahiano around fifty, wiry, slightly greying but with yellowish, bloodshot eyes beneath a heavy brow was blowing smoke from his pipe over Juliana's face and repeating incantations to the Orixá, Exum. A woman assistant, meanwhile, prepared a bath of herbs for Juliana to bath herself and cleanse her soul.

As the story goes, the creator, Olorum, formed the world by emanating seven energetic vibrations, called "Orixás." Each of the seven Orixás had a positive and a negative aspect, a masculine and feminine, a yin and a yang, resulting in a total of fourteen Orixás.

When Juliana had taken Marcus to a Mae da Santa in Salvador earlier in the year, he had been told that he had Oxalá, the Orixá of the original light, on one shoulder and Osun, of the streams and waterfalls, the Orixá of romantic love, on the other.

"You should always live near running water or springs," she had told him.

And when the Portuguese brought the Africans into Catholic churches to be baptized, the Africans intuitively recognized the seven Orixás in Jesus, Mary, and various saints. Hence, the Orixás also came to be symbolically aligned with Catholic saints, so that slaves could worship their deities under the guise of Catholic forms. Through reverence and worship of the Orixás, a person's physical surroundings become symbolically linked to the spirit world and the world of the gods to the physical.

<div style="text-align:center">~~~</div>

But when Juliana walked to the waiting aromatic bath, she noticed a goat tied up in the ramshackle house and realized what it was for.

"You're not going to kill that goat for me?"

"We must," replied the magician, "it is an important part of the rites."

"No," she objected in alarm, "you will not kill that goat."

The magician was puzzled.

"But we must - we need the blood of the goat to call the Orixás."

"No, not for me, I don't need the goat to be killed for me."

The magician nodded - and Juliana thought he had relented - but after returning from her lengthy bath she saw the decapitated head of the goat and screamed.

"I told you not to kill that goat!"

"But we had to," said the magician in growing irritation, "it's part of the ceremony and it has to be done, otherwise it won't work."

"Then I am leaving and I won't pay you! I told you not to kill the goat!" she yelled angrily.

The magician darkened menacingly and said to Juliana through clenched teeth.

"You will pay me or you will break both of your legs in a car accident."

Juliana's anger flared and she turned on the magician and screamed

"You're evil and you can go to hell," and promptly departed, refusing to hear more of the muttered curses that followed her to her car.

Back in Arembepe she told Silvana what had happened. Her friend turned white with fear.

"You must pay him, you must – please do Juliana, please - he is too powerful."

"No, never," she replied, "I told him not to kill the goat and he did it anyway."

The following day Silvana repeatedly begged Juliana to pay but she refused and she did the same the day after and still Juliana would not.

On the third day Silvana borrowed Juliana's car, had an accident and broke both of her legs.

She really thought
that Dylan wrote that song for her
She who made love to Surya
at Arembepé
And displayed her golden body
to the beach of Ipanema
She painted Chè and Shiva
and the god of Krishna Deva
He was
as was his want
so willing to believe her

Chapter 6

Back in the Holy Land

The train began to shudder and groan in its first efforts to steam out of the Madras railway station when Marcus noticed a book-trolly trundling along the platform. As it passed by his window a face was staring at him beatifically from the cover of one of the books.

"Hang on, I'll be back."

"But Marcus, where are you going? the train is leaving," exclaimed Juliana, but in an instant, she watched him leap off the train and run down the platform as she sat there wondering whether he had disappeared again.

Before long, however, with the train beginning to pick up momentum, Marcus came pushing through the heavy doors that separated the carriages with a book in his hand. Juliana sighed, turning her head towards the unfolding scenery of India as the train picked up speed.

An hour later after having his head buried in the book the entire time, Marcus' heart felt at peace.

"Juliana, you have to read this - all of the confusion I had felt about meditation and the path has just melted away."

Marcus and Juliana travelled around the coast of South India, stopping at tropical beaches and visiting holy places until they came to a place called Colva Beach at the southern tip of Goa.

The Portuguese architecture was still evident there in the simple but elegant houses that dotted the sandy streets behind the coconut tree lined beach and it was in one of these larger houses that sat lazily behind a wall of cascading bougainvillea flowers that a young monk from a monastery in Thailand, Kitti Subho, was to hold a meditation retreat.

Marcus and Juliana had now come full circle. Having met on a retreat a little over two years before, they were back in retreat again and just as in the first retreat in Varanasi they had been drawn together, now in this retreat they would drift apart - he absorbed in meditation, she into the arms of another young Australian.

In his first meeting with the monk, Marcus asked him if he knew of the Sage who had lived his whole life at the foot of Arunachala, the holy mountain in the south of India, the abode of Shiva in the form of fire. Kitti Subho replied,

"Yes, I have read his teachings, Marcus - I recognize him as a silent Buddha."

"Is it ok with you if I don't do your meditation technique?" asked Marcus

"Techniques are just a tool that have to be dropped at some point anyway," replied the monk, "and if you want to pursue the path of enquiry that the Sage used then you are welcome to do so."

Freed of the notion of having to become adept at a technique he never really felt comfortable with, Marcus was soon deep into meditation beyond where he had ever been before and experiencing more joy and profound peace within himself than he could have imagined. That he could see Juliana often talking to a stranger surprisingly didn't seem to bother him during the retreat so absorbed he was within. Each hour on the cushion became another journey into a silent unknown.

But coming to the end of the retreat he didn't notice where Juliana had gone and at first it didn't really disturb him either, but when sitting with some of his new friends around a fire on the beach, and he saw

Juliana emerge out of the darkness holding the hand of another man, the flood gates burst.

At first Marcus simply stood up, walked over to them and asked,

"Are you with him now?"

Juliana looked up at him with her beautiful almond eyes, her dark golden hair cascading over her olive shoulders that were draped by a sarong that fell around the beautiful curves of her body, her tanned skin glowing in the firelight, somehow exuding more beauty than ever if that were at all possible, and answered,

"Yes, Marcus"

Marcus kept walking past them straight into the darkness from where they had emerged, saying nothing. Five thousand years of pain boiled up from within and he began to run like a madman, and accompanied by a roaring sound as though the sea had become violent and angry, a sound which he came to realize was actually him and he kept running and kept roaring.

⌇

There were five days before the next ten-day retreat and most of the people remained in the house until the next one began and for five nights Marcus had to listen to Juliana making out with her new boyfriend where they slept together on the verandah - while he lay where he had meditated inside with only a window separating them.

And it was all he could do to stay whole, and to stay whole he had to remain constantly in the moment and that he did and continued to do, to stay completely within and in the present, for any chain of thought would give birth to instant pain and sorrow.

Over the ten days of the second retreat the suffering began to subside, to be replaced by periods of bliss as he fell in love with his inner self again, and while Juliana and her new found love remained at the retreat, he began to pay less attention to them.

By the end of the second ten days, he moved to a friend's house into a tiny windowless cell out the back where he slept on a mat and meditated, and began to read a thick volume called, 'The Life of the Buddha'. He walked to the beach and swam in the mornings before returning to his cell for the rest of the day to sit and read, sit some more and venture within.

A week later Juliana came to talk to him and they sat down together on the edge of a stone well outside of the house.

"You look beautiful Marcus, you look enlightened."

Marcus half smiled at that. Juliana had always wanted him to be more enlightened, more perfect, purer of spirit.

"I told Bia we had parted and she was worried about you," she said.

Marcus felt moved to hear that from his little friend.

"Tell her I will never forget her and that when she grows up, I will come to look for her," he said half-jokingly.

He looked up at Juliana as she began to speak again.

"Marcus, I knew I had to bring you back to India and let go of you after you ran away from me that time in Brazil - I knew you belonged here."

And Marcus knew it was true too.

⌒‿⌒

They did meet again, however. A year later Marcus was living on a house boat in Varanasi, and emerging from below the deck one morning he had noticed two children playing at the waters' edge, had looked more closely and then he had recognized them.

"Bia! Carlinhos!" he called out.

Bia had come running and skipping along the wooden planks that led to his boat and had thrown herself into his arms.

It was her eleventh birthday a few nights later so Marcus organized a party for her on the deck of the boat and there they sat with Bia in his lap the entire evening - he, his close friends on the boats, along with Juliana and her lover. Floating above the waters of the holy river beneath the stars within the very city that had birthed so many beginnings, and endings, of karmas recent and ancient.

It was precious company in a magical time and Marcus, who was learning sitar while in Varanasi had played the only song outside of his raga scales that he had taught himself - his own Varanasi version of Pink Floyd's 'Grantchester Meadows';

Icy wind of night, be gone.
This is not your domain.
In the sky a bird was heard to cry.
Misty morning whisperings and gentle stirring sounds
Belies a deathly silence that lies all around.
Hear the lark a harken to the barking of the wild dog on the shore
See the splashing of the kingfisher flashing to the water.
And a river of green is sliding unseen beneath the boats,
Laughing as it passes through the endless summers making for the
sea........

Only once more would Marcus see Juliana while in India and that was back at the place where they had fallen in love, in Bodh Gaya, and once after that in New York another six years later – in the street in Greenwich village. He would keep a small but sacred place in his heart for that sad-eyed, shamanic woman of illusions for the rest of his life. She died at only forty-seven years of age just as she had always said she would.

His feet played in the holy water
where her ashes swept by
alone within the currents
of darkened life
of illumined death
a fleeting caress
of her sad-eyed tenderness

Chapter 7

Travelling North

Marcus travelled through Gujarat and Rajasthan vowing that having loved and being loved by the most beautiful woman in the world he was now finished with women and would live the life of a celibate.

In Gujarat he journeyed into the desert and stayed in an old Muslim pilgrimage center where the Imam would cry from atop the minaret at dawn and sunset while Marcus wrapped himself in a white but colorfully embroidered blanket woven with camel hair that he had bought from a family of desert nomads. And as the Imam chanted from his tower he would turn to the desert and shrouded within his rough-woven garment, invite the silence of the chilly desert into the new found and joyful emptiness of his heart.

From there, he travelled to the holy places of Mount Abu and Pushkar, the birth place of Brahma the creator, except that each time he set out on a journey he would meet a woman at a train station or in a hotel or just in the street who would beg to travel with him and by the time he came to Pushkar, which in that time happened to be one of his secret places that westerners didn't know about, he was leading an entourage of three women, and a man from the retreat in Goa, Thomas, who he had run into in Mount Abu by chance.

They entered the little temple town with its sacred lake, the abode of Brahma, on the night of Shivaratri with all its inhabitants, of men, women, sadhus and children, all high on bhang.

There were no tourists in Pushkar then, no hostels bar the obligatory rundown government tourist bungalow and not a single sign in English or Hebrew. Marcus eventually found a sadhu friend of his and they camped with him in a medieval room overlooking the lake – a room lined with marble and with arched unglazed windows like you see in ancient romantic miniature paintings where a Prince would be courting his lover, glass of wine in hand - except that that was the last thing Marcus wanted then.

He would rise early while the others still slumbered and wrapped in his blanket, walk to the other side of the lake inhabited by sadhus practicing all those kinds of ascetic tortures that you read about. Sadhus who had withered arms raised above their heads for thirty years, sadhus sleeping on beds of nails, others who would never walk but only roll from one place to the other and still others who would just sit all day beneath a shady banyan tree and chuckle to themselves.

Marcus felt at home with them, adoring all that was an exception to the boring straight jacket of western society. He loved these timeless places, and he loved this edge of insanity with its still center of abiding calm and as much as he liked his company of friends he wanted to be alone once again and planned to leave by sneaking out unseen on one of the coming mornings. He wished to go back to his cave in Rishikesh and knew his sadhu friends there would be waiting for him and his cave, if Marcus returned, was understood to be his whenever he would reemerge from the vastness of India.

The morning he got up early to sneak out to the bus station he was seen by one of the women, an English girl whose name he couldn't even recall in the moment and of all three women, the one whose company he least enjoyed. She gathered her things and followed him out while the others still slept.

"Elsie," he remembered.

Marcus was too kind, or perhaps simply too soft, to order her to stay but regretted his weakness on the train journey north when he realized she had marked him to be her man and, remarkably, began haranguing him for not returning her love.

It was his train journey from hell and all he could think about was renunciation. He had had enough of women, enough of possessions and money and in that moment was struck with a fervent wish to throw it all away.

Eventually he managed to sleep in the crowded third-class carriage as the English girl continued complaining about everything. He awoke to find her slumped and snoring in his lap and on his other side a middle-aged Indian woman with her head on his shoulder dribbling profusely down his shirt. He looked up and saw hanging down between the slats of the luggage rack the most downwardly sagging balls he had ever seen belonging to an old villager dressed in a turban, and a stained white dhoti that had failed to contain its aging contents as its owner smoked and coughed and racked up mucous from his tarred lungs while his balls swung violently above Marcus' head to the rocking of the train.

"Fuck existence," thought Marcus.

The English girl woke up about an hour from Delhi and wiping saliva from her mouth straight away started to complain again - complained she was hungry and, 'why hadn't Marcus bought her some food?' complained that she needed to go to the toilet but the toilet was overflowing with feces and, worse, she asked Marcus where 'they' were going to stay in Delhi.

He turned to her and said as gently as he could that he wished to stay alone, that he had vowed to be celibate. That was a mistake because she began a tirade of abuse accusing Marcus of being conceited because he thought she wanted him for sex when she 'felt' they were destined to be together on a 'spiritual journey' and that she had so much that 'she' could help him with.

The train from Ajmir pulled into Delhi and they gathered their light belongings and took a rickshaw to Connaught place in the center of New Delhi.

"Where are we going?" she whined.

"I don't know," answered Marcus impatiently.

"What do you mean you don't know? you told me you know everything in Delhi."

"Yes, that I do, but right now I don't know what I am going to do with you," he responded with blatant irritation.

"Well, I need to eat and you've known I've been hungry for hours - why do you only think about yourself?"

"Come," said Marcus, leading her into a nearby busy local restaurant, or 'dhaba' as the Indians named them. He hesitated at the entrance while she walked inside in a crush of bodies milling around the counter. But Marcus stepped back on to the street and straight away disappeared down a lane way only to become surrounded by a large frenzy of beggar women tugging at his clothes before they collectively vanished down the next alley as suddenly as they had appeared.

In the space of a minute Marcus had managed to lose the English girl, his passport and all his traveler's cheques and money, his wish on the train having been wholly fulfilled.

Contemplating instant karma, he made his way to the park behind the Hanuman temple. Sleeping without money would not be an issue as he could sleep anywhere and had slept in this park many times before when not wishing to blow money and anyway, apart from the fact that you had to bathe under a tap in the open he preferred to sleep under a tree than sleep in the cheap dives on offer around Connaught place and Pahar Ganj.

But eating without money was another thing. He could beg like a monk but then he looked around and observed the many beggars and down and out people struggling to survive in India, thought that wouldn't be fair.

Finally, he decided that having nothing was not really necessary, so he made his way to the American Express Office nearby to start the process of getting his travelers cheques returned. It wasn't uncommon for travelers in those days to cash their money and cheques on the black market and then quickly claim them as stolen. Even passports were sold like that and as he waited in the office he looked around and wondered how many of the people in there were doing just that.

That's when the girl sidled up to him and in a west coast American accent asked,

"Hi, what's your name? I'm Cindy."

"Hi Cindy, I'm Marcus."

"You look a bit down Marcus - did you lose your money?"

"No, I am just meditating."

"Oh, there is no need to meditate and do all of that, really."

"Really?"

"Oh no, all you have to do is ask Jesus into your heart."

"Oh fuck," thought Marcus, "can this day get any worse?"

But Cindy wouldn't let go. She followed Marcus outside after he completed the necessary paperwork - one week, was what he had been told - one week with no money in Delhi and he would have to return the next day with a police report as well.

"You can come to our home if you like Marcus."

"I have to go to the Embassy now and try and get a new passport."

Cindy kept following him all the way to the embassy and gleaned from Marcus a bit of his history including the fact he had been living in Brazil so when he returned the following day to American Express with the police report and very hungry, the next girl to approach him with Jesus in her heart was a young Brazilian.

"Hullo. Are you Marcus?" she twinkled at him, "my name is Carolina. I am from Brazil."

"Amazing," replied Marcus, "what a coincidence."

In the end Marcus went with them, stayed in their house, sang Jesus pop songs, asked Jesus into his heart, participated in group hugs, resisted being bedded by Carolina, ate their food over the space of a week and left for Rishikesh the day he got his money and passport back.

Thanking them for the hugs and the apple pie as he waved goodbye to their downcast faces, he called back to their collective pitying expression,

"Don't worry, Jesus loves us all - even the sinners."

On the train to Rishikesh Marcus felt free and elated and alone at last, returning to his beloved cave on the banks of the swift flowing Ganges where the river of the Goddess swept out of the Himalayas and on to the plains. Except that no sooner had he crossed the ferry boat to Swarga Ashram on the other side of the river and stepped ashore he ran into Belle, one of the women he had fled from in Pushkar.

"Marcus!"

"Belle"

"I knew I would find you here."

"Really?"

"Yes, you told me all about Rishikesh when we were in Rajasthan, you don't remember? are you going to stay in your cave?" she asked.

"Yes, I am, Belle."

"Are you going there now?"

"Yes"

"Is it far? can I come with you to see it?"

"No, it isn't far - we go past the ashrams down river to where the path ends."

Belle was German, tall and quite pretty in a big boned, Germanic way with big round eyes - and brown hair he could only guess because it had been died red with henna and by its darkish tone, knew it to have been naturally brown.

⌘

As they made their way along the river past the line of "money" ashrams, as Marcus described them, memories came flooding back from a year ago when he had walked along here with Juliana and Carlinhos with Bia riding on his shoulders as she loved to do. He recalled how they had joked and laughed about the garishly painted Gods who had been "locked" in cages so they wouldn't cause trouble. Rishikesh had become a virtual spiritual Disneyland for Westerners since the Beatles had descended on the Maharishi's ashram and a mecca for Indians and westerners alike seeking to learn Yoga. Everywhere there were colorfully decorated walls with statues carved within, and standing sentinel without. Statues and carvings of Siva and Parvati, Rama, Sita and Laxman, of Krishna and Radha, elephant headed Ganesha, Hanuman the monkey God, and finally the ferocious Durga flaying demons with a sword from the back of her Lion.

The last of the 'money ashrams' loomed ahead – a particularly garish building lacking the artistic charm of the previous ones.

⌒⌒⌒

"This ashram, Belle, was built by a Rishikesh baker who figured out that the Swamis were raking in more money than him, so he dressed himself in orange, learned some yoga asanas and started collecting money from pilgrims to build his ashram - now he runs it like a kind of hotel and charges like a wounded bull to teach westerners yoga."

"I would like to learn more yoga asanas while I am here, Marcus – who would you recommend?"

"Well, certainly not him and certainly not Bal yogi back towards Laxman Jhula – unless you like hash cookies and tantric sex, that is – maybe Shivananda ashram, pretty Hindu purist over there."

Belle merely raised her eyes,

"Thanks, Marcus," before changing tack, "what happened to Elsie, Marcus? we all thought you must have eloped with her," she said chuckling.

"I killed her."

"You what?"

"I threw her off the train."

A confused smile crossed Belle's face.

"You're joking, right?"

"No"

"Come on Marcus?"

"Well, how many times do you have to imagine pushing someone off a train before it has the same karmic consequence of actually doing it?"

He turned to Belle and laughingly recounted the trip and how he had lost Elsie before being holed up in Delhi with the Children of God waiting for his money and passport.

Leaving the line of ashrams, Marcus led Belle along the path past a rocky shoreline where the Ganga swept and then roared away again as it dipped and thrashed its way violently past a point where forested hills began to rise up from the river.

"That is where the caves are Belle," said Marcus, gesturing with his hand past an enormous old banyan tree overhanging a raised half wall that curved around and butted into the rock face of the hill at which point a very old two-story hermitage lay in semi ruin.

Marcus pointed to the spot, saying,

"That is where a swami called Scorpion Baba sleeps and meditates when he comes to Rishikesh but somehow I have yet to encounter him – he gets his name from his power to cure scorpion bites by drawing a yantra on the area of the bite."

As he approached the caves, he saw old Swamiji - for that is all anyone called him - rise up from the stony landscape, and upon seeing Marcus, break into a gentle and toothless smile. Years before Marcus and his friend Graeme had travelled through the mountains with Swamiji on a pilgrimage. Swamiji came and gently embraced Marcus and then stepped back and bade Belle a more reserved hullo in accordance with his vows. The large frame and broad smiling face of Surendra with his easy laugh that rolled out from behind an enormous bushy jet-black beard now loomed in front of them and Marcus was crushed in a bear hug from the Yogi. Marcus noticed that Surendra and his sadhu nephew, Krishna Das, had been busy with building a new stone hermitage above the caves - they must have shifted a good ten tons of rock bare handed up from the river.

"Is my cave empty?"

"Yes, yes, empty"

As they crouched to enter the cave, wider than the others and deep, but only high enough to sit and not stand upright, Belle exclaimed,

"I love it here, Marcus."

Marcus didn't answer but felt his heart groan.

The next morning, however, Belle appeared at the front of the cave with her back pack while Marcus was still in meditation.

"I've decided to move in with you."

"I wouldn't advise you to Belle."

Belle slipped off her pack and brushing back her hair she lay back on the sandy floor and stretched her legs and arms alongside Marcus.

"Don't worry Marcus, I will just meditate and I won't disturb you."

"You really shouldn't stay here."

Belle sat up, plainly annoyed.

"And why not? you don't exactly own the cave and we are friends after all."

"Because everyone who shares this cave with me dies."

Marcus was scrambling for excuses and thought he had come up with a good one - it happened to be true.

"What? are you joking again?"

"No"

"Seriously now Marcus?"

"Well, there was Hans, who I used to share this cave with in the beginning - he was a real pain in the neck - he fasted himself to death because he wanted to prove to me that we could live on air."

"You're kidding me."

"No, I am not kidding."

"And then there was American Harvey."

"And what happened to… to Harvey?"

"Well, we were having a very spiritual discussion one night and I was emphasizing that in the end nothing, absolutely nothing that happens in this world really matters."

"And - go on."

"Harvey had been dealing acid in India and was carrying plenty with him and the following night he took some and while peaking, he ran straight into the Ganga right here in front of us - naked - and was last seen being carried away by the rapids - laughing and shouting, 'nothing matters, nothing matters, nothing matters'"

By this time, Bell's jaw had seriously dropped and her big eyes had grown into enormous orbs.

"And then there was a third one."

"No way"

"Not so interesting really - after staying in the cave with me she went back to Australia, lost the plot, ended up in a mental asylum and suicided."

"Nothing to do with me though," assured Marcus with his hands raised in the air.

"I don't know whether to believe any of this," said Belle with an obstinate look in her eye, "and anyway it won't happen to me - I feel good here."

Marcus sat there a few moments in silence and wondered what the hell was going on. He had vowed celibacy from the moment he had begun the second retreat in Goa, had told himself that he was finished with women but ever since leaving Goa he hadn't managed to be alone without one for more than a day and now Belle was spreading her mat and blanket a meter away and settling into meditation pose seemingly determined not to die.

A few days passed and then Tom turned up with another man who Marcus knew from Goa.

Now there were four of them from the retreat staying here in Rishikesh, and learning that Kitti Subho would do a series of retreats in the mountains over summer, they made plans to go together.

"Marcus, have you heard of Ananda Moy Ma, the Bengali saint?" asked Tom.

"Yes, but haven't read any books about her, why?"

"She is coming to Haridwar to one of her ashrams tomorrow and I am going to go down this afternoon - you want to come?"

"Sure"

"Me too," chimed in Belle.

So, Marcus and Belle rolled up their mats, each throwing a clean shirt and a toothbrush in their shoulder bags and headed off to Haridwar with the other two. Haridwar was just around thirty kilometers downstream and perhaps an even holier place than Rishikesh in the Hindu tradition. It was one of the few places in India that was privileged to hold the Kumbha Mela, the once in twelve-year spiritual mega festival that attracted millions of pilgrims, holy men and sadhus from all over India to bath and pray in the Ganga during the most auspicious of times.

Marcus loved the narrow Haridwar bazaar that snaked through the old city down to the river with its little hole in the wall shops stacked with colorful cloth, beads and malas, statues of the gods, shiny brass and dull clay cooking utensils, beedi and betel nut sellers and chai shops but most of all the shadowy corner where the rotund shop owner sat cross legged perched above an enormous vat of boiling buffalo milk stirring it slowly while serving customers lassis by the day, hot milk in the evenings - lassi drinks made by whipping rich and creamy buffalo curd with ice and either salt or sugar according to taste and with an added touch of rose water.

Marcus couldn't come to Haridwar without paying a visit to this shop.

Evening time in Haridwar was always a beauty filled spectacle down by the river. Brahmin priests sat on their little dais' perched above the water performing pujas for happy lives, for a child, for the loss of a loved one for success in business, for luck in marriage. At the crowded water's edge pilgrims pushed little leaf boats filled with rose and marigold petals and burning candles into the river in the fervent hope that the holy Ganga would carry away their sins.

Marcus and the others joined them doing likewise. It was beautiful with the candle lights dancing off the water to the backdrop of colorful temples and the little boats bobbing away downstream. Belle was enjoying herself, her face a riot of ashen Siva stripes sweeping across her forehead and red and yellow paste smeared over her third eye.

Marcus sat with his legs immersed in the Ganga but with a growing sense of ancient familiarity with the place - and for a few moments seemed to know the next verses of each chant as they droned off the lips of the nearby priest.

Arriving at the ashram of Ananda Moy Ma later in the evening they were told that all the sleeping quarters were full so they slept in the little park wedged between the ashram and the river.

Ananda Moy Ma was a Bengali saint renowned for both her inner and outer beauty. Another famous Indian saint, Swami Sivananda had once described her as 'the most perfect flower that India has ever produced'.

Despite her wonderful reputation Marcus had heard that she was constantly surrounded by pious old Brahmins who hovered around her with a mixture of fervent devotion and jealous possessiveness.

"Tell me about the book you are reading, Marcus," asked Belle as the four of them continued to lounge by the river.

"It's the Mahabharata," he answered.

"What is the Mahabharata? I don't know it."

"It has to be the greatest epic ever written in the history of the world - the story of the war between the ancient Kuru clans, and part of the story is the Bhagavad Gita."

Marcus took his eyes off the pages and looked over to Belle, asking her,

"You have heard of the Gita no doubt?"

"Yes," she said, but Marcus could guess she didn't know much.

"The Gita is the teaching of Krishna as spoken to Arjuna just before the battle began."

"And so, Krishna talked him out of fighting?"

"No, the opposite, Krishna convinced him to fight."

"But I thought Krishna was all about peace, that he was an avatar of God?" Belle looked almost offended.

"Krishna was teaching Arjuna that he had to fulfill his dharma and his dharma as a Kshatriya was to complete the war he had helped instigate - but to do so with detachment - understanding that all that would happen was already destined to happen," Marcus answered.

"Can you read us some Marcus?" asked Belle.

"Sure, Belle,"

And so, Marcus began to read,

"Says Arjuna, plagued with doubt,"

⌒⌒⌒

'How shall I in battle, slayer of Madhu,
with arrows fight against Bheesma and Drona,
the two venerable enemies, slayer of foes?
Instead of killing noble gurus
it is better to live by begging in this world
having killed gurus desiring gain here on earth -
I should enjoy pleasures smeared with blood.
Nor do we know which of these two is more important for us,
whether we should conquer or if they should conquer us,
those standing before us, the sons of Dhritarashtra,
whom having killed, we should not want to live.
"The blessed Lord said,
'You grieve for those who should not be grieved for
yet you speak wise words.
Neither for the dead nor those not dead do the wise grieve.
Never was there a time when I did not exist
nor you nor these lords of men.
Neither will there be a time when we shall not exist -
we all exist from now on.
As the soul experiences in this body
childhood, youth, and old age,

so also, it acquires another body -
the sage in this is not deluded."

Having slept the night under the trees and having being sung to sleep by the river they were awake in time to witness the commotion as Ma arrived by car, pulling up outside the large double doors of the ashram that led directly into the Satsang hall.

Tom had approached the ashram manager early that morning to make sure we could get in to see her but shortly after her arrival we saw the manager walking over to us in the park.

"I am most sorry to inform you but as there are so many, many people here Ma's attendants have told me there is no place for westerners today."

Marcus nodded his head in customary Indian manner.

"There is absolutely no chance of seeing her later?"

"No, I am very sorry sir."

"OK then"

Belle started to object, finding it hard to accept that we had come all this way only to be refused.

"How dare they discriminate against foreigners."

"Don't worry about it - it's India - things happen the way they are meant to," Marcus said philosophically, and throwing his blanket and bag over his shoulder, began to lead the way to the bus station.

As he approached the ashram doors there was a throng of Indian devotees around the entrance and Marcus thought it would be impossible to catch even a glimpse of the beatific saint as more and more people were pushing to get in.

But drawing level with the doors something made him turn in that direction and incredibly, in that moment, there was nobody in front of the doors and nobody else inside the hall visible to him except, sitting on a lavishly cushioned platform, was Ananda Moy Ma looking tens of years younger than her seventy-nine.

Marcus froze. Ma turned to him and placing the palms of her hands together touched them to her forehead and then, with a most fluid and graceful motion alike a lotus flower unfolding, she spread her palms towards Marcus showering pure love into his heart. He joined his hands in pranayama in response, bowing his head but when he raised his eyes again the doorway was once more filled with people pushing to get in and she was lost to sight.

"Thank you, Ma, thank you."

The perfect manifestation of God's love
is not to be grasped
as the palms of the lotus
unfold
her elegant fingers
tearing asunder
my heart

Chapter 8

Nothing to Search For

The five of them made their way up from the waterfall as dusk fell in the pine forest. It was July, and the monsoon was in full swing and streams and rivulets found every gully on the sides of the mountains they could do, to cascade and bubble downwards through the low-lying cloud and mist clinging to the steep slopes.

The path was narrow but not too muddy, bedded as it was by layers of pine needles and soft to Marcus' bare feet, soft to the feet of Georgina, Anna, Tom and Mick who followed him silently up the hill.

"What is that smell?" Marcus asked all of a sudden, halting abruptly.

The forest was descending into semi darkness and shadows.

"Bear," responded Georgina, "that's a Bear, no mistake," and then in more hushed tones, "I know it from my time camping back home in the Rockies - we had better keep moving and if he attacks, we run downhill, not up."

Marcus knew the danger. He had once walked curiously through the cemetery in the town that spread out around the bottom of the mountain and noted that one in three of the dead in that English graveyard seemed to have died from a bear mauling.

"Oh, very funny," piped up Mick who was trailing at the end.

"Mick," we are not joking exclaimed Georgina.

"Ha ha, as if," Mick called back carelessly.

Marcus turned around and observing the line of friends, every one of them in their early to mid-twenties, he saw that Anna was walking along with that slightly serious, slightly bemused look she often had, with the hint of a frown creasing her brow. Tom was glancing nervously over his shoulder while Mick, slightly rotund with a babyish face and thick glasses was half smiling, half questioning, plodding up the hill.

"Jesus," thought Marcus, "he will have no hope if that bear attacks."

For whatever reason, the bear mustn't have felt threatened by the troop of playful innocents and by the time they reached the dirt road that circled the top of the mountain they knew that the danger had passed.

"You guys were kidding, right," said Mick as they all sat down for a breather.

In chorus the rest of them replied:

"Noooo!"

"Oh, really - were we in real danger then?"

"Yeess!"

"Shite!"

⌒⌣⌣⌒

As the party got up to head back to the main retreat house, one of many grand old stone houses built by the British colonialists to escape the blistering heat of the Punjab during summer but now slowly decaying in the hands of their Indian owners, Marcus suggested to Anna that they leave the others and keep going the long way back around to his house. Marcus had his own crumbling bungalow higher up on a ridge that jutted out westward but with views from the front to the snow-mountains and glaciers that rose up beyond the narrow Chamba Valley. To the back, the plains of the Punjab stretched infinitely in to the haze of smoke and mist that shrouded India at all times.

Those were the plains over which countless armies had marched for glory and conquest over the ages. The Aryans, to conquer the tribes of Dravidians, and the modern Persians, by then converted to the beliefs of the prophet Mohammed thousands of years later. From the Punjab, the British had set off to subjugate Afghanistan before limping back again defeated and disgraced, but long ago, long before all of these armies, Karna had marched north and west to subjugate the ancient kingdoms of Gandara and Kham Bojja and had ventured within the foothills to the West to defeat the Bhailikars.

The army of Alexander the Great, whose campaign to unite the whole of the known world under his benevolent and iron rule had finally ground to a halt somewhere down there. It was told, that after a meeting with a penniless Sadhu, Alexander had understood the profound truths of which this ancient land had to offer and he was said to have asked to be buried with his hands turned upwards to show the world that the man who had conquered all had died with nothing.

As they sat down together watching the last of the summer light fade into darkness over the plains, Marcus gently took Anna's hand and said,

"I am going to miss our walks."

"And our talks," Anna responded smilingly.

She was German, petit, with tanned skin and straight blond hair that hung loosely either side of a pretty and always pleasant face. Raised in the high country of Bavaria alongside the border with Austria she had found her childhood affection with her grandmother rather than her conservative parents and had recounted to Marcus how her grandmother had taken her for walks through the woods and fields of Bavaria showing her the plants and herbs she used for cooking and healing - a rare survivor of an ancient knowledge that had been all but wiped out by the insanely cruel Christian inquisition that prolonged in Germany long after the Spanish had tired of the burnings and the screaming.

Marcus could have kissed her then and there if he had had the courage - or the will.

But in truth, he was as glad she was leaving as he was sad.

For six weeks they had been walking and chatting together – stories from their lives and stories that had brought them discoveries and knowledge from the past,

"Me too," he had responded to her, "I was obsessed with the Cheyenne when I was a kid," when she recounted to him her previous visit to America and that particular tribe.

And they had shared the cooking duties in the main house for one of the retreats.

At the end of each ten-day meditation there would be ten days of more relaxed meditation and talks before the next intensive began again - ten days on, ten days off and it was in those afternoons before the evening talk in the off days that they would wander off into the woods together, never even holding hands but making love in their hearts and minds. Why? Plato would have smiled to see them.

This was the day that Anna had to leave. Her visa had run out and her money was dwindling.

"Let's write to each other," said Marcus as he walked her to the gate.

"Let's, yes. I would love that," she replied, and while doing so took his hand in his, looking up at Marcus as they hugged goodbye, as he deftly averted the kiss that he saw coming, knowing that that would be the end of his resistance.

"I will send you one of my little paintings once a week," he called after her as she turned around to wave one more time before he could see the flash of her torchlight no more and was gone.

When Marcus descended the ridge to the main retreat house the next day, he encountered Belle sitting on the steps. She looked up as he approached.

"Hi Belle"

"So, did you guys make out last night?"

"What?"

"You heard me - did you and Anna make out last night?"

"No, we just chatted and then we hugged goodbye."

"You're an idiot, Marcus."

"But I'm celibate and we are all meant to be celibate during the retreats."

"You're an idiot Marcus."

Marcus responded by going into the meditation hall and sitting unmoving for three hours until his mind and emotions were as still as the sludge of a lotus pond.

Indeed, for the next few months Marcus sat on his cushion and meditated and sat by the window looking out over the monsoonal clouds while painting miniature water colors of winged dragons and winged angels and of clouds and rainbows that he sent religiously to Anna once a week - and the occasional one to Juliana.

He didn't walk so much in the woods anymore but then the first letter and drawing arrived from Anna. It was a drawing of them both holding hands and dancing in the woods with a bear.

Years later she would be able to tell him more about that - after she journeyed into the past beyond the life she was currently living, that is.

Six months had almost passed since they had begun the first of the retreats on that mountain and now the last ten-day retreat was about to begin, Marcus being the only one who hadn't left the mountain at all during that time.

Others had come and gone and returned again, or gone back home altogether to be replaced by new arrivals. During those precious months, they were Marcus' family and would remain so for years after. The familiarity between them, the light in their faces after so much meditation and the glow that surrounded them was something special.

Marcus, however, was unhappy. He felt he had not yet discovered himself and wanted desperately to be free, free from all of it. How could he leave the mountain without uncovering the secret of existence?

On a regular basis Marcus would host a group of people in his house to do the ten days of intensive retreat with him there and they would all descend for the talk at night, but the day before the retreat was to begin, the Monk appeared and asked Marcus to sit the final ten days in the main house. He didn't object.

That afternoon he was packing a few things to go down when Georgina walked into his room. She had been staying in his house for a while but she too was descending to the main house for the final retreat.

"Fuck me, Marcus."

"What?"

"Make love to me for Christ's sake, I'm as horny as hell."

"But Georgina, you're going to go straight back to America - and getting married!"

Georgina spread out her arms and grinned, her eyes wide with expectation.

"Exactly damn it - this is my last chance Marcus - after this it's all over."

"Then why get married if you're not ready for it?"

"Oh, fuck Marcus, I don't know - all I know right now is I am horny as all shit and I can't stand being around you without you fucking me."

"No Georgina, you're crazy - it doesn't feel right."

"Then just come here and give me a hug, damn it."

So, they hugged. A long sensuous hug with Georgina's soft breasts pushing against Marcus and he felt his sex start to swell, the thing oblivious to Marcus' spiritual path.

"OK Georgina, enough, please!"

They disentangled laughing. She placed her hand on Marcus' cheek and said,

"Have a good one Marcus."

～⌇～

By the eighth day of the retreat Marcus's third eye was exploding in pain. The migraine had steadily built up since about day five as he pushed himself to meditate unabated from four in the morning until twelve at night, such was his determination. The Monk told him to go for a walk around the mountain but he said, "no, it is just pain - I will handle it."

By the eighth day, as sometimes happened, the silence was beginning to break with people began to chat here and there, but not Marcus - he sat, he ate, walked in the garden and then sat some more for hour upon hour, unspeaking, all the time enquiring.

"Who am I?"

"Who am I?"

During the evening talk his body as well as his head became racked with pain with his mind free falling into darkness and despair and every idea of enlightenment, every hope of salvation, every yearning for peace was just so much useless babble. He wanted to get up and run but that also seemed fruitless and pointless - run to where, to whom?

That was when the words, "there is nothing to search for," came drifting into his consciousness.

There was nothing - no hope, no enlightenment, no Marcus. There was him - he who had always been here, simple, simplicity itself, nothing special. Free by his very nature, the very source of all things from where the idea of Marcus, the idea of the existence of the world and the entire universe arose.

Timeless, no past, no future and not even a present, he had always simply been, from time eternal – he simply was. He was that, that death could not touch as it was never born.

Yet somehow, he realized, the mind began recognizing itself as the source of itself - and he was amazed.

With him now in the form of a witness, the mind mysteriously activated itself again and began to reflect on this truth, "so this is enlightenment! but there is no-one who is enlightened!"

It occurred to him immediately that the path of meditation and all the retreats he had done, all the forms and techniques, the teachers and the gurus he had encountered along the way were also only a play on the surface.

It had been this inner knowing - this passion to return to itself that had been guiding him all along until the passion had consumed itself and he, the individual, had simply fallen by the way.

But there was even more that started to reveal itself to the greater mind – the mind as arising from the source of all things. He, as the witness, saw the life of Marcus continuing from that moment until its death, saw himself going back into the world to live life to its full.

His future was unravelling itself before him, not in every detail but as a road map of his existence. He saw in his dream life being loved and loving anew and felt it to be him but with a different sense of me although still experiencing loss and pain, joy and grief, in a long slow waltz to his death, but a death where he would merge into the peace of this eternal knowingness. In fact, all through the life that played out before him, his true self would always be there beneath the pantomime of his dream existence, sometimes fully conscious of itself, sometimes appearing veiled by the dramas of existence.

Marcus finally left the mountain and journeyed to Rishikesh along with two companions who had likewise understood that which had been revealed to him - Tricia and Matt. The three played for a while in the sands of the Ganges, staying together in the caves and here Marcus read to them from the Diamond Sutra, The Life of Ramana and the Bhagavad Gita - beautiful books of truth whose words dripped like nectar from their pages.

"I never really got the Gita, what, with all the war and killing," said Tricia one day.

Marcus laughed and remembered Belle saying almost the same thing.

"It isn't necessarily about war, Tricia, it is about following the dharma you have chosen to follow, completing your worldly responsibilities in the knowing of the supreme truth - and more than that, it has some beautiful descriptions of the ultimate."

"Read me some," she asked.

"Sure"

Marcus crossed his legs into a half lotus, picked up a hand full of white river sand in homage to the versus of the Diamond Sutra, allowing it to run through his fingers, and began to read. Tricia smilingly followed suit. The great river rolled past in swirling currents between huge boulders at this point, green and inviting.

On the far bank a sadhu was bathing and washing his ochre robes, meticulously laying them over hot flat stones before seating himself in meditation dressed only in his minimal underwear. He began to chant and fantastically, Marcus could hear the very verse he was about to read – or swore he could.

He randomly opened the Gita and began to read,

"I am the ritual; I am the sacrifice; offering am I,
I am the medicinal herb; the mantra am I,
I am clarified butter; I am fire; I am the oblation.
I am the father of this universe, mother, supporter,
grandfather, what is to be known, purifier, sacred AUM,
the origin, dissolution, state, treasury, seed eternal.
I radiate heat; I withhold and send forth rain,
immortality and death, and truth and untruth am I, Arjuna."

Chapter 9

The Serpent's Eye

Marcus set up camp in the forest on the ridge between the two valleys and it was here that the community had planned to build the retreat center. Still fresh from his time in India and full of the light of a great revelation into the mystery was his original self, the world was at his feet and this adventure had more or less fallen into place through a meeting with a girl who lived on the commune below and whose heart was set on building a forest retreat center.

She had asked him. He had said yes, he would help her build it. But there was no-one else yet, just them.

Marcus' parents with whom he had landed on his return must have expected him to linger for longer in the comforts of their home convinced that he would, now that his travels were over, follow in the path of his uncle whom they had named him after. His Uncle was a gay alcoholic who had lived with Marcus' grandfather until the grandfather had passed away. Marcus had liked him.

"But you don't know how to build," his father had said.

"I will learn."

"But where will you stay?"

"In a tent"

"Who is paying for the building materials?"

"Existence will."

"What do you mean?"

"If it is meant to happen it will find a way to happen."

~⌇~

The rainforest was very, ancient and there were giant Eucalypts too large for their arms to meet when they embraced the trunks together. There were trees of all sizes and he would soon learn which were best to cut for building. The ones which had the highest oil content would be most resistant to rot and to termites.

There were numerous giant ghosts scattered through the forest too, ringbarked during the great depression of the thirties in an ill thought government employment scheme to be left standing, naked of leaves, awaiting the day thirty years, forty years later when their resistance to rot and gravity finally gave way. Yet still, this part of the forest had never been properly cleared and somehow many of the giants had survived.

The great trees that had fallen were numerous and now lay across the forest floor adding a mystique to the undergrowth, their enormous trunks stretching out for up to thirty or more meters and covered in moss and lichens and decorated with ferns and luminescent fungi.

~⌇~

The first night after Susanna had left for the commune at the bottom of the hill Marcus sat there alone around the campfire being entertained by the light of the fire flies and the chorus of the cicadas.

A new sound came rumbling up from the gully a little way distant and to his mind it sounded like a cross between a pig and a motor bike and for a moment his hair stood on end until he realized it was a Koala on a search for a mate. Still, for just a moment, a wave of primordial fear, the fear of the lurking beast, had washed over him.

Kicking the camp fire dead with a layer of earth and confident that it would not spark again he went and brushed his teeth before laying down on his sleeping mat, first thoroughly checking that no deadly snakes or spiders had crawled into his bag.

It was in the twilight between awake and sleep that Marcus found himself outside of his tent looking back at it - in great surprise.

He looked around and yes, he was outside and, in the forest, just as if it were in real life and one of the fallen moss and lichen covered giants of the forest floor was transforming itself in front of his eyes.

The moss cover became smooth and glistened and the trunk began to move, a giant serpent head forming at its front end nearest to where Marcus stood and completely paralyzed as he watched helplessly what was taking place before his eyes. The trunk was soon fully transformed and the snake began to wind its way between the standing trees in his direction, opening its great fangs in malevolent threat.

His raw instinct was fear, flight and survival but there being no escape, he simply surrendered. In the moment of surrender he was no longer Marcus but the silent spirit that was the same as the origin of the snake itself and his fear dissolved into the great innocence as it does when all is lost.

"We are one and the same my friend and here there are no differences," he almost heard himself saying.

The giant serpent stopped dead in the moment of Marcus' surrender and Marcus sensed it asking him,

"What are you doing here in my domain," the serpent demanded,

Marcus' answer came in the form of an image, of the meditation retreat center.

The serpent bowed its head to him and began to recede backwards through the trees until it reformed once again into the shape of the fallen decaying sentinel.

Marcus sat bolt upright inside his tent again in a start.

Years later he asked of an Aboriginal elder,

"What is the deity that inhabits this ridge?"

"Why, the Carpet Snake of course, why?" she had answered immediately.

I spoke to you then
do you not remember?
your old dreams
your distant journeys

when my serpent's eye
watched over you
like a kindly mother

when my serpent's breath
had kissed your fear
that you fear no other

Chapter 10

Wild Rivers and Snake Venom

Doug wandered into the camp on dusk along with Gummy and Winiata, the trans Māori mariachi. Immediately Marcus noticed Doug's eyes that were no more than two narrow slits over a tightly drawn face.

Marcus didn't say anything at first but turned back to lighting the campfire now that the danger of searching helicopters had passed with the fall of night. Christina sidled her young body up to his while Adrian and Jen began taking down the light nylon tent flys that were strung across the campsite by day to keep their gully hideout hidden from the air.

Now they could relax and enjoy the fire and quietly contemplate the night stars above until Winiata found the mood to bring out his guitar and strum an innocent island melody and later they would fall asleep huddled together for warmth upon the soft brown peat floor of this most ancient of forests. With Christina on one side and Winiata, the other, Marcus would dream of the watching Thylacine as it paused to gaze upon the strangers for a moment before continuing its forlorn search for another of its kind.

But having satisfied himself with the success of his fire, he turned to look up at Doug who had parked himself on the other side of the flames to Marcus, his face lit up in the firelight and along with his intense and squinty eyes, giving him a red and demonic appearance.

"What the fuck are you on, Doug?"

Gummy chuckled, Christina looked up sharply to see what Marcus was seeing in Doug. Doug half grinned, half grimaced as he answered,

"Black tiger snake venom – we found one on the way back from taking the sacrificial lambs to the slaughter – caught it and milked it….," his voice trailing off as his face returned to its demonic grimace.

The sacrificial lambs were their name for the boatloads of protestors who now had to be ferried up the river in the night since the government had cleared out and made illegal, the main campsite. Met by Marcus and his small band and bedded down overnight within the forest before being guided along the secret paths by day to the dam building site, the protestors would appear out of nowhere to block the work of the bulldozers and chainsaws before being rounded up and arrested.

It was a game of numbers, a game played out on the national TV screens as school teachers, doctors, students, and all manner of citizens made their stand, purposely flooding the jails to breaking point to force the hand of the government to bring a halt to the work – a halt to the destruction of one of the last great wildernesses the earth still offered.

⌒⌒⌒

As a child, Marcus could see from their farm, the high bluffs of the Western Tiers rising up to the Tasmanian south-west where his father's best friend had told him stories of the wild rivers and of the giant beech and huon pine forests that had defied human intrusion since the beginning of time - until now.

And here, twenty years later, Marcus was himself exploring, mapping trails and testing the wildest forest in the world where he would encounter sudden dramatic changes in temperature, venturing out for two days at a time with nothing more than a tent fly and bags of dried fruit and nuts, chewing on the leaves of sassafras to sustain his energy.

He had to be careful not to fall through the false forest floors made up of a secondary vertical forest that had been so choked with rotted foliage compacted over time, that it gave the appearance of being the actual ground. As always, Marcus imagined that the Thylacine was quietly watching him, following his every step, his always companion upon a lonely trail.

~ ~ ~

Doug was rocking back and forth, muttering to himself. Gummy and the others were stoned. Christina wrapped her arms around Marcus' waist, laying her head upon his lap. Winiata finally pulled out his guitar. The music was somehow incongruous to the setting – perfectly and beautifully incongruous.

Some enchanted evening
When you find your true love,
When you feel her call you
Across a crowded room,
Then fly to her side,
And make her your own
For all through your life you
May dream all alone.
Once you have found her,
Never let her go.
Once you have found her,
Never let her go!

On the far side of the fire, Doug lay on his side emitting a distinct hissing sound as he slithered out of the firelight to wretch somewhere out in the darkness.

Marcus, felt Christina's soft breath fall into sleep. He would be the first to rise in the morning to kick dead the campfire and string the tent flys over his companions, after which he would go out alone to reconnoiter and sabotage what he could at the work site a couple of kilometers distant from their camp.

After doing his work, Marcus decided to venture on through the near impenetrable forest along pathways that followed faint animal tracks before tracing bubbling watercourses to find their destination above the confluence of the two great rivers - to a place beside the Franklin where stood a truly magnificent stand of ancient myrtle-beech. Here the ground was covered in thick green moss where the wildest of rivers slowed to a comparatively sedentary rush. Once there, he sat alone, alone except for the Thylacine and the whoosh of the passing waters.

The government had not only brought in the helicopters but also ex Vietnam army vets to try and find them. They never did. Marcus made his prayer to the lost spirit at his side, Doug had made his to the spirit of the Tiger Snake and Marcus was sure that that spirit never left Doug for the rest of his crazy life.

Together, their prayers were blessed by a river running free.

By the wildest of white waters
a gnarled myrtle beech
four hundred years has sensed
that shadow passing by

If she was ever present
she must be its source
of time
of love
of time's dream

and of the lost but lingering eye
of the very last
of my gentle Thylacine

Chapter 11

Reg's Secret

Marcus pulled the XT on to its stand, unbuckled his helmet and unzipped his leather jacket as he strode into the old cedar lined halls of the council chambers. Portraits of deceased and past mayors stared down at him in disbelief while photos of councilors long gone stood in rows of two, suited and correct save for a slight crumple of a collar here, a misplaced hair vainly trying to cover baldness there.

He wondered what he would wear when it was his turn to be photographed and left for eternity to stare down the newcomers to city hall. A few hours previously he had been stark naked working his vegetable garden. In the years before he could never have imagined he would be here in these timbered halls, thrust into the politics of the city after the machines of destruction came first for the forests and then for their own home-made houses on the communities that spread through the rolling hills to the north of the provincial city.

That was the life he had envisaged, a life of meditation and communal living, an idyllic dream of a new age. Yet his semi transition into one of the city's lawmakers had been a seamless journey for him and he never questioned it once his new journey had begun.

One hour ago, he had eaten a counter meal at the Tatts hotel and finished it off with a shot of whiskey, a good settler for public speaking.

"Must be in the blood," he thought. His ancestral home of Skye was famous for its whiskey. His father, still the hereditary chief of his

Scottish Clan, always had a bottle on the go while his mother's cherished nightcap was whiskey and milk.

But in that moment, the slight nerves in his stomach were in anticipation of the storm he was about to walk into behind the heavy wooden doors that opened at the top of the stairs. He could hear voices up there and as he rounded the bend in the stairs, he saw more than a few familiar faces from the local community milling around on the landing with fists full of papers and council agendas and giving last minute instructions to the councilor they hoped would help them solve their problem, fix their road, get their development passed.

As he reached the top of the stairs most of the faces turned to him, the odd one giving him a stony stare but he was more than a little pleasantly surprised to hear a gathering murmur of greeting and approval. Even from people he didn't know.

∼◡◡◠

Just yesterday the Council general Manager had summoned Marcus into his office.

"You're treading on thin ice boy," he had said in his bush drawl with a half-smile crossing his face.

"And just what are you trying to tell me, Paul?"

"I think you know Marcus."

"No, Paul, please enlighten me."

"You really don't quite know who you are dealing with boy," Paul had asserted.

"Well, Paul, yesterday they were very nice to me - they offered me a job across the other side of the world in their new hotel acquisition in Spain."

Paul nodded, his face turning a bit nasty at this point,

"You would have done well to take it son."

"But I don't speak Spanish Paul, a bit of Portuguese but no Spanish."

At that point Marcus had laughed at the general manager and rising from his seat had said.

"Thin ice, Paul, has the habit of taking down the whole fucking dog team and sled."

～⌣～

Marcus was quite aware of who he was dealing with but Marcus held no fear for his safety. He didn't feel it even if the threats had started coming. It was already too public as his interview about the close relationship between the mayor and his developer friends had been aired on national television last night. But Paul was just trying to scare him but like the leopard who had followed Marcus through the jungle all those years ago he reckoned that if they growl, they just want to warn you off. If they really intend to kill you, they don't warn you.

～⌣～

Fred Harris, the mayor, had grown up in this small city and in his younger days as a local cop, Fred had ruled the streets with fear. Fred had been a Z force commando during the war and Marcus had met a few of his victims from those early years after Fred had joined the police force.

Charlie was one of them. Charlie was a firewood deliverer these days but his brain had been partially damaged by a bit of Fred's tough street discipline in the old times. Charlie still hated Fred with a passion but many of the cities' people thought Fred was the type of cop the place needed.

The town was like that. There were those who hated him and those who loved him and Marcus could guess that there were plenty of old ladies sitting in church on a Sunday who harbored dark secrets about nights with the "Black Prince" as Fred was known back then.

Fred, it had been related to Marcus, had pretty much taken any woman he wanted and if there was a husband or boyfriend involved, well, they just had to grin and bear it. Until the day when Fred had been quietly transferred to Sydney after an incident with a woman in a jail cell and while stationed there, Fred had worked his way up to the rank of Chief Inspector at the notorious Darlinghurst Police Station where the cops had strong links to the underworld scene of crime, drugs and prostitution.

Marcus had no idea at the time as to whether Fred had been up to his neck in all of that but it was said there just didn't exist an honest cop in that place during the sixties and seventies.

Marcus had been friendly with the previous Mayor, Bob Sculthorpe, and had helped Bob win the mayoral vote a few years ago. Bob had been a conservative head of the chamber of commerce coming into council, but within the year he had had Bob drinking tea with Rainbow Guy at the outlandishly illegal seven story Rainbow Temple in the hills and together they had gone a long way to uniting a community previously divided by the protests.

Reg, however, was about as conservative as you could get and Marcus had been at odds with him countless times but back in the drinks room after meetings, he would treat them all as he would any other person. Reg had surprisingly opened up to Marcus one night. They all knew that Marcus had a strange spiritual life - didn't really understand it but they respected his sincerity.

"I'll tell you a story Marcus - maybe you will understand," Reg had said out of the blue one night.

"Sure, Reg, I'm interested."

"Well, it was when I was fighting the Japs on the Kokoda trail."

"You fought on the Kokoda trail?" exclaimed Marcus.

The Kokoda trail was the most legendary of second world war battlefields for Australians. The hardships that the "diggers" suffered in the jungle fighting, the malaria, the mud, the heat and the sheer bloodiness of the conflict was told in many stories. Every child in the country had been raised on stories of the Kokoda.

"We were patrolling in the jungle when we were ambushed by the Japs - there was an exchange of fire and people were diving for cover -

I jumped into the jungle and found myself staring at a Jap soldier who had his gun pointed at my chest," Reg paused and looked at Marcus intently with his wide-open goggly eyes, comically magnified by his thick glasses, "you know what Marcus - an amazing thing happened - I was staring death in the face and all of a sudden, I had never seen so much beauty, the jungle, the trees, the flowers, it was all so beautiful - it was all, well, love."

Reg was reliving the ecstasy and his eyes drifted as he did so.

Marcus was smiling broadly.

"So, what was that, Marcus?"

"God, Reg - in the absence of you there is only God - you checked out - thanks Reg."

"By the way Reg."

"What Marcus?"

"I take it you lived."

Reg laughed and unbuttoning his shirt, jabbed at his chest

"Here is the scar, look - the little Jap bugger shot me right here – you want another beer, Marcus?"

"A shot of whiskey thanks Reg."

"Did I ever tell you the story about the fella I met at my school reunion, Marcus?"

"No Reg."

"Well, there I was…"

There was a mischievous glint in Reg's eye and he tended to start leaning his head forward and squinting when he told a joke.

"And I saw this gorgeous woman and I had to think for a while - she looked kind of familiar but I couldn't place her so I went up and said,

'You look familiar but I can't remember who you are?'

'Well, I remember you Reg,' she had said, 'my name is Roberta but back then it was just Rob.'

'Fucken Jesus Rob! what fucken happened?'

'I had a sex change, Reg.'

And so, I looked at him - big tits and all and I asked him.

'So, did it hurt?'

'What do you mean 'did it hurt?'

'The operation, making your tits bigger? turning your dick into a cunt?'

'Ah no, not so much, that part didn't hurt.'

'So, what part hurt then?'

'Oh, the part that hurt was when they made my brain smaller and my mouth bigger'…"

Reg started guffawing and splashed a bit of beer over Marcus' shirt.

"Thanks Reg, I'll go home and tell it to my wife - she'll love it."

It was in Marcus' nature to make friends and influence people but if there was a confrontation to be had he wouldn't back off and he could meet fire with fire, sometimes too readily.

"Good on you Marcus, about time someone stood up to 'em."

Marcus returned the compliment from the older man in the pressed slacks and an open necked lemon-yellow shirt. He knew him from somewhere but couldn't place him.

As he entered the chambers a silence fell over the heavily wooded hall.

The Mayoral throne lorded over the u-shaped benches of the other eleven councilors, behind which were lined wooden pews like those you would find in a protestant church. The onlookers and the petitioners sat in those.

Heavy wooden panels adorned all of the walls and hanging from them more portraits of past mayors. There was a single pew behind the place where Marcus sat and on to that he dropped his helmet and leather jacket before removing his agenda from his back pack and sitting down.

He glanced up, just for a moment, and as he did so a few faces that had stared stonily in his direction now averted their eyes. Except for Kevin, the Taxi driver and Labor party stalwart who gave him a wink.

Kevin had been with him on this and so had the bespectacled doctor who sat on Marcus' left. The rest of them were either silent or hostile.

Fred began with the usual apologies. There were none. Then, the reading of the minutes, duly passed. The Mayoral minute, Fred calls for his minute on the Manchester building development to be held behind closed doors and the public is cleared of the on lookers and petitioners.

But those who remained close to the thick oak double doors with the stained-glass panels at the top of the stairwell heard Fred lose it.

What they didn't see was the large and hulking frame of Fred with his slicked back and carefully dyed jet-black hair striding down from his throne in the direction of Marcus with his fists closed.

Nor did they see Marcus rise to his feet, a couple of centimeters taller than his furious adversary, place his arm around Fred and turn him back in the direction of his mayoral chair.

The following day Marcus rose with the sun, meditated on his verandah until the warmth of its rays forced him to strip, walked out into his garden naked and began planting marigolds in amongst the newly planted lettuce and broccoli. At around nine, he heard the conch shell blasting from the communal hall at the top of the commune. Washing off his hands with the pure spring water he wrapped himself in an orange sarong and headed up the hill to the gathering, meeting his beautiful little daughter on the way as she came out of her mother's house to take his hand.

The morning mist was rising wispily up through the forest as a kookaburra called laughingly to its mate. It was just the pleasant dream after the insane one after all, but for how long would it last?

How much love
a heart can give?
and how much milk
a breast to share?
And where to place
all the things they want
on a mantle full but bare?

The wounded child
in a scarred man's body
from womb to end's door
But how many crowns
of thorns and gold
'til he breaks upon the shore?

A king no more

Chapter 12

The Master, The Messages, The Revelation

Marcus sat before the Master near the front of the hall, tears streaming from his eyes. Where had he been? He had planned to stay for just two weeks but he knew he could not leave this man, not now.

Back in India after many years, nineteen in all, he had left behind his political involvements in Australia.

Plans, it was often said, are what makes God laugh the hardest, and after India, Marcus had thought he would be on his way to Paris where his young French wife awaited him.

But the visit to this Master had been a long time coming. Seven years since first hearing about him from an old friend, the Master was one of the few living disciples of the sage of Arunachala and now, finally, Marcus was seated before him and overcome with ecstatic and tearful joy.

Marcus had only one fundamental question to ask that still tormented him,

"How was it so, that having understood the nature of his true self, he still was so subject to human frailty and suffering?"

His relationship with Genevieve had been both passionate and troubling.

Days later he put such a question to the Master but the master did not answer him at all, only smiling at him and after some time he had asked Marcus to repeat his question.

But Marcus couldn't find the question anymore, such was the power of silence emanating from the Master. All he could experience was that deep silence that uttered no word and harbored no thought.

Genevieve came to visit him in the end, running out of patience for Marcus to appear in Paris but there was a story to that that unfolded two months later.

In the space of a few days, Marcus had first received a message from his brother that his mother was in hospital with a heart condition and may be dying, another from the mother of his two daughters who lived in Bali saying that she had to go to America urgently and that Marcus must come back to be with his children and then finally, a message from Genevieve demanding to know why he hadn't come to Paris.

With all of these pressing demands calling him from three different corners of the globe, Marcus decided he would just have to deal with them all as quickly as possible.

He approached the Master thinking that the old sage would give him his blessing but instead the Master rebuked him severely, saying,

"You held your true love in your arms, yet now you wish to abandon them for all these women? go if you wish."

The old man summarily dismissed him with a wave of his hand.

Marcus bowed silently, got up and sat back in his place in the large, fully packed hall. He was stunned and in shock. How could he abandon his dying mother, yet how could he abandon his master, his self, his truth?

In the end he did nothing. He retreated to his room and remained there for five days in silence feeling completely broken and torn apart. And that is exactly how he allowed himself to be. Broken, cast out, and in complete despair. And into this despair he dived and swam until there was nothing left but nothing itself.

On the sixth day Marcus ventured out to the Satsang Hall to see if any messages had arrived, half dreading bad news, half expecting furious admonitions from wives past and present. As he approached the table where the old Indian man handed out faxes and mail, he wondered what his reaction would be if he heard that his mother had died.

He loved his mother and she adored him but she demanded much from him and their relationship was such that they couldn't spend too much time in each other's company. But the love between them was strong, almost passionate and at seventy-two years of age she was still a strikingly handsome woman. Marcus recalled the newspaper clippings of her wedding with the photo of her dazzling the onlookers in her white wedding dress and clutching a bouquet of flowers with the caption reading,

"The most beautiful bride Tasmania has ever seen was today married in St. John's...."

Marcus was handed three messages and he opened them slowly and was relieved to read from his brother that his mother had recovered and was now out of hospital. He placed the message on the table and opened the next one. The mother of his children hadn't needed to rush to America after all. He began to smile.

Opening the final fax from Genevieve his smile broadened and broke into laughter as he stood there shaking his head.

A few people nearby looked over to him smilingly, curious of his mirth. Genevieve was coming to India, she said. If he wasn't coming to Paris, she would come there to see him and find out what the hell was going on.

⁓⌣⁓

Seventeen years younger than Marcus, the couple had been married a few years ago in a romantic wedding in the forest beneath a waterfall to the tune of Edith Piaf's, 'je ne regrette rien rien'.

Marcus' mother who loved all things French and even spoke French in honor of her ancestry had been overjoyed at the union, but the marriage had not been easy, Genevieve had been only twenty-one on the day of their marriage.

Dark haired and extremely pretty with large dark eyes and a sharply intelligent mind, she had been a gifted student who had graduated from the Sorbonne in Paris at only sixteen years of age. Two years later she arrived in Australia to study to be a pilot and had won all the awards at the flying school before graduating.

Genevieve was smart, playful, loved to party and took life incredibly seriously. And like Marcus she had a fiery temper to go with her high ideals. The last nine months of their marriage had been an on and off affair with first Genevieve and then Marcus taking other lovers.

Marcus, holding the message from Genevieve in his hand knew then that this would be the point in their marriage where it either blossomed or else fell apart as their pathways perhaps took different roads. Genevieve had not shown any great interest in the deeply spiritual side of Marcus but had adored him for his political involvements and his integrity and resolve to get things done and not, 'just talk about it like all the French people she knew'.

He headed back to his room and wrote a letter to the Master, sealed it in an envelope and wrote on the outside, *'Not for Satsang'*.

In it he had recounted to the Master all that had transpired and thanked him a thousand times for his far-sighted rebuke - and he told him about Genevieve's impending arrival too.

But in the Satsang hall the following day the Master picked up his letter and started reading it aloud - except that he playfully added bits of his own. Marcus rose from his seat and laughingly went before the Master, sat in front of him and could do no more than to laugh and laugh. When he returned to his seat, he noticed that thoughts were passing but not touching the mind nor were the thoughts remaining to manifest new thoughts.

He was in unhindered and deep peace and his mind was simply functioning without volition, without care and in the absence of fear. He remained like that for the rest of the day and into the night when no sleep came, and nor did it seem necessary.

The following day and night were the same until around two in the morning when an extraordinary thing happened. From seemingly nowhere, from emptiness, arose an accusation that was accompanied by a sense of dread.

"You have killed someone," the voice told him.

At that point Marcus' mind clicked into rational thought mode once more as he began desperately to search all the memories of his life to find out whom and for what reason he had taken someone's life. The accusation of him having killed was so strong and so convincing that Marcus knew he must find that memory. He trawled methodically back through all the recollections of his adult life and could find nothing. He dug and sifted back through the memories of childhood and found nothing.

But, as his memories continued to regress, he experienced himself being reborn and the next moment he realized that he was remembering when he was an old man living and meditating in a cave, practicing yoga and being in deep states of absorption. A woman approached his cave and left food outside and as she did so she glanced inside to where he was sitting and she joined her hands in pranayama.

The process continued back and back as it does in the picture frames of a movie until he saw himself as a middle-aged man, still in orange robes, already living the life of a hermit until finally to a time he was a young Brahmin priest sitting erect, tall and elegant with his forehead shaved and long jet-black hair swept back in a tail, and chanting Vedic hymns alongside the Ganga.

He saw both beauty and pride in that handsome young man but somehow the aspect of pride stood out the most.

The memory he had been searching for came as a shock. The young Brahmin standing over the dead man's corpse as it lay bloody on the ground. What had this man done? But he couldn't find that memory but only another where he was running, and running in terrible remorse and, tearing off his sacred thread, he had disappeared into the mountains to never again be seen.

But this wasn't the end. Although the memories became more

distant and less explicit, he realized that there was a long history of war and violence in his long ago past. Many warriors had preceded this life he had just seen, warriors who had fought for their lands and for their gods.

Marcus felt it was like the universe, the cosmos of which he was, was somehow saying to him, 'not yet, this is not your time, not yet."

Genevieve came to India in the end but she felt no connection with what was going on and focused only on the poverty and suffering she saw in India. She stayed for a few weeks and then returned home and though Marcus knew it was not going to last he left India for Paris when he heard that Genevieve had fallen ill. From Paris they travelled back to Australia together where they finally both agreed to part.

Genevieve was too young to be married, had more adventures in the world to follow and other dreams to fulfill but they loved each other nevertheless and parted in as romantic a way as when they had originally married.

Marcus and Genevieve went to a party together and later left for the beach of Byron Bay, made love in the moonlight, sang to each other 'Je ne regrette rien rien', and set out on their separate destinies.

I
am no more than your ordinary self
no less
than your divine self.
how can it be any other way?
when the one be forever one,
not two

And who within this empty room
is judging who
to be free?
and who beyond this brimming hall
of vain attainment
is judging who
to be bound ?

Chapter 13

Gorky Park

Marcus held the letter from Genevieve in his hands, hands somewhat soiled from having fed and washed his horses in the afternoon. She sounded like she may be missing him, reflecting as she was on the time that they had journeyed around Europe in her mother's grand old Peugeot.

Back then, Marcus and Genevieve had travelled from the South of France up to Rotterdam where they had caught the ferry to the north of England before driving up to Scotland.

At Marcus' ancestral home of Skye, they had joined his parents in the Clan festivities and it had been while standing in the ruins of the ancient family chapel that the second vision had come over him.

The Chapel stood on an Island bordered by a rocky stream and with the adjacent voices muted by the water bubbling away on either side of him, Marcus had become drawn to that stone as his mind began to assemble its ancient story.

With Genevieve at his side, he had been staring at the gravestone of a long-gone ancestor, carved in the Viking fashion of a King holding his longsword to his breast. The vision had been fleeting but it had been enough to remind him of his father holding a letter from a Polish Count who claimed to have traced their family from Lade in Norway during the ninth century, all the way forward to the line of chiefs on Lewis and Skye.

"Do you remember that letter – the one from the Polish Count?" he had asked, but his father seemed to have forgotten. For some reason, Marcus had been the only one in the family who had deeply immersed in its history since his grandfather had shared his old books and stories with him when a boy. Books of colorful tartans, of Scottish heroes and their ancestor heroine, Flora Macdonald, who had sheltered Prince Charles Stewart for a few nights in the old family home that now lay in ruins beyond the cliffs of Portree.

He and Genevieve had travelled on from Skye back to the Continent where, somewhat auspiciously, they had met up with her part Polish step-father in Warsaw.

Travelling on to Moscow just a few months after the fall of communism and with the country still in chaos, Marcus had been reminded that Moscow too had been established by the Vikings on their trade route to Constantinople although the chaos that was Moscow in that turbulent year gave little indication of prosperity, but rather one of desperation and confusion on the faces of a people who in some streets were lined three deep while holding a single item of clothing, a kitchen utensil or a pair of worn shoes to sell for the cost of a meal.

"Guys, I have to go to Vladivostok for a few days – you will have the keys to my apartment - and my driver while I am away."

"DHL business or 'agency' business?" Marcus had asked to a flash of anger from Genevieve. But Chris, their American host in Moscow and a past lover of Genevieve from a former posting in Paris, pretended to ignore the implication.

"DHL want to set up shop in Vladivostok," he calmly replied, and throwing his suit coat over his arm and picking up his baggage, headed for the door.

To Marcus, Chris' real occupation was all too obvious. Politically to the conservative right, schooled in Russian at a Washington DC college and working for a global American communications company. What else was needed to be said?

"Thanks, Chris, safe journey," smiled Genevieve. And after hearing Chris' elevator close outside the apartment door, turned to Marcus, admonishing, "hey, you don't have to say that."

"Maybe, but it is kind of funny, us being hosted by a CIA agent in Moscow, don't you think?"

Genevieve was not as amused so Marcus had changed the topic.

"Genevieve, I read in this little English Moscow newspaper that The Animals are playing a live concert in Red Square tonight – let's go – they were one of my favorite groups back in my teenage days – and before, in the afternoon, speaking of music, let's go to Gorky Park."

"Gorky Park? Music?"

"Gorky Park, yes - The Scorpions, 'Wind of Change'," laughed Marcus.

Together they had set off for the expansive gardens of Gorky Park in the center of Moscow, leaving their driver at the main entrance.

What the two had no idea of, while lazing around the park, was that in that same afternoon the entire Baltic division of the Red Army would be dumped at the gates of Gorky Park, tens of thousands of decommissioned soldiers, the majority of whom were mere teenagers, hundreds of them drunkenly embracing Marcus and Genevieve as they had slowly made their way back to the front entrance. Fast forward another ten years and a host of Russian arms dealers and foot soldiers of the Oligarchs would be trying vainly to recall who that couple were in the photographs with them and their former comrades in arms. Hope for the world had seemed even possible in those days.

Marcus tossed the letter back on the table with the memories to pick up the other letter, the one he felt just a little bit nervous to open – the one that would begin the rest of his story.

Follow the Moskva
Down to Gorky Park
Listening to the wind of change
An August summer night
Soldiers passing by

Chapter 14

The Viking Runes

Marcus had thought often of Bia over the years and felt truly heart warmed upon opening her letter and particularly about her wish to meet this Master of his. He lovingly folded the paper and placed it on his pocket, pulled on his riding boots and went to saddle his horse, calling him from his verandah.

An hour later, he was sitting in the sun in front of the local store opening a bottle of beer, his horse tied to the post in front of the store where he always won a few pats and strokes from children if they happened by. He pulled out the letter and read it again, recalling that it had been seven years ago that he had suddenly felt the need to contact Juliana again – the exact time that Bia had said she had died.

But it was months later that Marcus finally decided to call her and it would be the first time they had spoken since her eleventh birthday - when she had sat on his lap on the houseboat in Varanasi all those years ago.

She wanted to come but was re-thinking the idea. Her children had decided they would rather go skiing in Colorado with their grandfather and her partner was too busy with his new business to think about traveling.

"I don't feel confident traveling to India alone Marcus."

"Have you booked a ticket?"

"Yes"

"What date?"

"The twentieth, of January"

"Where?"

"Delhi"

"I arrive on the eighteenth, of January in Delhi, Bia, and can wait for you there and take you wherever you wish to go."

"Will you take me to see your master?"

"Of course, but we can also travel a bit first if you want."

"I would like that, thank you Marcus - maybe I will think again about my plans."

When Marcus put down the phone, he was left with the strangest of feelings that he had just been speaking to his wife. Her voice had seemed so, so familiar and her presence over the phone so natural to him as though he had already been with her for years and years.

He decided to consult his runes. It wasn't something he did much, preferring to leave the future alone to surprise him according to its will. But in the odd chance he wanted to get guidance he decided on the runes because of their connection to his long-ago ancestry and besides, they worked for him more accurately than the tarot or the I Ching.

Marcus wrote the names of Genevieve, with whom he still had contact, Tara, a lover he had been with in India just recently, and Bia.

He shuffled the grey stones in their red velvet bag and placed one on each name.

The rune that appeared on Bia's name was the one that simply said, 'partnership or marriage.'

He shuffled them again.

"OK," he thought to himself, "lets' make sure this is right."

Again, he drew the marriage rune for Bia while different runes from the first reading were drawn for Genevieve and Tara. Marcus was taken aback. He could only remember once before having drawn exactly the same rune for the same question if some doubt had lingered about the reading.

As if making an effort to confuse himself he placed the three runes back in the bag and shuffled and drew once more and again, the marriage rune appeared over Bia's name. The chances with twenty-five runes of drawing that particular one three times, and being placed over the same name out of three was too eerily impossible.

Marcus felt humbled. Whatever destiny had in store for him appeared to be out of his hands entirely. Destiny and free will. He had a pretty good understanding of its relationship but somehow the humanness in us all seems to desire at least some free will in our choices.

But behind Marcus' doubt was this. Since breaking up with Genevieve and having being heartbroken before in marriages and relationships when he had been promised eternal love and commitment it had always proven to be a mirage, and now, in his early middle age but looking many years younger, Marcus appeared more beautiful than ever to women and he was enjoying it. With his disillusionment with marriage and with his overriding devotion to his journey into the unknown there was plenty of resistance to the idea of another committed union.

But this was Bia and he had to admit that he had more than once wondered what could be if he ever met up with this girl with whom he had loved as a child. And now she was coming to India alone to meet him. And the runes had spoken.

Could this really be?
between the roots
and the water
between the mouth and its hunger

Through the portals
of forgotten lore
while courted by a mantra
of the Goddess' love

There within the depths
of Mimir's well
their secrets foretold
by Odin's ruined eye?

Chapter 15

The Train to Pushkar

Marcus noticed he began to feel a little nervous as he passed the second day in Delhi wandering around some of his old haunts, getting his ears cleaned out on the grass in the middle of Connaught Circus by one of the many Indians that scraped and cobbled together a living shining shoes, hawking peacock feather fans, hashish and hair combs, and, cleaning ears.

He met up with a young Indian friend whom he had known over the years and who had evolved from a shoe shine boy as an eight-year-old to a shopping guide and now in the act of proudly showing Marcus his new auto rickshaw. Marcus even used him for shopping sometimes knowing fully well that Sajit was taking a cut and taking him only to the shops where he had something to gain but that was just part of the deal. Sajit would bargain hard for Marcus and Marcus would join in, turning his back and walking out if he didn't get the price he wanted, and then Sajit would soon come after him telling him the shop keepers had lowered their price.

It was, in fact the bargain that India offered and its relationships with wealthier westerners in total. Your rich, I am poor, now let's screw you for as much as possible while making you feel good and loved and then we will have a nice cup of tea together.

"Take me to the Railway station in your new Rickshaw then Sajit," said Marcus.

Sajit beamed with pride and said,

"For you Marcus, I no charge."

"Oh yes you will," smiled Marcus.

They set off for the station where Marcus purchased two tickets for Pushkar. He had revisited Pushkar a couple of years ago and had been shocked by the change. Now it was no longer a remote and sleepy little temple town on the edge of the desert but full of westerners, many of whom were Israeli and there were new guest houses and cafes selling veggie burgers, omelets and shakshuka with garish signs in English and Hebrew. The former peace of the town was often broken by the roar of Enfield's as they thundered through the narrow streets. The building by the lake that housed the marble room where Marcus had stayed for free some twenty years before had now evolved into one of the more expensive hotels, the Pushkar Palace. But somehow, he had still loved it so it was there he would take Bia before heading to the bustling city in Uttar Pradesh where his master lived in a simple suburban cottage.

Climbing back into Sajit's rickshaw, Sajit asked him where he was going.

"Pushkar in Rajasthan, you know Pushkar?"

"I heard, but not been - you going alone or you take friend?"

"I take friend."

"Where is friend?"

"She comes to Delhi tonight."

"She coming airport?"

Marcus smiled, anticipating the next question,

"Yes, Sajit, she coming airport but she is lady and needs nice car I think."

"Oh, OK then I can organize car for you - my friend, good clean car - I come too Marcus - greet you friend to India."

"No"

~‿‿◠

Marcus waited outside of the old Delhi Airport. It was a cold mid-winter night and, in those days, they didn't let you inside to wait for passengers arriving off flights.

He was dressed in a long black overcoat with a white woolen scarf wrapped carelessly around his neck. Tall and blond with medium length hair swept back from his tanned face, Marcus had checked himself in the mirror in his modest room back in Pahar Ganj and thought to himself that he looked pretty good in that outfit.

Now as he waited through the second hour, he tried not to harbor any expectations of what might be.

Bia was effectively married anyway and he tried to suppress his intuition and forget the casting of the runes. He would be happy just to see her again no matter what happened and also, she could not possibly be thinking of having an affair with someone who used to be her mother's lover.

He tried to push it all out of his mind.

He started a conversation with an East End born Indian girl with a cockney accent who was waiting for her sister to arrive on the same flight from London. They were best friends within minutes.

"Who are you waiting for" she asked,

"A girl I have not seen in twenty years."

Thinking of that Marcus did the math and realized that in another nine days it would be Bia's birthday and so it would be exactly twenty years since they had last seen each other.

Devina looked up at Marcus a bit surprised and remarked.

"That's a long time but I'm sure you will still recognize her - people don't change that much."

"True," replied Marcus, "but they do when the last time you saw them was as an eleven-year-old."

"You're joking!"

"No, I am not joking."

"So, what's the story?"

"A much too long one," answered Marcus, deciding that he only wanted to confide so much in his new best friend of a half hour duration.

Devina took a different tack.

"Where is she from Marcus?"

"From Brazil, I knew her family many years ago when I lived in Brazil."

That sounded normal enough, Marcus thought, but Devina clearly picked up on Marcus' excitement as he shuffled his feet and rubbed his hands to keep away the cold. Her eyes widened mischievously.

⌒〜〜⌒

The first passengers were coming off the London flight. Marcus could see the baggage labels of British Airways as people fell into the arms of loved ones. Would he be able to recognize her? Every girl who looked anything like South American he scrutinized carefully beginning to worry that they might end up missing each other in the burgeoning and growing throng of people, hugs, tears, taxi drivers chasing fares and unbelievable amounts of baggage that Indian travelers managed to haul on to flights. Typically, it was chaos now.

"Is that her?" asked Devina gesturing to a girl pushing a baggage trolly towards them while Marcus' eyes had been searching in an altogether different direction.

He turned in the direction of where Devina was nodding and saw her and knew unmistakably that it was Bia. She was already smiling broadly and the light that lit that smile ricocheted off Marcus' heart and he felt himself beaming in return.

Devina, nudging Marcus cheekily in the ribs, said laughingly,

"She's beautiful Marcus - have a great time with her."

Devina had no doubt.

Bia pushed her trolly to one side and threw her arms around Marcus' neck and they hugged. It was just like all the other times when they had met up again in that other lifetime when Bia would run to him and throw her arms around him.

He gently pushed her away and holding her with his hands on her arms they gazed smilingly into each other's faces with a familiarity too deep to fathom.

⌣⌣⌣

Marcus and Bia took the cab to the five-star Ashoka where Bia had booked a room and while they chatted a bit, mostly they just smiled and held hands and stroked each other's arms. It was loving, playful, intimate and sweet but still Marcus could not know what, if anything more, would happen. He was happy to be with her for now and she with him.

Reaching the lavish hotel, they checked in and took the lift and shared it with two Australian businessmen who were in the mood to talk. 'In Delhi to design a golf course' they proudly informed their companions in the lift.

"What do you do?"

Which meant, what is your line of business.

"I am an international arms smuggler but a crap golfer."

It got a laugh, a slightly nervous laugh. Bia smilingly shook her head as if recollecting Marcus' warped humor.

Marcus didn't stay long in her room. She would be tired and jet lagged so they hugged and he told her he would be back the next morning, late.

"How many days did you book the hotel?" he asked her at the door.

"Just tonight, Marcus, why?"

"Because I have train tickets for Pushkar for tomorrow night - do you think you can handle it? It's an overnight train and we have a sleeper cabin to ourselves."

Bia smiled, nodding her head.

"I think so - no, I'll be fine - where is Pushkar?"

"In Rajasthan on the edge of the desert - you're going to like it and I have booked a nice place for us to stay."

"Marcus, I am in your hands."

Marcus entered the lift to the lobby and met the same two

businessmen heading down for drinks.

"Nice lady, she's your girlfriend?"

"I'm not sure – once upon a time she was like my daughter but who knows how things could turn out?"

But this time, they looked at him convinced he was borderline mad, not sure where the conversation would take them. Marcus couldn't stop beaming.

"Drugs," the businessmen concluded.

He came back to Bia's hotel at around eleven the next morning and found out from reception that she was awake and had eaten breakfast so he called her.

"I will come down and we can sit around the pool," she said.

Which they did, but Marcus still had the uncontrollable urge to touch but didn't have the same excuse as the night before when they had just met up so he offered her a foot massage. Massages of any kind were always welcome after a long flight, he figured.

He massaged, they chatted, he asked about Juliana. She told him some more of her mother's battle with cancer. She asked him about his children, he asked her about hers. Neither of them mentioned her husband. She asked when they were going to see his Master.

"After Pushkar I want to take you to Rishikesh - I thought it would be nice for you to taste India again, and visit some cool places before heading to Lucknow - Lucknow is not exactly a beautiful city."

"Rishikesh?"

"Do you remember Rishikesh, Bia? you were there with me when we travelled together, the whole family."

Bia nodded.

"Yes, I remember – and I remember playing outside the sadhu caves."

"We can visit them again, one of them still lives there - I visited him last year"

They couldn't take their eyes from each other. Marcus was still finding it surreal on the one hand but completely familiar on the other.

Bia checked out of the most expensive hotel in Delhi soon after and they took a cab to the seedier area of Pahar Ganj, where Marcus was staying in a reasonable but much cheaper place.

He walked Bia up to his room slightly apologetically, carrying her bags. Fortunately, she wasn't traveling too heavy.

"I already arranged with the hotel to pay for just half a day so we can rest up here until the train leaves and it is only a short distance from here to the station - hope this is OK for you," Marcus asked, conscious of the fact that Bia was probably accustomed to higher standards since her childhood days in India.

Even then they had sometimes stayed in five-star hotels but on other occasions had slept in stoic ashrams and temples. Traveling with Juliana he never knew where they were going to stay next – it had been fun, with the unknown ever present at every turn.

Bia looked a lot like Juliana, especially from the front, but dark haired and with more of her father's profile. Her features were doll like, her body petit but her eyes were deep and brown and, well, wise. She was calm and moved with grace, perhaps more controlled than her mother, a bit of her father there noted Marcus.

She lay down on his bed.

He lay down next to her propped on his elbow.

She rolled over to him and embraced him, wrapping her arms around his chest and whispered in to his ear.

"I can't resist you - I knew from the moment I saw you that I might be in trouble."

Marcus was taken by surprise; he hadn't really expected this, or had he?

"No-one can find out about this she added."

"Oh, so this is going to be a secret affair," thought Marcus to himself and then, stroking her face, he smilingly reassured her.

"I don't think that's going to be a problem - I don't even know anyone you know."

Bia smiled in response and held him tighter.

They lay awhile in each other's arms pondering, perhaps, what would come of this.

They made love that night on the train, ensconced in the sleeper cabin but the beds were single and maneuvering not so easy.

But it mattered not. Bia was of medium height and though petit and fine boned her lithe body disguised a softness and serpentine sensuality that you would normally expect from a more voluptuous form. And she moved with the ease and grace of a woman comfortable with her own carnality and the pleasures it could gift her. Finding her mouth, Marcus closed his eyes and melted into her full and kissable lips.

"Was this the best kiss of his life?" he asked himself.

"Everything about this woman felt good, her lips and skin both smelt and tasted delightful, sweet and subtly scented."

The train clacked and rolled in unison to their lovemaking and afterwards they slept, and dreamed, awakening in the first light of dawn to the sounds of the metallic brakes screaming and groaning their way to a stop in the Ajmir station.

On the short bus trip through the sparsely treed and arid rocky hills that separated Ajmir from Pushkar, Bia leaned her head on Marcus' shoulder, holding his right bicep with one hand and passing her other feelingly along his forearm.

"I love your arms," she admitted with a delightful smile - I have to say, I have a thing about nice arms."

In response, Marcus playfully placed his arm in her lap and replied, "All yours"

In Pushkar they stayed on the top floor of the Palace Hotel with a view to the sacred lake and for three days walked casually and lazily around the streets and temples of the now busy town that bustled with travelers, priests, desert nomads and sadhus. They made the now mandatory camel ride into the desert and when it suited them, whenever the passion arose again, they retired to their room and made love.

On the third day after another particularly slow and sensitive love making, Bia turned to Marcus saying,

"I don't think I can keep going on like this"

Marcus was a little taken aback and quickly replied.

"Oh, that's ok, we can just be friends if you like"

There was a pause as each tried to understand what was passing through the mind of the other, the first awkward moment of their days together.

Bia then looked at Marcus intently, a serious expression that softened into a smile as she said.

"No Marcus, I mean I cannot go back to my husband - it's too late, I want to marry you - I want you, I am in love with you."

Marcus remained silent while Bia's eyes scanned his face, searching for a clue to what was going through his mind. In fact, a thousand things were racing through his brain and a thousand emotions through his heart as Marcus observed the passing show from an inner place of calm.

"In truth, I have been ok with the idea of this being a love affair," he thought to himself, "I have many women, beautiful women I could love and be loved by now if I wanted - do I really believe in marriage anymore? am I really in love with Bia?"

The last thought surprised him because this was different, he realized. All the other times that he had fallen seriously in love, and there had been, in truth, only four or five times out of a score of a myriad lovers and two short marriages when he had fallen totally in love, his emotions then had been stronger and that feeling of love sickness that swept all rationality and reason from the hearts of afflicted lovers was not present this time.

But then he reflected, and he felt with clarity that being with Bia was the most natural thing in the world. It felt, well, right.

His thoughts went back to his feelings of fear and insecurity with his past loves and how, since being with the Master, he felt stronger within himself, less buffeted by those fears of loss.

Marcus recalled the casting of the runes and saw too that on his path of freedom a focus and commitment in his love life would be best for him. His mind went back to a time in Varanasi, ancient Khasi, the city that somehow linked their fates together, a palm reader telling him that he would not stay with Juliana but would marry a wealthy woman later in life who was still a child. At the time Bia was skipping around just outside the palmist's room.

He looked at Bia. She was beautiful but more than that she was incredibly sane and intelligent and he realized that in part, he had fallen in the past for impossible women and his choices had been just a form of self-destructiveness. What really scared him was that he knew Bia would possibly be forever but he had sworn off 'forever'.

Around other beautiful women he questioned whether he could trust himself but he thought on that count he could. He hoped he could, because he knew that to betray this woman would not only break her heart but break his as well.

As the setting sun shone through the arched window and lit Bia's gentle and perfect face his heart cleared and his mind crystalized in the realization that this had never been anything but written in the stars a long time ago.

Bia was his soul partner and all those other loves had been no more than the search for her. And in seeing that, he suddenly felt a surge of love for all of them and asked their forgiveness and in turn, thanked them for their generosity.

"Yes," he said.

"Yes what?" she asked, her pensiveness falling away from her face.

"Yes, I will marry you," he smiled.

She threw her arms around him and whispered

"Forever?"

"For however long it is written," he answered.

"What do you mean, Marcus?"

He held her hand and looked seriously into her eyes, saying,

"Every time I said forever in the past or someone said forever to me it turned out to be a lie," he answered, "I don't want to ever lie to you, Bia - we don't know how long we are meant to make this journey together but I do know that you are my wife," he said.

The runes being cast
three times in all
the cards laid out
and the stars aligned for fate

Of the lover's tantric tryst
the first word of the story writ
with the ink still drying
upon the very last

Chapter 16

The Sands of the Ganges

In Rishikesh the fires of their passion for each other grew into an inferno of delicious love making.

Marcus and Bia were exploring each other relentlessly as she took him inside of her and together, they loved each other to seemingly unfathomed depths of succulent and delicious pleasure. He adored her taste. She delighted in his maleness. They slowed to a gentle rhythm and kissed each other's mouths for an eternity while he gently and slowly probed within her exploring her most responsive places while she tightened, slid and squeezed her sex around his in response, drawing out and prolonging their passion until sweetly sated. He licked her tears of love from her cheeks.

He lay next to her playing with her hand and told her.

"You are an amazing lover."

"And so are you," she replied with tender sincerity

"You're the best lover since…," but then he stopped himself.

"Since my mother," she laughed and they both giggled.

"Do you remember she used to tell us we should get married when we get older?" asked Marcus.

Bia rolled her eyes saying,

"You were not the only one - she used to tell me I should marry Caetano Veloso when I was a teenager."

"They were friends weren't they," Marcus remembered.

"Yes, and I used to hang around Caetano a lot when I was about fourteen," and then smilingly added as she caressed Marcus' forearm, "he would have made a terrible husband - her first idea was better."

"I love his music though," added Marcus. "I still have one of his old vinyl albums in Australia."

And then he began to sing,

They are chasing me
In the hot sun of a Christmas day
But they won't find me
In the hot sun of a Christmas day
I walk the streets
In the hot sun of a Christmas day
Everybody's blind
In the hot sun of a Christmas day
I miss my girl
In the hot sun of a Christmas day"
She seems to love me less
In the hot sun of a Christmas day
Machine guns
In the hot sun of a Christmas day
They killed someone else
In the hot sun of a Christmas day

It was about the time in Brazil when the military dictatorship was imprisoning and murdering protestors and revolutionaries and many musicians and artists whose work the Generals considered subversive were being deported, Caetano and Gilberto Gil amongst them. Juliana had spent time with both of them during their exile in London.

Marcus sang a few lines of another of Caetano's' songs written in English while feeling homesick for his native Bahia during a cold English winter, a song to his musician sister,

"Maria Bethânia
Please write me a letter
I wish to know things
Are getting better, better, better"

"You're not in tune," she interrupted.

"Then sing me something in tune," he asked, pretending to be offended

"I can, ok, I am a trained singer," she answered.

"And what else are you trained in apart from singing and love making," he teased.

Bia breathed in seductively at that and kissed him for an eternity on the mouth while moving into his lap and passing her breasts sensuously over his chest before abruptly disengaging when feeling his hardening response, saying,

"Chega, enough! - astrology, I did an astrology course with the best astrologer in Brazil,"

"And?"

"And graphic design. I design cd covers and book covers."

"And?"

"Ah, I did medicine for two years but couldn't handle it when it came to slicing up body parts."

"Really," exclaimed Marcus, "I don't mind that at all. in fact, I love dressing wounds and giving injections - I do it all the time with our horses."

"You have horses?"

"Yes, my oldest daughter, Bri, you're going to love her, she competes in competitions and we have three horses on our farm - you like horses?" he asked.

"On our family farm in Bahia we have many horses and I have been riding there - mostly during holidays - since I was a child."

"I love women who ride horses," said Marcus as he took Bia in his arms and kissed her while stroking her thighs, his fingers searching for her delicious wetness. Bia began to respond eagerly but Marcus pushed himself away, teasingly saying,

"Chega, enough."

Bia flashed him a slightly annoyed, yet loving look.

"Now, are you going to sing for me?"

"Really? you really want me to sing?"

"Yes, I really want you to sing."

Bia closed her eyes for a moment and catching her breath and straightening her posture and sitting cross legged in her nakedness upon the tangled sheets and pillows she began,

"Se você disser que eu desafino, amor
Saiba que isso em mim provoca imensa dor
Só privilegiados tem ouvido igual ao seu
Eu possuo apenas o que Deus me deu
Se você insiste em classificar
Meu comportamento de anti-musical
Eu mesmo mentindo devo argumentar
Que isso é Bossa Nova, isso é muito natural
Só não poderá falar assim do meu amor
Ele é o maior que você pode encontrar, viu!
Você com a sua música esqueceu o principal
Que no peito dos desafinados
No fundo do peito, bate calado
No peito dos desafinados
Também bate um coração!

She sang with feeling and moved her hands in gestures to the words of the music and she sang in perfect tune.

"Wow, that was beautiful,"

"You liked the song," she smiled, slightly shyly.

"You really can sing and it makes me want to kiss those perfect lips that sing in perfect tune," said Marcus as he leaned across and began kissing her mouth before descending down to her breasts and stomach with more soft kisses and caresses. He reached down past her neat strip of black hair that mantled her wet sex and while moving his tongue within her she gasped and whimpered and then sliding her moist naked body over his she closed her full lips around him and drew his sex deep into her mouth in turn and elicited from him a shudder of uncontrollable spasms as they pleasured each other ecstatically.

The next day on the banks of the Ganga Marcus gave Bia his promise of eternal love with a necklace of green peridot stones that he passed over her head and hung around her elegant neck. Bia was moved to the point where the beginnings of tears moistened the corners of her brown eyes.

"Thank you, Marcus, thank you - it's beautiful - I love it."

The cold January waters of the mother swept by in currents and eddies between enormous grey boulders.

Marcus and Bia held hands sitting comfortably in the sun warmed grains of deep white sand and closed their eyes.

'As many as the sands of the Ganges.'

It reminded him of the most repeated stanza in the Diamond Sutra.

He remembered they had lain in this exact same spot more than twenty years before. He still had the photograph somewhere.

The sound of the river gurgled by and everything emptied into silence as their thoughts were carried downstream by the sacred waters, the giver of life and the receiver of death, as the goddess began to slow her pace and widen her girth and spread out into the plains of India to where they would journey the following day and somewhere in the past the rivers flowed and the goddesses of the rivers exalted.

In the torrents of her past
the Goddess' eyes fatally upcast
to the reddened lust
of a darkening sky

Remembering King Santanu
and of waters run dry

The children of the Kali yuga gave
to her fickle currents
their exceptionally enchanted
but fleeting lives

Forgetful of King Santanu
and of waters run dry

Chapter 17

The Spinning Fan

They were seated in the hall a few rows back from the Master who was now eighty-six years old, a heavy-set man with one lazy drooping eye who had once been a wrestler, a revolutionary fighting against the British occupation and an Army sergeant.

But one who had dressed up at night in a woman's sari bedecked with lip stick and jewelry impersonating Radha and he had done that to attract his beloved Krishna. And Krishna had visited him regularly but all this had changed when he journeyed to visit the Sage of Arunachala who questioned him saying,

"When Krishna comes you are happy, but when Krishna leaves what remains?"

With those words the Master had awakened to his true unblemished and original nature.

He had passed some years after his retirement in places such as Haridwar, Rishikesh, Chitrakoot and Brindavan and wherever he went he would change people's lives and they would want to stay with him and follow him but without saying where he was going, he would quietly disappear and leave them waiting for his return.

Now he was too old to run and hundreds of earnest people and more than a few mad ones gathered in his lion like presence to have their ideas and concepts devoured and laid waste.

Marcus liked him for his terribly politically incorrect sense of humor, the fact that he loved cricket (he once had dragged a television into the hall during a match and made everyone watch it instead of him giving Satsang), and he loved him more than anything for the fact that the Master was none other than his own inner self.

Bia turned to Marcus, after sitting in silence for an hour and whispered to him,

"This man is so beautiful."

He was very happy to hear her say that. Especially after the events with Genevieve's visit. Bia had tuned into the Master very quickly. and he felt that yet another sacred thread had been sown into the fabric of their deepening bond.

⌒ᴗᴗᴐ

Bia dreamed that night of her mother smiling above her in joy. Marcus watched her as she dreamed. He loved those early still hours when without any intent or direction he allowed his mind to empty into silence. Bia stirred and lazily opened her eyes, a soft smile on her face as her dream melted into the wakening dawn.

"Marcus," she said, rolling over to nestle her head in his lap, "I had a beautiful dream with my mother - she was beaming and she was so happy that I was here with the Master - it was so real."

"I totally believe it was."

"Was what?"

"That it was real."

"Yes, it wasn't anything like an ordinary confused dream."

"These are not ordinary dreams Bia - they are visitations and visions that transcend time."

Bia rolled on her back looking pensive with a Mona Lisa half smile across her lips, her dark hair loose over the pillow. Marcus liked her best in that natural state and had the thought of laying alongside her and taking carnal advantage of her soft morning nakedness. For him, the morning love makings were best of all and in those days, they made love afternoons, evenings and mornings but today he saw that Bia was in a different place. She wanted to share her dreams not her flesh so he breathed in and redirected the serpentine energy, that had momentarily descended to his loins, to ascend once more in to the heart.

~∿~

Marcus left Bia in the bed one morning. She was feeling off color and having done everything he could in the way of massage and tender loving care he would bring home the doctor after Satsang but he was running late. He turned over the kick starter of the old Enfield and the power of the single large cylinder kicked it right back and struck his leg bone with and it hurt.

"Ow, fuck!" was what Bia heard while lying in bed inside.

He kicked again taking more care but now the motor hardly gave a splutter.

He was running late.

He tried again and no luck and his irritation made him curse.

"Fucking hell! - start you fucking piece of shit!"

Bia was listening to Marcus' shadow side and starting to comprehend the full package. She threw on a robe and made her way outside.

"Can I help Marcus?"

Marcus looked at her slightly embarrassed but still dirty with the bike.

"Yeah," he said sheepishly, "this is me too - I' don't have much patience with things I don't know how to fix - hang on I will try and roll start it."

He managed to get up enough speed to roll it down the slope out of the driveway and ran the bike down the street before throwing his leg over the saddle and releasing the clutch. The engine coughed into life as a pig darted across in front of him and he moved up the gears swinging around a cow munching garbage in the middle of the street while a three wheeled rickshaw high revved in the opposite direction missing him by centimeters.

And that was another thing he appreciated about the Master. Like him, the Master could get ferociously angry. Marcus had himself experienced it when Genevieve had gone with him to visit the Master in his house a year and a half ago.

Genevieve had responded to the Master rudely and arrogantly and the Master had roared at her to get out of his house, had grabbed Marcus' arm and told him to,

"Get rid of that bitch! - you stay with me - you are my son."

The Masters large hands and massive arms still had the strength of the wrestler that he had once been. Even at eighty-four years of age.

Marcus had well understood that he and Genevieve were not on the same path at that moment while in the Masters' presence but he had sat there and refused to 'get rid' of Genevieve in that fashion and he had stood his ground with the Master arguing, but all of the time this had been happening, with the Master at his most fearsome and Marcus at his most stubborn, he had felt a beautiful tranquility just below the surface. The argument they were appearing to have, was only a dance taking place above the still center of being that connected their inner selves as one and the same. It was surprising, beautifully surprising and made it so clear to Marcus in that moment, the absolute illusory nature of the pantomime of life.

"Then you do it your way," the Master had finally said.

"Yes, I will do it my way," Marcus had answered, "or maybe her way," he added.

The Master had henceforth ignored him until finding out the next year that Marcus had indeed done it his way.

⌒⌣⌒

"This was how it was," thought Marcus, "we are all just riding the waves of our personalities to the end of our days and it is useless to try and change them and even more fruitless to try and change others - what needs to fall away will fall away in the face of seeing its innate falseness, not by fighting it and trying to transform it into something better or a personality that is more convenient for other people to bear - when we become completely exhausted by a flaw in our personalities that continues to give us and those around us pain, we will be ready to surrender it naturally," he considered.

The Master likened enlightenment to switching off the fan. When the fan is switched off, the illusion understood, the momentum keeps the fan spinning for some time, perhaps even several lifetimes more until its energy is exhausted.

Marcus envisioned the Goddess Kali chopping off the heads of the demons and as each head hit the ground a new demon would sprout. Finally, the Goddess had to resort to swallowing all of the demons into herself.

The Master, however, when angered by someone and often to the bewilderment of the other disciples as to why he was angry, would produce remarkable transformations in people or mysterious events would take place that completely changed circumstances. Marcus had understood that very well during the week he thought his mother was dying, had decided to leave and the Master had surprisingly and severely chastised him in the hall.

⌒〜〜⌒

That evening, after the doctor's visit, and Bia had started a course of antibiotics and complementary herbal medicine Marcus asked,

"Bia, do you remember me getting angry when you were a child?"

"You mean when you used to fight with my mother?" she asked.

"And when the horse used to escape from his stable and gallop round over my garden beds," he added.

"I remember you being very loud but you know, I always felt sorry for you and blamed my mother for starting those fights."

"Really? well that's probably why you used to find me out in the garden all sad and give me a hug when that happened," answered Marcus as he rolled over and caressed her cheek lightly, feeling more deeply in love with this woman. He felt he could be himself. He felt accepted for who he was and it would prove to be one of the strongest foundations of enduring love and respect he would feel for her for years and years to come.

In fact, most people viewed Marcus as a calm and extremely laid-back guy, a sweet man, a fair man and it was true for he was all of that. It was just that in those odd times when he wasn't, he really wasn't.

A past love had once said to Marcus,

"You are impossible to live with and impossible to live without."

Bia stayed with Marcus in that sprawling and busy city for the rest of her two months in India before the day of her leaving. Her children's summer holidays were over and so was her time in India. They would meet again in Rio in another two months.

She was apprehensive about what awaited her back home. A partner of six years who would suddenly discover she was about to marry another man. A father who would learn that her new love was none other than the lover who had appeared in his house with his estranged wife more than twenty years ago. A large and wealthy establishment family who even way back then had been divided about Marcus' presence. How would they be now?

Bia however, was set on her course. She wanted Marcus.

She was dressed very differently than she had been during their travels. Smart and elegant in a tailored woolen jacket.

"It probably had an expensive label on it too," thought Marcus but his eyes lingered on her appreciatively as she turned and waved to him before disappearing in to the immigration check.

She walks into the silver bird
she waits for the storm

A long time ago
a hammer had rent the sky
with its fury
and a ship had sailed
out of the bay
on those other journeys

as his longing eyes
had likewise
followed her away

Chapter 18

The Bandit Queen and The Temple of Love

Marcus returned to the city that grew drier and dustier by the day, now that they were heading into the end of March. He moved into another house he had stayed in before and into a room with air conditioning.

In their shared bathroom, Marcus met a pretty and fun woman from New York, Edna, who became his new best friend within the day. Forgetting to lock his door he had found her peeing on the toilet.

Showering and lightly dressing he drifted into the living room where the whole household were taking chai.

There was a heavy-set ex Californian policeman who now went by the name of Raj and practiced Tibetan pulsing, a form of healing with hands, a blond woman he had not met before pleasing to the eye and the house manager, Gayatri, small, lithe and feisty of Mexican American heritage with big brown eyes that flashed from beneath her thick jet-black brows.

"Marcus, come and have some chai," invited Gayatri.

"You have met Edna but have you met Tatiana yet? she was here last year but she just got back yesterday."

"Hi Tatiana, I am Marcus," taking her hand gently in his without shaking as was his customary way of greeting women.

Marcus thought he noticed a hint of seductiveness in the way her eyes danced with his for a few moments.

"Your name sounds Russian," he remarked as he seated himself on

133

the cushions that surrounded the low set glass table.

"Yes, not so difficult eh," she responded giving away her accent in the process.

"And you?" she asked, holding Marcus' attention with her cool expression while narrowing her gaze to the point where Marcus felt like a bull in a sale yard being assessed for blemishes. It was hot and the fan whirred nosily overhead. Marcus was shirtless.

He didn't really mind. In fact, he enjoyed this game.

"From Tasmania," he replied, always ready for the look of puzzlement from his new acquaintances as he said it, and to add emphasis,

"From a sheep farm in the middle of Tasmania," he laughed.

Tatiana was a bit thrown.

"What is Tas…., how do you say it? what is this place?"

"Well, if you go from here to Antarctica, you might find it on the way," responded Marcus as he sipped his chai and helped himself to some cookies on the table."

"Marcus your bad," interrupted Edna.

"Sorry Tatiana, Tasmania is this place at the bottom of Australia and they are all inbreeds and convicts," explained Edna in all of her New Yorkness.

"Convicts?" pleaded Tatiana, not quite understanding.

"Yes, convicts, like what you put in your gulags, prisoners, bad people," explained Edna while laughing in Marcus' direction. And then,

"Marcus, are you still in love with me?"

"Of course, Edna - how could I not be – you're just so…beautiful, and sweet, I love you."

"Oh good, for a moment there I thought you might be angry with me."

"I love you too," she winked, blowing Marcus a kiss from her Madonna like lips.

In fact, that is who Edna reminded him of. Madonna, short, sexy, with dyed long blond wavy hair. Prettier than Madonna, decided Marcus.

Raj was grinning and shaking his head in bemusement, taking in the banter having put to rest his book on tantric healing.

Gayatri then leveled the conversation as she turned to Marcus asking,

"So, Marcus, when are you going to meet up with your Brazilian princess again?"

And turning to Edna and the others

"Do you guys know this story?"

In the following days as they came to know more about each other Marcus discovered that Raj had an Egyptian girlfriend born in the UK, but Raj believed in open relationships from his time on an Osho commune.

Gayatri, he already knew had an on again, off again relationship with her German boyfriend while Edna had a partner in New York who she was also in business with, importing fashion accessories from Bali. But she was at the crossroads with her man, trying to figure out if she really wanted to be married or not.

Tatiana, it turned out was married to a Russian businessman but baulked vaguely when asked about his business.

"Arms dealer," thought Marcus immediately, "sugar daddy."

In the nineties the majority of Russians getting rich were those dealing in arms pilfered from corruptly guarded weapons depots and he learned too that Tatiana had made the most of her freedom the last time she had been in the city.

It was quite the cocktail of disparate sexual energy in that house he had entered.

The Master had fallen ill and was not going to attend the meetings in the Hall for the next week or two at least. His health was managed by a German woman doctor who rarely left his side and worried incessantly about her responsibility and burden. Her biggest headache was keeping the diabetic old man away from sweet meats and sugar which he loved. On one of his rare trips overseas he had been carrying a kilo of sweet meats with him as a gift for the disciple in whose house he would stay but was told by customs at JFK airport that he couldn't bring them in to the country.

Another of the Master's idiosyncrasies was that he totally abhorred wastefulness so he had sat down in a chair and devoured the whole kilo before proceeding through customs.

So, when the Master was ill, the followers would play and people would begin to disperse to places like Rishikesh, Haridwar or Varanasi or some to Brindavan. All holy places within a day's journey of the Master's home.

Marcus' household decided on doing something a bit different. Marcus and Raj both had 500cc Enfield's and they found another Israeli friend who rode one to join them on the road to Khajuraho, one of India's most famous temples and renowned for its erotic tantric carvings of sexual acts performed in a myriad different posture adorning every wall, inside and out.

～∾～

Taking it easy, they calculated, Khajuraho would be about a two-day ride.

The Israeli, Avi, clearly smitten by the attractive Jewish girl, coaxed Edna to ride with him while Tatiana jumped behind Marcus without saying a word. That left Raj to carry the young Russian Cossack dancer, Stepan. Stepan, noted Marcus, was also along for the ride because of Edna. His eyes devoured her constantly and to Marcus perception, she didn't mind at all.

"This will be interesting," he thought to himself as they roared off on the throaty old bikes thumping their single cylinders through the chaotic avenue that led through the middle of the town. He quickly realized that the testosterone of the group was transferring itself to the bikes as Avi set a mad pace through the streets and out into the open road. Marcus and Raj followed with matching speed but Marcus would let the others go ahead, if the passing moves completely exceeded sanity, to catch the others after choosing his openings. Riding like this, one lapse of concentration was death on the Indian roads that basically had one rule - the biggest and the bravest rule.

Marcus saw a gap open up between a lumbering gaily painted truck and an onrushing bus that careened almost sideways on a ridiculous tilt along the highway and he gunned his bike through it.

"I am glad I am riding with you, you ride well," said Tatiana as she moved her body forward and hugged Marcus tightly, passing her hands over his chest and leaning her head on his shoulder as she did so.

Marcus' body enjoyed the attention but his heart and his head managed to remain sober. Something told him that this journey would be more than just a test of survival on the chaotic roads.

About half an hour after leaving town, sober was the call for all of them as they came across an upturned truck with smoke and steam hissing from its engine, one wheel still spinning in the air. The driver had already fled, observed Marcus, as he parked his bike and checked the cabin.

He saw the two bodies strewn along the road verge behind the truck, the bicycle a twisted tangle of metal and rubber still lying on the road and he figured that the accident must have literally happened no more than two minutes before at the most. Normally a crowd would gather quickly but so far only two farmworkers had appeared from the nearby field leaving their oxen shackled to the plow behind them. Between the field and the road grew large clumps of elephant grass and Marcus figured that the driver was probably crouched in there somewhere and would remain in hiding until nightfall knowing fully well that if the villagers caught him, they would beat him to death on the spot. If the police caught him, they would beat him half to death before robbing him.

The others gathered around the stricken men as Marcus rushed to his bike for his first aid kit.

"Don't bother," said Avi, looking down at the bodies, "they're fucked man - if they are not dead yet, they soon will be," and looking up at his companions, exclaimed with rolling eyes, "life can be a bitch, no? poor fuckers."

Raj lent over them and passed his meaty hands over their heads and felt one of the men's pulses on his neck, saying,

"This one is alive."

At that moment the other younger man, no more than a youth really, began to groan but was clearly not fully conscious. Both had multiple lacerations and head injuries. Marcus reappeared with his kit, Tatiana was just watching silently, as was Stepan, both expressionless, but Edna had tears in her eyes and with her hand over her mouth.

"What can we do for them?" she asked.

"Here, come and help me," said Marcus, "we can only do what we can but I don't feel like driving away without doing anything."

"Me neither," said Edna.

Marcus set about bandaging the men's heads, applying antiseptic to the wounds before doing so and he handed Edna two small bottles of homeopathic arnica, for bruising, and rescue remedy, for shock, to squirt between the men's lips. Raj was placing his hands on the men, moving from one spot to the other. Cars, buses and trucks rumbled past, slowing to avoid the upturned truck and slowing to see the entertainment - a bunch of crazy foreigners trying to save two dead men.

Stepan managed to wave down an empty three-wheeler and with the help of the two farm hands and the driver, the four foreign men carefully loaded the severely injured victims onto the back seat, handed the driver a hundred rupees to drive to the nearest hospital in Kanpur and wiped their hands and consciences clean.

"You think that fucker will take them to the hospital or just dump them by the road," pondered Avi delicately.

Tatiana slid on to the seat behind Marcus, who asked her,

"You ok?"

"I have seen dead men before today, don't worry,"

Marcus didn't think she was being cold. He felt she just didn't know what to feel anymore, but he believed her.

Avi roared off into the highway, swerving to avoid a bus as he did so, and they set off for Kanpur at the same breakneck speed.

Marcus found himself praying for Edna's safe return, he really liked her. After a while Tatiana nestled into Marcus' back once more, her arms around his waist.

In Kanpur they had to stop again. Raj needed to find new plugs for his bike. The rest of them sat around a dingy chai shop taking in the scenery while Raj and a grimy mechanic tinkered with his bike across the road.

If you have never had to stop at the outskirts of an Indian provincial city, it is like this. Dust, garbage and ramshackle workshops line the sides of the road interlaced with hovels made from an assortment of torn plastic and strips of tin and held together by flimsy poles and frayed nylon rope. Buses and trucks roar past other such vehicles standing by the road with bonnets up or wheels off waiting for repair. All of it is covered with layers of grease and dust and finally complemented by the presence of the odd cow, a few pigs and the obligatory mange ridden dogs scratching around for morsels in the dirt. Their chai was brewed in a blackened and battered aluminum pot, the multiply used leaves boiled with copious amounts of sugar before the Chai-Walla carelessly threw a cup of what could have been mistaken to be milk into the vile mix. It tasted like crap.

"Hey Marcus, nice restaurant, maybe next time we can bring our parents," cracked Edna.

"Next time you're going to have to dress better for the occasion Edna - if you want me to take you out."

"Oh, fuck this, what does Raj need to do man - we need to get going before it gets dark," interjected Avi, his patience wearing thin.

Part Chilean, part Russian Jew, Avi was shortish with broad shoulders and while not the prettiest portrait in the gallery nor the politest at the party he had a good heart and a total devotion to the Master. His intensity and borderline madness made Edna laugh.

Stepan answered him saying,

"Hey, Avi, screw you, relax - let the ladies enjoy their tea."

Stepan was lithe with the body of the dancer he was, tallish but not as tall as Marcus he had an angular face with a slightly hooked nose, full sensual lips and a lazy eye that seemed to wink at you as he spoke. He was still quite young and had been in the military until he had been delisted with the entire red army as it was recalled from the Baltic states in ninety-two, four years ago. The same year Marcus had been in Moscow with Genevieve.

Marcus had been there in Gorky Park at that very moment the soldiers had disgorged from the lines of buses to be literally dumped and left to their own devices. Two hours later there were around forty-thousand drunk kids in uniform wandering around singing and throwing up and Marcus and Genevieve had to have their photos taken with half of them as they made their way slowly back to the gate. Most of Stepan's former army friends were now making money in the weapons trade and had tried to bring him back into the fold only recently.

Half an hour later the three Enfields crossed the Ganges River and were heading south out of Kanpur but another hour further on, as dusk descended on the plains, they realized they had taken the wrong highway and were entering the ravine country along the Yamuna River.

They gathered around their map at a lonely traveler's stop, one of those places that served simple food and chai and even had rope beds lined up out the front for drivers to sleep on under the stars, beds that Marcus had slept on more than once during his journeys.

They found a minor road on the map that connected the highway they had taken to the one they wanted to be on and decided to try it rather than backtrack to Kanpur.

A few kilometers further on they found the road and turned east again. Night was settling in and the road became patchy, narrow and twisty as it snaked through rocky ravines and the going became slower and slower.

"The ravine country," Marcus thought, "what had he read about it?"

It was after ten at night when Marcus noticed the lights on his bike begin to fade and the engine begin to lose power until finally it rolled to a stop just as they entered the only village they had so far encountered since leaving the main highway.

"Damn, but maybe my luck is with me," thought Marcus.

The village was small but large enough to have a few small provision shops and a barber but that was about it. He couldn't see any sign of a mechanics workshop and only two parked motorbikes were to be seen and no cars at all. A single truck was parked just in the front of them and over to the left an old tractor and trailer sat in front of a small temple.

Tatiana dismounted wearily from behind him and loosed her long blond hair while adjusting her jeans. She wore only a white cotton embroidered shirt with an open neck that revealed more than an Indian sari top. A cotton prayer shawl hung carelessly around her neck.

The villagers had never seen anything like her and soon were emerging from every corner and every small hut and shop that could be seen and by the time Marcus propped up his bike on the stand there would have been two hundred brown faces staring at them with big white eyes from out of the gloom.

Marcus realized that they had probably never even seen a foreigner before.

"Where the hell are we he wondered?"

Tatiana remained cool and turned to the crowd asking, in her distinctive Russian accent.

"Chai, you have chai shop?"

Silence. More people gathered. Maybe three hundred now as Marcus saw a few sleepy children edge their way into the throng to catch a glimpse of the 'firangis' who had dropped out of the sky in the middle of the night.

"Chai hai?" called Marcus, and in response came a voice from somewhere in the crowd.

"Chai pinao?

"Harji, mehra doste chai pinai," confirmed Marcus.

Then there was a babble of voices and Marcus saw the man push his way back through the multitude. Thinking he could speak Hindi, half a dozen voices immediately began jabbering and gesticulating to him, but his Hindi was not good enough for that. He knew enough words and key phrases though from living six months in a village many years ago.

At that moment the other two bikes came roaring back into the village having realized that Marcus and Tatiana were not following anymore.

An agitated Avi pushed his way roughly through the gathered villagers followed by Raj, Stepan and Edna.

"What happened? what you stopped for man?"

"My bike broke down, I think it's the battery – and hope it isn't the alternator," replied Marcus.

"Fuck, what will we do, fuck!"

"Maybe I will ask if anyone has a battery for an Enfield for starters," replied Marcus coolly.

Then Avi suddenly felt the crowd closing in around them and lost it.

"Hey, what you doing man, get back, give us some space," yelled Avi as he went to push the nearest villager away from him but Marcus grabbed Avi by the shoulder and with irritation in his voice snarled at Avi.

"Just cool it."

And then turning to Raj said forcefully,

"Raj, get Avi out of here and you and he take the girls with you and wait for us outside the village. Stepan, stay here with me."

"Good idea," agreed Edna.

Tatiana, cool as ever, simply yawned and said,

"I need my chai."

Avi became agitated with her,

"You stupid - you want to wait for a chai? how about you stay here and get raped by all these fuckers then."

Tatiana rolled her eyes. At the same moment a little grizzled old man in a white kurta and dhoti came pushing through the crowd with two chipped and stained glasses of chai and seeing there were now six firangis hesitated.

"Bahort danyvad papaji," thanked Marcus as he swiftly took the glasses from the old man's hand and handed one each to Tatiana and Edna and turning to Avi said,

"Avi, this is India, not unlike the fucking Gaza strip - you keep your cool and so will they - you lose it and so will they - it is that simple."

Not that Marcus had never lost it with the Indians but he had learnt when to and when not to. When a tantrum could work for you and when it might just get you killed. In front of an Indian mob was definitely one of them.

"Hey man, I am just wanting to protect the girls here."

"Understood, then take them out of here now."

As the four of them left for the parked bikes the villagers politely made way for them in that Indian manner that meant, that 'space' did not preclude body contact and plenty of squeezing past. Some of them eyed Avi a bit suspiciously and with a hint of disapproval, noted Marcus, but mostly they were just being entertained by something they had never seen before. Not a single woman in the crowd he observed.

The moment Avi and the others departed Marcus turned to the nearest men and boys and started asking their names smilingly, shaking every hand he could reach while Stepan stood there with his amused half smile namaskaring to them with his palms raised. He was having fun, good.

"Battery," Marcus pointed to his stricken bike.

"Battery karab hai."

"Dussehra battery hai?" which basically translated as,

"The battery is broken - do you have another one?"

Marcus still prayed it wasn't the alternator.

One of the men started explaining something to Marcus in rapid Hindi all the while gesticulating to somewhere out in the darkness. When Marcus said he didn't understand the man started shouting louder.

Marcus simply nodded. Stepan chuckled. The man threw his hands up in the air at the stupid firangis and left.

The old grizzled man returned with four more chais, once again a bit confused as he realized that the others had now disappeared.

Marcus took two chais and handed them to the two most important looking men at the front keeping the others for himself and Stepan, sat down and began passing off names of Indian and Australian cricketers to his delighted audience. And waited for a miracle.

Around midnight the crowd had dwindled to around a hundred. Stepan asked,

"So, what we doing - we going to just stay here? what about the others?"

"I'll tell you what," replied Marcus, "if nothing happens in the next fifteen minutes, you go find the others and head off and I will find you on the road tomorrow maybe."

"You be ok?"

"Sure, someone will offer me a mat in a hut, no problem."

Something did happen, however, as two men appeared in the dim light of the solitary street lamp. One was wearing western style pants and shirt and he walked straight up to Marcus and Stepan introducing himself.

"Hullo, my name is Gopal - I am son of village chief - I can help you with speaking English - what are your good names?"

"Thank you, Gopal, namaste."

"I am Marcus and this is Stepan."

"And what is your country?"

Marcus spared him of the "Tasmania" response and said,

"Australia, and my friend is from Russia," and continuing, "I am from the same village as David Boon," the Australian cricketer of course.

And then Gopal came straight out with it, a little smile slipping from his lips as he spoke,

"And do you know whose village you are in?" and before Marcus could offer a guess, continued, "you are in the village of Phoolan Devi."

Gopal puffed up with pride as he spoke the name of the most notorious and internationally famous bandit queen, most known for taking out her revenge on a neighboring village of high caste Brahmins where she had been gang raped as a child. She had lined them up and shot and hacked to pieces every male in the village as her gang had looked on.

"Of course," thought Marcus, "the ravine country of the Yamuna."

Phoolan Devi had terrorized the ravine country for several years with her gang, one of who was her loyal lover. Terrorized in particular, the Thakurs or Brahmins, but here, in this village, these were her people.

Here, although presently held in a high security prison cell, she was still loved and revered. Their own female Robin Hood, their vengeful Kali who had broken the centuries old caste-based oppression they had had to suffer through time immemorial by way of a series of ghastly atrocities of her own.

Marcus remembered reading articles in the Indian newspapers. Of how police would only venture into this area in small armies and armed to the teeth, the most dangerous country in all of India.

Nonchalantly, Marcus then asked Gopal,

"Ah yes, Phoolan Devi, this is her village? and you are her friend?"

"Yes, of course," nodded Gopal feeling pleased and with an Indian waggle of the head.

Stepan was looking at Marcus completely puzzled and lifted his upturned palms in a shrug silently pleading with Marcus to fill him in. Marcus subtly signaled with his hand to be patient while saying to Gopal,

"If you see Phoolan Devi, please tell her from me that myself and my friends are very, very honored to have visited her beautiful village."

"Yes, yes, of course - we are also very honored to have foreigners visit our village - this is first time."

"Little wonder," thought Marcus but then curious to understand more, asked,

"And there are still dacoits operating here?"

"Yes, yes - just last night there was truck driver killed outside our village," gesturing in the direction Marcus had sent the others.

"And why was he killed?" suddenly a little unsure of whether he should have asked. But Gopal was enjoying himself and proud as punch.

"He made mistake."

"Oh"

"He would not pay our tax."

By this time Stepan was starting to get the picture. Marcus turned to him and they both smiled and nodded comically to each other. Gopal continued.

"Do not worry your good selves - your friends will come to no harm."

And then gesturing to Marcus' bike parked across the street from where they sat on the concrete platform surrounding the sacred Pipal tree, so typical of Indian villages and towns, where a man was installing a new battery in his bike.

"They walked to other village two kilometers away - one man there was known to have a bike like yours."

"You must thank him for me Gopal, how much was the cost?"

"No cost."

"What do you mean, 'no cost?'"

Gopal simply shrugged and said,

"Please take it, it is our gift."

Marcus decided he didn't really want to know how they had acquired the battery after all and instead he walked over to the little temple and prostrated before Durga seated on her Lion within, leaving two, hundred-rupee notes at her feet.

"I see you are religious man," nodded Gopal approvingly.

"Yes, very, I especially love the Goddess Durga whom I worshipped in my past life," replied Marcus leaving out the fact that he had also been a Brahmin in that life.

The old Enfield fired up, fully charged, and as they thundered out of the village of the Bandit Queen, Stepan threw his head back in laughter, shouting to the darkness,

"Faarrrkkk"

They found the others two kilometers from the village in a clearing of stunted trees. Avi was pacing while Edna and Raj were seated next to each other on the ground. Tatiana was laid out on her back with her arms folded beneath her head resting on her small pack. It was one in the morning.

Avi strode up to them excitedly.

"You guys got the bike fixed. Five more minutes and we were out of here. I was telling the others you were dead already."

"That's nice of you Avi, but we have new friends back there who we can get to kill you if you like," teased Stepan as he climbed off the bike.

"What you mean?"

"Well," explained Stepan, "they killed someone right here the night before."

"No shit," said Edna.

"No shit," confirmed Marcus.

"It's the village of Phoolan Devi, the bandit queen - we rode straight into it - you heard of her?"

"You're shitting me? sure I've heard of her man," put in Raj.

At that, Avi turned on the others, with voice raised.

"I told you it was fucking dangerous here and we should leave - I told you but no, you just said, 'chill Avi, chill, don't be paranoid.'"

"Chill Avi," laughed Edna.

Avi walked angrily over to his bike and fired it up. Edna threw her pack on, laughingly ruffling his hair and hopped on behind him. Avi grinned sheepishly at her. Tatiana slid on behind Marcus, immediately resting her head on his back and wrapping her arms around him as they rode off into the night swinging around pot holes as they went.

The afternoon of the next day, after numerous obligatory chai stops at dusty road side haunts where timeless India stood still in the haze of the relentless sun the bikes rolled into Khajuraho. There was not much of a town but a few houses, some shops, mostly souvenir shops, and a varied collection of scattered hotels. Marcus and Edna were all for getting a room with attached hot bath. They were sweaty and caked in dust from the trip but the others had less money and in the end the bond was such between them that they opted for a six-bed dormitory in a cheap and sprawling pilgrim rest house that had endless empty rooms, peeling paint on the walls, and with stained porcelain and rusty taps in the communal bath room.

Four of the beds were pushed together in a line along one of the walls of the narrow rectangular room. Along the other wall where the door opened were two more beds end to end turned the other way leaving a narrow corridor in the middle. It was basic to say the least. Two fans hung from the ceiling and the beds at least had clean but stained and frayed sheets and pillows.

"This is going to be interesting," thought Marcus, observing the arrangement of the beds.

The six of them paused as they entered the room and looked at each other all wondering the same thing but it was Edna who broke the deadlock, tossing her bag in to the middle of the four beds pushed together and then grabbing Marcus' laid it next to hers, saying,

"Ok that is the parents in the middle, now the rest of you kids can sleep where you want."

The Russians moved in fast. Stepan promptly lay down and stretched out in the space next to Edna while Tatiana placed her things on the bed in the corner next to Marcus', drew out a towel and shampoo and without saying a word nor with a hint of an expression on her face, made her way out the door.

"Hey, what about me," objected Avi looking decidedly pissed at Stepan.

"Hey, there's room for all the kids on the big bed with Mom and Pop, Avi," laughed Edna.

As young and pretty, as she was, "no more than thirty," Marcus thought, Edna had decided to be the Jewish mother for the night.

"No fucking way, you think I'm gonna sleep next to a guy," objected Avi.

Laid back Raj, meanwhile flopped tiredly on one of the single beds saying, in his southern drawl,

"I guess this will do me fine then."

⌒〜〜⌒

Marcus walked out on to the balcony, come corridor, to smoke a beedi and take in the view of the surrounds from the second story of the guesthouse. He passed by the bathroom door and heard the girls in there giggling. He could only imagine what and about whom they might be laughing. It was nice to hear Tatiana laugh though. Avi followed him out leaving Raj and Stepan resting on the beds. He drew up alongside Marcus and joined him as they slumped over the rusty and peeling metal railings to see the famous temple rising above some trees about three hundred meters away.

"Marcus, can I say something to you?"

"Sure Avi"

"You know what Marcus - I've felt you are giving me a really hard time lately and I feel a lack of respect coming from you," he paused and then finished with, "and it doesn't feel good."

Marcus reflected on the journey since the previous night in the village of Phoolan Devi, and realized he had cut Avi short on several occasions when they had stopped for a chai break, losing patience with the 'Israeli way of speaking' to the Indians.

"It shits me the way you speak to the Indians, Avi - it's what I don't like about a lot of Israelis but it doesn't mean I don't like them, it doesn't mean I don't like you - you see I don't dislike people, I don't hate people, but sometimes I just hate what people do - and sometimes I say so."

"Well," responded Avi, "I want us to get along."

Marcus drew the last puff of his beedi, stubbed it well and tossed the organic butt over the edge of the railing and turned to face Avi.

"Thanks for saying that Avi - you have a good heart - I like you even more," and smiling Marcus drew Avi to him and gave him a hug. Avi responded awkwardly and looking into his eyes Marcus saw a sensitive man beneath that crude exterior. From that moment on his patience for Avi was pretty much limitless for all the years they would know each other. Avi was ok – mad as batshit, but ok.

Marcus turned back to the view and pondered the situation. He enjoyed so much this sense of community, this tribal group they were bonding into as they worked through the dynamics and relationships in the midst of adventures and small difficulties. Being part of a tribe, a band of brothers and sisters was where he felt most at home, just as he had done in those early days on the community before it had all gotten too insular and too conservative in its radicalism, and during his time at the Franklin River and way before then, the months in the Himalayas doing the retreats.

It made him think of Brazil and Bia and he remembered how it had been tough for him in Brazil when with Juliana. He had only had her and Bia and when Juliana was not speaking to him, he had, well Bia as a little kid, but he didn't have a tribe. Many of Juliana's friends had been jealous of him or antagonistic and some members of her family and ex in-laws openly hostile. What would he encounter this time? More of the same perhaps? It was the first time he started to have doubts.

He had two gorgeous women with him who both seemed to like him. Smiling to himself he wondered if they had decided something in the bathroom already. He felt apprehensive. Bia, he was convinced, was where his destiny lay, but could that destiny be altered by chance and random surrender?

Marcus got his answer that night.

They had all gone out to eat together in a local Dhaba and Marcus noticed Stepan was flirting seductively with Edna and Edna was enjoying it. Avi was clearly a bit envious but was making light of it while Marcus too felt a twinge of jealousy about Edna. He liked her but he wasn't about to compete for her in this situation because he didn't know what he really wanted or else he didn't want anyway. And he owed Stepan - in a fashion.

He guessed Tatiana had claimed him already while the girls were in the bathroom and in different circumstances it could have been like that.

Like at the Franklin River campaign when they had been a tribe and Marcus had slept with several women in succession and even in the same bed and sharing open sleeping bags on the floor of the forest with Winiata, the beautiful Maori transvestite, and Christine, his young girlfriend at the same time, sharing the warmth and the love beneath the trees. There hadn't been any real jealousy then. They had been a band of brothers and sisters on a mission. Although then he hadn't been passionately in love either and that was the difference.

In the room that night as they lay down to rest there was plenty of banter and play. Edna rolled over to Marcus and put her arms around him and kissed him goodnight spreading kisses over his cheek but Stepan rolled her back towards him while Avi sat at the end of the bed complaining that he was missing out.

"Just lie down and relax with us Avi," teased Marcus.

"No, way, you think I'm going to lie next to a man - hey Edna come over to my bed I have more experience than that fucking Russian."

"No Avi"

"Oh, Edna come on, please, make me happy."

"Go to bed Avi."

"Come on Edna, be my girl."

"On the bike I'm your girl, be happy with that."

"Yes, fuck you Avi, it is my turn to seduce this beautiful lady."

Stepan began to kiss and caress Edna with growing passion and Edna responded willingly.

"Oh, screw you guys," said Avi as he joined Raj on the outer who just lay on his back with his eyes open.

Tatiana meanwhile had silently wrapped herself around Marcus' back. He didn't mind that at all and took her hand in his and squeezed it. He indulged affection and sensuality and Tatiana was a very attractive woman, long and slender with bright blue eyes, firm breasts that Marcus could feel pressing between his shoulder blades while she began to kiss the back of his neck sending a tingle of pleasure down his spine. He felt her hand move deftly under the sheet along his naked torso searching out the gap between his belly and his sarong. His body opened in response and he felt himself shiver with forbidden excitement as he rolled over and took her in his arms. She closed her eyes and moved her mouth towards his but instead he kissed her delicately on her forehead, whispering to her,

"I can't do it, Tatiana, I am a promised man – but hey, I'm happy to hug you and hold you until we sleep."

"Ok, I would like that," she replied sweetly and hugged him fiercely, squeezing her legs tightly together, her body shuddering uncontrollably for a few moments before she lay quietly beside him taking his hand in hers and kissing it gently.

It had become perfectly clear to Marcus in that moment. He was Bia's man and he was able to resist even this extreme temptation with a clear mind and heart. It felt right. Their bond was too strong.

Stepan and Edna kept up their play for some time but after a while the heat seemed to fade within that little tryst as well and eventually, they all slept, albeit fitfully, and dreamed of naked lovers carved into temple walls that contorted and writhed and came alive and spread themselves about them kissing their lips and sucking deliciously on their breasts within the twilight zone of their consciousness.

⌒‿‿⌒

Mid-morning the following day and Marcus was sitting, meditatively, leaning against a wall inside the main temple when Edna appeared and seeing him there sat down opposite him, resting her gaze on him. She had a serious expression on her face.

"So, what do you think, Marcus,"

"Think about what, Edna?"

"You still love me?" she asked teasingly as she broke into a little smile before changing back into her serious face, "no, I mean what is this all about, the six of us coming here, the crazy attractions between us and this place?"

Marcus remained silent for a few moments and allowed himself the space for his answers to find form and then after a few long moments replied,

"Well, there is no chance at play here - look, the Master stops giving Satsang and then people either stay or travel - some went to Rishikesh and Haridwar, some to Brindavan and so on, depending on what their needs were."

Edna looked at him questioningly, asking,

"So, what's the connection? are you saying we came here for a reason?"

"Of course, we did - look at us all, look at this temple, all these erotic carvings in the worship of Tantra - Tantra is not just about the yoga of sexual and spiritual union but is about facing the Maya, the world, the Illusion, entering into it, embracing it and letting it go in surrender to the divine - understanding it to be just a manifestation of the divine through the acceptance of it rather than the rejection of it."

"Go on, you have me interested."

"So, look at each of us - I am about to enter into a marriage and am

153

confronted with the realization that this marriage is for real and maybe even forever and that is suddenly challenging for me - I am attracted to you, to Tatiana and to other women I will meet in the future no doubt - so somehow this whole situation, this meeting and journey with all of you to this place creates the perfect crossroad for me to have to make a choice and in the world of illusion, the maya, I made that choice, but in the world of the eternal self, the unchanging, that choice has already been made, the script already written and it is all just a dream of the sleeping Vishnu," Edna was silent and attentive, "and you, Edna? you are at the crossroads of a relationship you are not sure if you want anymore - I don't know all of your story but I guess that you too feel that a decision has to be made, yet somehow it seems to have been made for you."

"I'm still not sure, Marcus."

"I think you will stay with him," said Marcus and then moving on,

"And Stepan, did you know that when I first came to the Master, I had a hot affair with a girl from Kenya - well, she had been with Stepan before and he had to go away to get a new visa in Nepal and when he came back, he found her with me - I had thought it was all over between them, but he was really cool about it, and as you well know his sexuality is intense and Stepan and myself have this brotherly karma between us around that energy - we have history," Marcus smiled, "it is like we compete but don't mind sharing."

Edna looked around her at the walls, surrounded by eroticism on all sides and pretended to fan herself, saying,

"Stop, Marcus, now you're making me feel hot and sweaty."

"Tatiana, Ravi, Raj - they all have issues around sexuality and relationships."

"So great, here we all are," said Edna, adding in her New York twang,

"In the world's first ever, original porn cinema."

"And I love you all," added Marcus.

"I love you too, Marcus,"

Edna went silent for a time, the two of them closing their eyes to the lustful, erotic carvings that surrounded them. Eventually, she opened her eyes and while gazing out through the opening at the side of the temple towards the hazy blue March sky of Central India, asked,

"Are their tigers out there?"

Marcus laughed,

"Sure, there are tigers out there – did I ever tell you about the Tiger I used to fight in my dreams,"

"Another time sweetheart,"

"The Tiger still watches us as we sleep, Edna."

And, yes
it was quite surreal
to ride thru the valley of the shadow of death
with a biblical Jew
to that temple of flesh

And, when
to recall her name
lingering there within those halls erotic
whispering anew
upon his dying breath

Chapter 19

Paris, New York and a Ticket to Rio

Genevieve was waiting for Marcus at Charles De Gaulle airport after the flight from Delhi. She greeted him with a smile and a hug and led him to the underground holding his hand.

He was doing a favor for her, helping her renew her residency in Australia while they were still legally married and as his round the world ticket had a stop in Paris before heading to New York, well, he liked to help, he liked her.

She took him to her mother's loft, the place his ex-mother-in-law used when she came to Paris from Provence to visit her daughters. It was a small but very cozy little place on a top story in the Rue De Lille, just one block from the Seine on the South Bank across from the Louvre, the very heart and soul of Paris.

Marcus settled in and Genevieve left for her apartment in the ninth district which lay just to the north of the city center where the Jewish rag trade thrived. When he had stayed there with Genevieve on previous visits to the city, he had always walked home to her apartment along Rue De Saint Denis because Saint Denis was one of those streets that gave you a wonderful kaleidoscope of Paris all in one. Chique cafes, scattered shops and patisseries, owned mostly by Jews and Arabs, and further along, whores plying their trade along the sidewalks.

He decided to go for a walk and found himself sitting on the Pont de Neuf listening to some African buskers and watching the River Seine slide by like he would the Ganga in India.

Nothing to do right now and nowhere to go. After each song he would flip a coin into the buskers' guitar case and then stuff his hands back inside his pockets to keep out the spring evening chill before turning his attention back to the river. They were playing an eclectic mix of popular songs with an occasional song in their native tongue and Marcus guessed they would have been from one of the old French colonies, maybe Senegal. He thought of Senegal first, knowing it to have been the longest held French possession in Africa, and had been under their dominion for almost three hundred years. He also thought of Burkina Faso because that is where Bia had almost travelled to with her cousin when her family had opted out of joining her in India - before Marcus had offered to meet her in Delhi.

"What if she had gone to Burkina Faso?" he wondered, "what would our destinies have held for us then?"

He had picked up a pile of faxes from Bia on his return from Khajuraho and had sat there reading them while Tatiana had sat alongside him reading a fax from her husband. Marcus had wondered aloud if her husband had mentioned how the gun running business was going and she had playfully swiped him with the fax paper in response, saying,

"Yes, he wants to know if you can make some contacts for him in South America."

Bia had broken the news of Marcus to pretty much everyone who was close to her. Some with trepidation, some with open excitement. Her jilted partner was completely pissed and was not talking to her anymore and worse, he was bad mouthing her to all of her friends. Her father, on the other hand, had been incredibly accepting. Marcus had not expected that at all.

But the grandmother had gone straight to see the priest, while her aunties had maintained a somewhat shocked indignation. Of the cousins, a few had remembered Marcus and had good memories of him playing with them when they visited Bia as children. A mixed bag of reactions awaited him, and he wondered if he was just repeating an old story that he had never truly let go of.

～ ⌣ ～

The buskers took a break from their music. Four of them in all, playing a variety of instruments, guitars, shekeres a xalam and African drums. Two of them dread locked, two of them with shorter heads of hair, they were probably all in their thirties and forties, dressed like, well, African buskers with a predominance of green, red and yellow clothing. One of them sat down next to Marcus and pulled out a plastic container of home cooked food that let loose a steamy aroma of spices and the rich food made Marcus realize he was hungry.

It reminded Marcus of the time around eight years ago he had eaten in a South London African restaurant. The type that sprang up in someone's home and were spread by word of mouth that were the health department's nightmare and who closed them down with fines that were never paid before the same people would open again in another relative's house.

That was the time that Marcus, as a youngish looking thirty-six-year-old who had almost never had a lover over thirty since being with Juliana, had found himself being seduced by the big momma of the premises who must have been over fifty and weighed about two hundred and fifty pounds but who had exuded so much sexuality as she sat herself next to him and flirted outrageously, that he had found his sex hardening of its own accord - and to his complete astonishment.

He had heard of withered old shamanic women having the same power. After that experience he believed it fully.

～ ⌣ ～

"Voulez-vous manger avec nous mon ami ?" asked the busker with dreads wrapped in a Rasta style woolen beanie that struggled to contain the matted locks. He turned to Marcus while holding up the container of food.

"Il sent bon," replied Marcus and then struggling to find more French came out with.

"Mas je ne mange pas votre diner."

"Mais sil vous plait, mon ami."

"Ok, obrigado."

"Damn," thought Marcus, "now I am starting to speak my bad Portuguese again, my even worse French is going to hell."

"Where you be from, mon?', the busker asked as he produced another plastic container from his jumbled cloth shoulder bag and began making a meal for Marcus.

"Tasmanie," he replied.

"Tanzanie? are you from Tanzanie?"

"Non, je suis Tasmanien," there was a pause, "an Island off Australia."

"Ah bien, Australien"

Whereupon Marcus sat on the Pont De Neuf dining cebu guinaar, a delicious, spicy Senegalese stew of chicken and vegetables and couscous with his new best friends. It tasted sensational and he stayed there chatting and answering questions about India and asking them about Senegal until they pulled out the huge spliff whereupon he decided to head back to his loft. Ganja was not his drug.

Genevieve came around the next morning telling Marcus that she had had a serious fight with her boyfriend who was seething with jealousy about Marcus being in town. Marcus remembered what it was like and felt a twinge of sympathy for the suffering fellow male and simultaneous relief that he didn't seem to wear that kind of pain the same as he had in the past.

They spent the week together, or at least the days and sometimes the evenings as well, doing what had to be done at the embassy with all the paperwork and then going to art house movies and galleries and she even took Marcus to a party with her instead of the boyfriend.

Genevieve was punishing him mercilessly for his jealousy.

And she was enjoying Marcus' company. It was nice to be there with her as a friend and seemed like a perfect signing off from their previously tempestuous marriage. She was somehow softer, sweeter, even a bit humbler maybe. One of her girlfriends swore to Marcus she had changed since returning from her confrontation with the master. It made him wonder.

And Bia knew he was there and knew what he was doing and Genevieve knew about Bia so in Marcus' mind, all was good.

Marcus' next stop was New York where he moved in with Edna into her apartment in Soho for a few days, just around the corner from a loft where he had stayed with an artist friend two years before.

On that previous visit he had helped his artist friend put together styrofoam and chrome rod sculptures for her first exhibition and had expected they would be a complete flop but he was totally wrong and the next time he had seen the sculptures they had appeared in a stylish art magazine with an interview of his friend discussing her next avant-garde project. She was now one of the latest darlings of the quirky Manhattan art scene. Marcus decided not to visit her this time.

"Do you still love me, Marcus?"

"More than ever, Edna, but where is your boyfriend, I thought you lived together?"

"He moved out to stay in his workshop because you were coming."

"Really, why?"

Edna tilted her head and raised her eyebrows, a half-smile passing her lips.

"He thought he might be in the way of us," raising her eyebrows as she spoke.

Marcus studied Edna trying to figure out where this was leading to. She was so pretty. And dressed smartly now she was back in her Manhattan stomping ground. In the end he didn't go there. It seemed like a situation where no-one knew exactly what the other wanted or expected, including the boy-friend.

"How long you want to stay Marcus?"

"Just a few days - I have to buy a ticket to Rio and then I'm heading to Baltimore for a couple of days to visit my God daughter."

"God daughter? you have a God daughter in Baltimore? I can't keep up with you Marcus - come on, tell me the story, there has to be a woman involved right?"

"Yeah, there was."

"Well?"

"It was the first time I came to New York - I came as part of a non-governmental delegation to the UN conference on disarmament in nineteen-eighty-two."

"And what else haven't you done?"

"Haven't gone over the Niagara Falls in a barrel yet," and then added,

"But I did cross a ravine with a raging torrent beneath it in the Himalayas using just two cables for support - had to crawl across them like a crab and as I got to the middle, they started to separate..."

"Ok, no tangents, Marcus."

"Well, we were supposed to be billeted out to the homes of people in New York but when I found out my billet was out past Queens somewhere I decided to look up an old girlfriend in the Village and see if I could camp with her."

"So, you stayed with her and you started having it on with her again?"

"Nothing of the sort, when I got to the Village, I realized I didn't have her phone number with me and all I could remember was the street she lived in."

"Oh cool, so here you are first time in New York and you are lost in the Village without the proper address - what did you do? sell your body?"

"Not quite"

"Not quite? Marcus, normal people check into a hotel!"

"I didn't have much money and I was going to stay for six weeks."

"So?"

"So, I walked up and down her street checking the names on the post boxes inside the lobbies of each building."

"Marcus you can't get into buildings without a key."

"I waited for people going inside and asked them to let me in."

"And they let you in? Marcus people in New York don't do shit like that - we don't trust anyone."

Marcus shrugged. Edna shook her head in disbelief.

"Anyway, I couldn't find her name anywhere, and it was getting dark but then I saw this little store that sold Tibetan imports and knew she would visit that store so I walked in and asked this black guy at the counter if he knew her."

"This doesn't happen here, Marcus - it just doesn't happen."

"But he knew her and called her but she wasn't home, but before long we were good friends and he told me to hang in and see who came by."

By this time Edna had surrendered.

"So, after a while this black chick comes into the store and the guy introduces us but she doesn't even say hullo, she just glances at me out of the corner of her eye."

"At least this sounds more like it," laughed Edna.

"The guy tells her I am looking for somewhere to crash but she still doesn't say anything and they continue their conversation about some mutual friend's drama but finally, she is finished and walks towards the door,"

"No," exclaims Edna.

"So, she gets to the door and then turns around, really coolly, and says to the guy, nodding in my direction, not even addressing me, 'he can come stay with me'."

Edna is smiling, shaking her head.

"So, I walk out after her and to cut a long story short,"

"This is already a long story," cut in Edna.

"To cut a long story short, I offered to massage her."

"That is just, so 'new age', Marcus."

"She complained of having a head ache - I had already cleaned the kitchen and wanted to offer something else in return - she said, 'you can massage my head and neck but don't touch my back - I can't handle anyone touching my back.'"

"So, you snuck your way down to her back, right?"

"Of course - that is where her issue was."

"What issue?"

"She had been whipped in a past life."

Edna's big eyes bulged.

"And I suppose you told her that?"

"Sure, I did."

"I don't believe this - I just don't fucking believe it - here is this Tasmanian white guy, walks into a black chick's apartment not even knowing her and tells her that she has been whipped in her past life - what did she do next? throw you out on the street I hope."

"No, she cried and we made love."

"Really? where was she from? California?"

"No, she grew up in Harlem - right here."

"She was from Harlem and she didn't put a knife in you? ok, so where does the god daughter come in?"

"A few years later she has a kid and asks me to be the god-father."

"Thanks Marcus, I need to get some air, let's go do some shopping - I need the therapy after that."

They walked out on to the street and turned into Broadway where Edna dived into a delicatessen. It was packed with people so Marcus handed her some money to help buy food and told her he would wait outside and soak up the last rays of sunshine.

A homeless black man approached him and asked him for ten bucks. Marcus told him he didn't give money for people to buy crack but he would buy the guy a hot dog from the stand on the corner so he walked down with the homeless man and bought him a hot dog, asked his name, and began a conversation.

The man became a bit emotional.

"Man, some people give me money just to get rid of me - no one wants to talk to me."

"I love everyone," replied Marcus, but then added, as he nodded towards a man walking past in an Armani suit carrying a briefcase and a superior smirk worn across his face, "except maybe jerks like him – them, I just acknowledge their existence."

They both laughed, and the man took Marcus by the arm saying,

"I like you, man, can you give me some money now?"

"No, but I'll buy you another hot dog if you like."

Edna appeared next to them with a large bag of groceries cradled in one arm and without looking at Marcus spoke to the homeless man,

"I am so sorry sir, is my friend bothering you - I am so embarrassed if he is."

"Edna this is Ray, I told him you might be able to score some crack for him."

"Oh, come on, man," complained Ray.

<hr>

Marcus managed to find the cheapest return business class ticket to Rio after following a tiny little classified he spied in the 'Village Voice'. It took him to a single little room on the third story of a shabby building in the East Village where, who would have guessed, sat an Indian man behind an almost bare and chipped desk that contained a single folder and the remains of a curry.

Behind the man was an old travel poster of Paris showing the Moulin Rouge and a line of can-can girls with legs kicked up in unison and their tutus opening the way into the frilly decor of the man's lurid fantasies. It was the only decoration in the whole room. Marcus handed the man a hundred dollars and looked closely at the ticket - and hoped.

<hr>

It gave him three days in Baltimore where he stayed with Janet and Mike and the kids in the predominantly black inner-city neighborhood.

His god daughter Robbie was eight now and had been looking forward to his visit for weeks.

The first night while Marcus was in the upstairs bathroom brushing his teeth, he heard gun shots out the back. He killed the light of the bathroom and looked out into the tiny back yard just in time to see a man swinging over the back fence with a gun in his hand and lie down in the bushes hiding.

"Er Janet," he called out from the door of the bathroom, "there is a guy in the backyard with a gun."

"Just stay away from the window and he will either go away or someone will kill him," she called back as she tucked the children into bed.

"Ok, no problem," and he went back to cleaning his teeth in the semi darkness.

The next day he took Robbie around the Baltimore harbor, taking her to visit the aquarium, the playground, the museum and finally the shops where she bought a giant Mickey Mouse from the Disney store that was way bigger than her. Hyped on chocolates, lollipops and ice creams he finally gave her back to her mother, sticky, over excited and manic. Janet took one look at Robbie and turning to Marcus said, shaking her head.

"You're putting her to bed tonight."

So, he did, reading story after story until finally, his voice cracking, Robbie fell into slumberland, cradled in his arm with a contented half smile across her full little lips, her tight and curly African hair, spongy on his skin.

～ ～ ～

Back in New York with Edna again, Marcus insisted on inviting her partner to come and have dinner with them. He would pay as a 'thank you.' And they did and Marcus saw that her man was feeling uncomfortable so he began the conversation talking about his pending meeting with Bia in Rio and by the end of the night everybody was relaxed. And his ticket to Rio turned out to be fine. Business class was cool. Edna and her partner would stay together happily and have three beautiful children.

> *In the city*
> *they say never sleeps*
> *there are subways that take you*
> *to a place of no destination*
> *but somewhere you must find*
> *over coffee or wine*
> *your heart of hearts*
> *that you may send a letter*
> *nevertheless*
> *with a story that ends,*
> *'With love from New York'*

Chapter 20

Nothing is Forever

Bia was there as he walked through customs and out the frosted glass doors. The way she danced up to him with that sweetest of smiles and threw her arms around him was just so her, so familiar.

Marcus was back in Rio, for the first time in twenty-two years.

"Come, Marcus, I am going to take you to the mountains."

"To where?"

"To my house in the hills past Petropolis - it's where we often go for weekends and you won't meet my children just yet - I left them with their father for the weekend so we have each other just for ourselves."

They made their way up the steep valley, Bia's little Suzuki four-wheel drive bouncing and lurching up one of the worst roads Marcus' had been on. Giant granite monoliths rose up on each side of them and up ahead Marcus caught a glimpse of the tallest of all of them towering up at the head of the valley, Maria Comprida, as it was named.

Lots of things bore the name of Maria in Brazil. He noticed the flowers that grew along the edge of the rainforest, the Mata Atlântica, and remembered they bore the name of Maria too. 'Maria Sem Vergonha', or Maria without shame, named such because they always flowered, they always displayed their beauty, the flowers that had no shame in this catholic world.

To Marcus they symbolized Brazil and all of its sexual contradictions. The country where women wore bikinis that provoked to show more than had they been entirely naked, where widows still wore black, where honor killings still scandalized the news on a regular basis, where virgins were worshipped and where during Carnival, no man had a wife and no woman a husband.

And where women went to confession and knelt before the priest with plunging necklines sobbing tears of remorse forming rivulets trickling through the valleys of their full and heaving breasts. The foliage was lush, the mountains phallic and the sea a seductive azure.

Reaching the top of the valley, the land flattened and broadened and finally they passed through a large wooden security gate and entered a little paradise of neat and fine houses nestled within tropical gardens dotted along the crystalline stream that bubbled through a succession of natural pools made from the river rock. Each side of the top of the valley the monoliths rose skywards from the edge of sloping green fields where a handful of horses and cows grazed in tranquility.

This was yet another facet of Brazil. The road that led to this place was abominable but at the end of the road lay idyllic luxury. A very pristine condominium where wealthier people from Rio, many of whom worked for the giant television company of Globo, which dominated news and entertainment in the country, passed their weekends in a carefully preserved natural environment.

But there was no money for the road because that was public and public moneys were pilfered and drained like water into the pockets of corrupt politicians and public officials and by land developers who could bribe their way out of paying for public amenities and road improvements. The country was a beautiful mess.

"Come Marcus, not now, I want to take you for a walk - you're going to love it."

Marcus released Bia from his arms after a passionate kiss in her bedroom that left his fingers tingling with the feel of her soft flesh and silky skin beneath the light clothing where he had begun to explore excitedly.

She took him by the hand and led him outside of her pretty cottage and through the exuberant garden to where it flattened in to a lawn dotted with flowering azaleas and hibiscus that randomly blended with native trees that had been left untouched around the garden's periphery. They crossed the stream at the bottom of the garden via a rock wall with a shallow pool behind it and Marcus, taken by the purity of the water could not resist leaning down to drink.

"It's good to drink," confirmed Bia.

"Amazing water," he commented after quenching his thirst, "after New York, Paris and India this is actually water, alive water!"

Bia held his hand and led him up a little path until they came upon a larger one that headed directly up the valley. The monoliths rose up in front of them and before long the valley narrowed, the path became steeper and the forest closed in around them.

"This is the Mata Atlántica," Marcus, "it used to cover most of the entire coast of Brazil and it is the eco system that has more species of plants and animals than any other in the world."

"It's beautiful - it's very alike our subtropical rain forest back in Australia - you'll notice when we get there," he smiled at her while drawing her nearer to him.

Bia had already told Marcus in the car that she had decided to go and live with him in Australia.

It was a huge decision for her to make. She had never once been there and leaving her large extended South American family would be a major event. And she had two children too. A boy, Sol. fourteen, almost fifteen whom she had birthed when only sixteen herself and a daughter, Rosa, nine-years-old.

Marcus wondered what it would be like joining the families together. He had three daughters, one of whom had just left home but the younger two were only eleven and eight and they would all be thrown together soon.

⌣⌣⌣

Marcus and Bia crossed the now narrow and swift flowing stream several times as they made their way deeper into the forest until it opened out into a moss-covered floor where a few forest giants surrounding a fairy like glade. A giant blue monarch butterfly spread its wings and danced through the branches of the trees.

"Oh well, there goes a tornado in America," quipped Marcus as his eyes followed the butterfly."

"Tornado, what do you mean?"

"Haven't you heard, Bia? the fluttering of a butterfly's wings in China can cause a tornado in America - an old proverb about the laws of chaos and cause and consequence."

"I like it."

Bia started unbuttoning her shirt until it hung open revealing her low-cut white bra and then reaching round her back pulled the bra sideways and deftly unclipped it, sliding it off to reveal her largish nipples and smallish but shapely soft breasts. She then moved towards Marcus and pushing her hips gently into his began unbuttoning his shirt until their naked excited skin rubbed delicately against each other. Marcus thrilled at the sensation of her nipples passing over his and after a long and drawn-out kiss, perfect lips to perfect lips, he withdrew, asking

"Are there Jaguars here?"

"Maybe, maybe no, but I want to devour you first," she murmured while nibbling his ear.

Her hands slid down to the button of his jeans and quickly released it and the zipper in one swift movement. Marcus felt her long fingers close around his growing sex and slide from root to tip with the expertise of an angel playing her harp.

"I love him, I love his shape and his size," she whispered.

Marcus untied the cord of her loose cotton pants and slid them down over her rear and dropped his own torso as he did so to pass them over her feet while burying his lips over the mound of her sex, still covered with her panties.

"And I love her, I love her smell."

Then slipping her last remaining garment over her small perfect feet he began to taste her, fully drawing her to him with his hands around her ass and using his tongue to explore her as he rapidly remembered her most sensitive and pleasurable spots. Bia exhaled sharply as his tongue found its mark and the wetness of her began to drip around his open mouth and he drank her and swam ecstatically within her.

"I want you inside me," she gasped

"Now!"

Marcus released her after one last passionate kiss of her sex and quickly spread their garments over the soft moss for Bia to lay. She sank on to her back with her legs apart and her fingers tightly wedged inside of her, her eyes glazed with pleasure and moistness.

"Come inside me Marcus," she pleaded and lent forward to draw his hardened sex to her.

Marcus felt his organ had already become wet with the excitement as Bia's hands moved over it and passed his own wetness fully around him before taking his to hers. The sensitive end of his hardened sex as it entered her swollen ready labia sucking him tightly inside of her shot waves of almost unbearable pleasure through his spine. She drew his body to hers sliding her sex around and slowly devouring his, and arching her back, thrust him inside of herself with the force of her legs around his buttocks.

Cradling her weight around his neck she moved him patiently and rhythmically deeper within until the very tip of his sex slipped perfectly into her deepest and most secret inner sanctum of flesh. She squeezed it longingly.

Holding Bia beneath him with his elbows to allow her to move and do with him as she wished he was sure he had never in his life felt anything like this.

If there were no adequate words to describe God then Bia's sex was God. He groaned, she exhaled and panted in time to her movement. Lips closed on hungry lips they drank and devoured their fill of each other from every opening and pore on offer.

The Jaguar watched from the shelter of the forest, still, forever still.

Bia sat by the stream as a shaft of sunlight broke through the canopy to light her skin golden, her dark hair hung loose past her shoulders and danced above her breasts as she washed herself, a sweet smile for Marcus as he sat on a rock next to her.

"I love you, Marcus."

"And I love you too."

"Stay with me forever."

Marcus paused for a few moments, staring into the water as it bubbled past.

"Nothing is forever."

A look of sudden hurt passed over her face and she glanced sharply up at him.

"Only our true self is forever - everything else passes, everything else has its time to begin and its time to end," he continued.

"I mean until we die, Marcus."

"I know that's what you mean but how can I promise that?"

"I can."

"Can you really? every time someone made that promise to me before it didn't happen and I told myself I would never make that promise again."

"I am not those other people, Marcus."

"I know Bia, you are my partner from lifetimes it feels to me, maybe but how can I make that promise to you when I don't know for sure if I can keep it? if I make that promise to you now and break it, it would be the worst betrayal - I would rather never promise and allow fate and destiny to take its course and trust that whatever happens on our paths in the future is how it is meant to be – but Bia, I love you and I adore you and it feels right to be with you," he affirmed.

Bia nodded, not entirely sure of herself or Marcus in that moment. A moment of doubt but she was a calm person who took things in and mulled them over intelligently and she moved on.

If there was any lingering doubt in their minds, there was certainly none in their bodies or hearts whenever they came together in those days and for the years to come and each time, they made love they would lie together at the end and say to each other
   "Was that the best ever?"
And they would totally mean it.

On the far side of the mountain
he had played with a child
On this side
a woman grown

Always a river gliding by
and people waiting
for messages and prayers
and fashioning answers

In leaf boats of marigolds and rose petals
lit with candles
'Is it forever you
for whom I await by the water?

Chapter 21

The Witch from Panama

Marcus slept fitfully the first night back in Rio. It had been a long time since he had encountered one of the large predators in his dreams but this time there was a stark difference – the predator had at first been watching him, but suddenly it was he doing the watching and he wasn't fighting a tiger, or being stalked by a leopard, but was witnessing through this feline's eye a great battle taking place upon a frozen lake. For a moment he feared for the great warrior in the midst of battle but his fear transformed into surrender and his surrender to the white of the frozen ice.

Marcus stayed with Bia in Rio for the next five months in the very same house he had stayed with Juliana during their first year together twenty-three years before. It was Bia's house now, and there he came to know her children. Sol, a quiet boy with a wonderful smile, a wizard with electronics, long and lean and gentle. Rosa, feisty and discontented but an honesty about her that Marcus liked and the older she grew, the more he came to love her.

He met the entire extended family at a gathering at an uncle's enormous and lavish house in the heights of Jardim Botánico and decided that would be the last time he made the effort.

Most of Bia's generation were fine with him but the older generation with the exception of her Uncle Edu who he knew from years before, and Bia's father, who welcomed Marcus with awkward graciousness, were frosty and anything but gracious. They were a large and wealthy family.

The grandfather, now dead, had been a minister in the Federal government and the founder of the family bank - Bankers and Industrialists who had expanded their wealth and influence over generations from their origins of old money accumulated from the sugar cane plantations of Bahia, the type that had cared for their slaves as well as they had cared for their horses, they were correct in their business dealings, socially liberal and highly educated and held a disdain for the crass corruption and politics of the nouveaux riche.

Not bad people, but they carried their airs of lofty superiority highly and Marcus later understood that he was not the only one who married into the family who struggled for their approval.

And in this family, nothing was said in the open. Hurts and slights would remain locked in the metal trunks of their sub conscious and the keys thrown away while the civil facade was maintained, and woe behold anyone who dared to open it, as Marcus would one day discover.

Bia had already borne the brunt of her aunties' disapproval for having being too honest in telling her grandmother about Marcus. She adored her grandmother and she, Bia, had been the patriarch's favorite granddaughter as a child so perhaps this just added greater impetus to the old woman's hasty visit to the priest in prayerful hope for God's intervention.

Bia herself would try to keep a foot in each world. In her family's world she was the blood of their blood, and for the family, to them she primarily belonged and the expectations, while not necessarily spoken, were seeped into her consciousness and learned in the very way she carried herself, the way she set each foot studiously before her as she ventured into the world.

But in Marcus' world she was the spirit that moved between bodies and time, that died into and reformed from the original self to birth again and for Marcus her family was but a station on the way where he had found her so they could continue their journey from where it had been left.

Marcus had his own family and he loved them and cared about them all and they were seriously good people but he never felt any real dependence. They were his family, yes, but not his rock. His rock was periodically the abyss to where he would throw himself whenever his path felt blocked, too solid, too secure and into this abyss he would plunge to his awful regret until the regret itself died into nothingness.

Knowing this he could promise her nothing, yet with her was where he knew he belonged.

Bia was ready for the journey, and perhaps in knowing where one foot remained, she was ready to distance herself, if not entirely remove herself, from all that she knew to follow him. To the other side of the world.

They had passed the balmy winter morning at the Arpoador, the point at the end of Ipanema beach before the seas swept around the rocks to Copacabana. The Arpoador was the best surf break on the beach where middle class kids on new surfboards vied for waves with black kids on battered boards from the Favela Contagalo above. Hawkers selling ice cream, chá mate, sarongs, hammocks and embroidered blankets of the Nordestinos, peanuts and coconuts, patrolled the beach with cultivated and natural humor.

Old and young alike, fat, perfect and thin displayed it all and left little to the imagination. Marcus' attention moved intermittently from the waves and nothingness to the theater and flesh and back again.

Heading back home along Rua Marques São Vicente in Gávea, Marcus and Bia had just received word that the witch from Panama had shown up in Rio and wanted to visit them.

She was middle aged, voluptuously bordering on fat with jet black hair and gleaming eyes. Short in stature with round doggy cheeks, a face still attractive with lips painted thick with red lipstick. Her eyes locked on to Marcus in that penetrative gaze that wanted you to understand she missed nothing.

Marcus had known her in India when with the Master and her arrival in Lucknow had sent shock waves through the community as she bewitched the Master with her outrageous personality and fearlessness and terrorized his attendants telling them they were killing their Master with their neediness and their bad medicine. In a previous life within her life, she had been the personal healer and soothsayer for Manuel Noriega, the former dictator of Panama who had been ousted by the Americans the moment he dared display his independence and hence outgrow his usefulness to them.

That was before her visitation by the Sage of Arunachala. Such visitations had occurred frequently enough to people like her who had never before heard of the Sage and some even, who had never before had an interest in spiritual matters, and these mystical encounters invariably had led them to India and the Master. In that she was no exception but everything else about her was, an exception.

She dined with them that evening in their home and after dinner they sat around the large living room with its double-glazed glass windows looking out on to a well-lit tropical garden.

In the middle of the conversation, she looked up at Marcus and said, "You know why you keep coming to Brazil?"

"To find Bia," replied Marcus.

"More than that"

"To lead Bia into another life," he said assuredly.

"True, but you already know that although in the end she will have something important to teach you and you will have to be humble to receive that teaching."

Marcus smiled. He was painfully aware of his tendency to pride. He had seen it starkly in his vision of his past life. The young erect Brahmin, beautiful and proud, which had him wondering, in turn, where that life had evolved from. The origin of all this pride.

"No, there is more," said the witch.

Marcus looked at her inquisitively as if to say, "please go on."

"You lived here before, a long time ago but you looked nothing like you do now - you were small and dark."

"A Native American?" suggested Marcus.

"Yes - so now you know - I don't know why I had to tell you but I did."

"Nothing like that is a surprise for me," replied Marcus, "thank you."

"You were a powerful presence then too," added the witch.

And as Marcus led her to the door and down to open the gate to her waiting taxi the witch leaned up to Marcus and whispered, now that Bia had remained inside.

"Keep away from her family."

"That may not always be possible."

"Then don't get involved. keep your wild spirit at a distance."

There are omens
and strange tidings
on the névoa do mar
the sea spray's whisper
through the lips of the Orixá

Do you think you
in your vainest thoughts
be Oxala, Oshun or perhaps Iemanjá
a God in full command of his realm?
really?

Chapter 22

I Found You in a River

For two months, Marcus had waited for Bia to arrive in Australia with her daughter and during that time he had met up again with Raj and his Egyptian girlfriend and then Genevieve had arrived from France and yet another young Australian friend whom he had met in Lucknow had come and stayed bearing an open heart but Marcus' resolve to not stray had been firm in spite of many possibilities.

Again, Bia's presence oozed with that intimate familiarity of which he remembered.

"Marcus, during the time I had to wait in Brazil, I went to visit a psychic astrologer to ask her about you, about us,"

"And?"

"She told me that we had been together for many lifetimes in the past, that we had met in ancient times when you had not been my husband but my guardian,"

"And you died young?"

Bia looked startled.

"Why, yes, how did you know?"

"It's ok, just go on with the story - I will tell you when you finish."

"Well, she said that I had died during times of war and that you had been out of the city but had returned to find me gone,"

"Yes, I was heartbroken, but tell me the rest, because I am sure I know it."

Bia composed herself again, glancing at Marcus who was finding it difficult to hold back telling her of his own dream vision he had had all those years ago.

"So, for many lifetimes you sought me out, we met again and again and in those life times we married but each time I died young and you would be lost in grief again until in the last life you chose to live as a hermit to try and understand your suffering and I lived that life elsewhere too – I am sure it was in Palestine or Egypt."

Marcus drew Bia to him and recounted to her his dream that had come to him shortly after Juliana's death.

"Bia, I know that same story - it came to me also – I know and feel every part and every line and the songs and the verses too – I found you in a river a long time ago."

Bia looked at Marcus as equally stunned as he.

"And Bia," he finally added, "in a few weeks we will go back to see the Master but first we will stop and visit the place of the Sage of Arunachala, the Shiva fire mountain."

Through molten streams
of samsara
the circle forms anew

O'er the divide of oceans
of time
of times end
of death
and death's birth

And of Gondwana's fiery separation
when a holy mountain
had traversed the sea
ablaze with infinity

Chapter 23

Of Trees and Streams

"Marcus, are you serious when you say you want to buy this farm?" questioned Bia.

"Yes, I can see it - I can see how it can be - it has a great water source and it has the land and it is right in the valley where you wanted to live."

They had driven through this valley a few times together and Bia had commented on its beauty.

"But the house, the farm buildings, it's depressing," objected Bia.

Marcus looked around and he could see exactly what she was seeing. But where she saw buildings in a semi ruinous state and rotting fence posts strung with rusted and broken wire, he saw a blank canvass that had it all.

"Trust me, this is it," assured Marcus, "the price is good too."

"Ok"

"Ok what?"

"I trust you."

They hugged. That was it then, and they had signed the contract the following day.

The farm was a hundred acres of gentle hill and grassy flats with just a few pockets of trees. A few invasive Camphors and some native trees lined the banks here and there along the degraded streams that rounded each side of the hill to meet and form a permanent stream at the very end of the farm. But the upper streams were silted up and choked with grass and weeds and flowed only when it rained to recede into stagnant water holes during the drier spring and beginning of summer.

Nestled in the center of a green valley of rolling hills that intersected the towns of Mullumbimby and Byron Bay, the farm, to Marcus' eyes was all that he had dreamed to have.

'Little Arunachala,' as they called Mount Chincogan, rose up in its perfectly conical form behind the township of Mullumbimby in the distance.

The town lay at the outer edge of the ancient Caldera that millions of years ago was the largest active volcano in the southern hemisphere during the time of the dinosaurs when South America, Australia and India together had formed the giant continent of Gondwana. They had drifted apart in those times of the earth's infancy and during that continental drift the part that was India had exploded in a fury of volcanic eruptions, and it had been during this journey north to Asia, that the mountain of Arunachala had been born.

Marcus considered himself a child of Gondwana, living as he did between the three habitable lands of the ancient continent and sometimes when asked where he was from, if he didn't say, "Tasmania" he would say, "from Gondwana."

～⌣⌣⌣～

Marcus and Bia would transform that house with mostly her money and his design and vision, his sweat and labor, into a grand and elegant homestead and he would remake that farm into a manicured horse stud with new fences and native rainforest plantings along the streams.

In the years to come those trees grew up into a forest and as they grew their canopies reached out over the streams and shaded out the grass and weeds, the streams re-appeared and began to flow again.

The smaller outbuildings, the old piggery, the cream shed and the falling apart storage shed, Marcus rebuilt into cottages for guests, for Bia's son, Sol to have his own place and for travelers to stay for free and help with the plantings and the horses, and the farm became a paradise with sweeping gardens, organic vegetables and fruits, and beautiful horses.

Friends came to stay from overseas, friends from their time in India, and people would drop by for cups of tea and coffee almost every day. Conversations would range from horses and gardens to Advaita philosophy to herbal medicine and politics and everything in between and included total nonsense imbibed with fits of hysterical laughter.

⌒‿‿⌒

Five teenagers in all, Bia's two and Marcus' two daughters, one rebellious and the other the most passionate about horses, all lived with them.

They held parties, Satsang, bhajans and choir rehearsals, invited friends for trail rides to the beach and had teenage sleepovers. Their farm became a hub of life and a wheel of fortune in miniature through the seasons and the years. They lost count of the numbers of people who stayed with them and they almost lost count of the years that passed by and for sure, Marcus and Bia lost count of the number of times they made love.

Farm life was busy with horses to break and train, repair work and pasture slashing to be done and not forgetting the teenagers to manage.

The last part was a challenge for Marcus. He realized that apart from his oldest daughter who was a pretty easy-going kid, he had never been around teenage girls that much, having being virtually imprisoned inside an all-boys boarding school in Tasmania at that age.

His anguished and sometimes frustrated efforts at training them to be human could sometimes boil over into raised voices and he would later wonder how necessary it had been, as each of them blossomed as they grew.

"Get the fuck up there and clean up your mess!", he shouted.

The girls looked up at him indignantly, saying,

"What's your problem, there's no need to shout."

"Well, I already asked you sweetly three times and politely another three, it seems like you didn't hear."

But he loved them all, regardless and got up at four and five in the morning to drive them to horse events every weekend of every winter.

Marcus was a liberal parent and gave them no rules around drugs, alcohol, love and sex but plenty of education and for the most part they responded with varying degrees of intelligence. He had to pick a thirteen-year-old drunk and semi-conscious from the lawn of one of her friends once but hey, she lived and learned, albeit slowly.

"Anyway," he considered, "the sooner they had boyfriends the sooner their hormones would settle and then everything would become the boyfriend's fault and not his."

His basic tenets were don't get pregnant, don't get diseases and don't sleep with anyone who doesn't genuinely like you.

⁓ ⸎ ⸏

"You see the way the bat flies," he said one day to Manuela as they went out on a trail ride one evening.

Shortly after sunset the sky would fill with large fruit bats as they lifted en-masse out of their giant fig tree roosting homes to darken the sky with their giant wings and this evening, the sky was dark with them.

"What the hell are you talking about Dad?"

"About bats and the way in which they fly."

"What about the bats?"

"They never fly straight, but jag left to right, up and down."

"So?"

"So, they are almost impossible to shoot with a bullet."

"Dad, why the hell would you want to shoot the bats?"

"I don't - but that is why people use shot guns on them these days and why the American Indians painted bats on their horses."

"Dad, I really don't get it."

"So that bullets wouldn't hit them - that is the old relationship with bats and horses you see, and here we are riding along with bats flying all about us."

"You're crazy"

"Do you remember what you always wanted when you were little, Manuela?"

"Maybe, no, what?"

"A crystal ball and a wand."

"What has that got to do with bats and horses?"

"Nothing, but don't forget that that is what you wanted when you were little."

Manuela rolled her eyes.

It was a time of horses and children teaching him patience and forbearance but every now and again his anger that had been developed as a survival tool in boarding school, and as a survival tool probably even before then, would explode and everyone including the dog would disappear for the fifteen minutes it took for him to calm down, knowing that by then he would be his normal easy going and loving self.

Bia never enjoyed those moments but she loved him for so much else she readily accepted them as part of her man, her beloved. In those times she did anyway.

But there was one thing that Marcus didn't like about Bia. She was at times jealous of him around other women.

Marcus only allowed that jealousy to determine his friendships once and that was when she first moved to Australia and Genevieve was there and Genevieve wanted to maintain her friendship with Marcus. Bia couldn't allow it. He never allowed her to do that again. But in turn he loved her too much to stray far from her with his eyes, less even in his heart and never at all in the flesh.

A stream
and a bed of roses
a white house
children at play on a sloping green lawn
an elegant wife
and a large red dog

There are horses thundering through the grass
at play
and above, in the night
a vast Australian sky

Chapter 24

The Frightened Horse, The Child

As Marcus calmed down, he felt the exhaustion seep into his muscles. His frustration had boiled over to anger and the anger had left a frightened animal eyeing him in the corner of the yard. It had left him, a supposedly wise man of many small deaths, feeling defeated. Not by the unwilling horse but by his own weakness, his own rage, his own inability to control the rage in the face of adversity - his personal cloud that obscured the natural order of things. Or at least that is how he saw it then.

At other times he just accepted the way he was but he couldn't accept frightening the horse like this.

"Whose rage was this? a dream rage? but a dream rage that left wounded dreams and scattered thoughts and emotions - nothing needs to change; it is what it is, but the present scarred by the past demands it nevertheless, and each time it burns my heart I say to myself enough, no more - but it will burn away in its time, not ours and it will present us with its path not ours - when we have truly had enough it will."

But he couldn't help wondering what had been its source. Just who was this warrior that would come riding out from the past to haunt his dreams? But it was this same warrior that rekindled the knowledge that he desperately sought in that moment.

He looked up at the chestnut quarter horse mare and asked her,

"What next? where to from here?" feeling a wave of compassion for her followed by another of regret.

Images from a time long obscured elevated itself from his consciousness but in this movie emerging from the fog the horse was white. It appeared he was drifting, almost dreaming but it allowed him to discover the way out. He had to learn, he had to learn so much more and the horses would teach him more than he would teach them.

⌘

And they did and so too did his daughters and Bia. The love between Marcus and Bia flowed back and forth like the tide yet there were times when Marcus didn't feel in love with her in the romantic sense, when she was just Bia, his wife, and if he had had those feelings in the past with other women it would have been a signal for him that this was not 'it', but with Bia there was this undercurrent of enormous respect and gratitude that quickly cooled his wandering eyes.

Then every so often he would see her in a different light and see her in all of her beauty and fall completely in love with her again and when making love her beauty grew to be almost unbearable to his sight and touch and every time they did, they both swore it was the best ever.

When they had been apart, when Marcus or Bia had travelled overseas without the other and they met up again more often than not they wouldn't make it back to the house before their passion demanded them stop in a secluded spot on the way.

"Did you miss me?" she would say, and Marcus would reply with a grin,

"No, of course not, but I'm happy to have you back."

They made love in the bushes when at parties and dances and they made love in the car on the way home. Whenever the passion was fierce, they would find a place, find a way.

There was more than one moment when she would look at him after a long kiss and say to him,

"I'm yours forever."

But Marcus wouldn't respond. He had no plans of leaving her but he wouldn't break his taboo and he would never say forever as much as she longed for him to say it.

Now as her pregnancy grew along with the roundness of her belly and the fullness of her breasts she glowed.

This was the pinnacle of Bia and Marcus' family life and it was finally crowned with the birth of their boy.

Bia and Marcus drove to the closest beach, just ten minutes from their farm. The same beach they would gallop their horses when time and weather were kind.

A long stretch of pristine white sand that ran for close to eight kilometers between the seaside towns of Brunswick Heads and Byron Bay.

Until you came into Byron Bay itself the entire beach was backed by a nature reserve of coastal banksias and melaleuca bushes that abounded with wallabies, potoroos, echidnas, death adders and abundant birdlife. Flocks of white cockatoos would fill the sky intermittently, rising up as one from the coastal scrub with its scattered rust colored tea tree lakes.

It was a sunny autumn day and Bia walked the beach wearing only her bikini bottom, her full pregnant breasts proudly displaying her womanhood as if she were an effigy of a pagan goddess unearthed from the sand.

The moment a sea hawk swooped low above them and a pod of dolphins appeared in the surf but twenty meters from shore was the moment the first contraction gripped her ready uterus.

"Marcus, it's happening."

Bia stooped to lean over, her hand on her belly.

"Really, did you see the sea hawk just fly over you?"

"Yes"

"Marcus, I think we have to go to the hospital."

"No hurry, the baby won't be born until one in the morning."

"Don't tell me that, that's fifteen hours away."

He laughed.

"Everything will be fine - he is going to wait until the sign of

Aquarius is on the ascendant and I think that's about one in the morning."

They drove the hour into the Lismore Hospital, calling Bia's friend, Kate on the way.

"I don't know if I can do this much longer."

"Well," said Marcus," you are going to have to hang in there until one o'clock in the morning."

"Don't say that- what makes you so sure?"

"He is going to be born with Aquarius on the ascendant, remember?"

Bia groaned.

The mid wife organized some gas for Bia and the nurses wheeled it in.

But the gas wasn't enough to quell her pain and she didn't much like the effect.

Marcus and Bia's friend and female back up, Kate, then helped themselves to the gas.

But after a while the pain and irritation grew within Bia's body and mind.

"Come on guys, your giggling isn't helping me, please. I want an epidural."

So, they stopped sucking on the gas and called the doctor and Bia had the epidural.

From that moment on Marcus knew he had to be with her holding her hand, reassuring her, massaging where it felt right. Bia was nearing transition and Marcus knew well that during the transition between regular contractions and the pushing stage, the mother's mind could dig into some dark spaces.

At five minutes past one in the morning Niko was born.

"Let me see him," pleaded Bia.

"Oh, he is so cute, look at his lips pouting - he was frightened."

And he was. His little lips were pouting and trembling and his whole look said,

"I was scared."

"This boy is so sensitive," thought Marcus.

Rosa, Kate and Bia were oohing and aahing.

"He looks like a Chinese banker," said Marcus as he took his son in his arms.

"He does not," objected Rosa.

Rosa had been wonderful the whole night. Marcus adored Bia's daughter. Beautiful, almost Arabic in her looks, she had an inner strength and serenity about her now. Such a transformation from the troubled and demanding little nine-year-old he had first met in Brazil five years ago.

They moved Bia to a private hospital on the other side of town in the early hours of the morning where she could rest up a couple of days in her own room.

"I'm going to let you sleep, and Bia, I will take little Niko for a walk.

"Ok," she drowsily responded.

He lent over her and kissed her.

"I love you and we have a beautiful boy."

"I love you too."

Except Marcus didn't just take Niko for a walk around the hospital. With few staff around at five thirty in the morning he walked the well wrapped little bundle passed the reception and straight out the door.

"Now you can see the sky little man, and the trees and the birds."

He walked to a park and sat on a swing rocking back and forth and sung to his baby, drawing just enough covers from his face so his little eyes could see the sky and the branches of the giant fig tree that partly shaded the playground.

"This is planet earth, Niko," he said, before asking him, "do you recognize this place Niko? you see that up there, perched on the branches right above the pond? that is a kingfisher - it is a bird that can heal your wounds if you place its feathers in your hair - and you know why, Niko? because when the kingfisher dives into the water, the water closes all about him and in no time at all, the wound of the water is healed."

The kingfisher dived into the pond. Niko's eyes widened and blinked.

Marcus was well aware that new born babies could not recognize things close up, but their vision could see things at a distance. That is why they like to be outside and not indoors.

The air was cold and sharp in that autumn morning and Marcus held his bundle to him tightly. Niko was awake, open eyed and still staring at the branches where the kingfisher had returned with a small goldfish in its beak.

After time spent bonding in this way with his child, Marcus started to realize that he was starving.

"When was the last time I ate?" he thought to himself.

Leaving the park, he turned down a street away from the hospital and found the bakery and walking into the bakery saw by the clock on the wall it was already past seven.

Inside, a gaggle of older and middle-aged women were already up and about purchasing bread and buns for their family's morning breakfasts and as Marcus walked in with the tiny baby of course all eyes turned to him. The smell of hot cooked bread and pastry was making him feel ravenous.

"My goodness, that is a little one."

"How adorable, what's your name?"

"How many weeks?"

"Weeks?" Marcus responded, "he is only six hours old."

There was a chorus of astonishment and shock.

"What are you doing outside with such a tiny newborn?"

"Where is his mother?"

"Sleeping in the hospital."

"I can't imagine they would let you take him out."

"But he told me he wanted to see the sky - could you please give me six hot crossed buns."

And two days later back at the farm Marcus took Niko with him for a walk to see the farm while Bia slept. He could never resist pulling weeds where he saw them, and clearing around his trees, his precious trees. With one hand holding the baby and the other pulling weeds he later returned Niko to Bia covered in bits of dirt and grass.

"Marcus where have you been with him this time?" exclaimed Bia in feigned shock.

"Oh, the bits of dirt?"

"It's good for babies to get dirt on them when they are young - exposure to microbes is good for their immunity," he said laughing.

Bia shook her head at him but the love in her eyes made Marcus feel like her King.

Marcus slept in a different room for the next few months and Bia would bring Niko to him around three in the morning from when he would try and keep him happy for the next six hours to let his mother sleep.

It wasn't long before he had Niko on his lap while slashing the paddocks with his tractor before breakfast.

In pursuit
of our own mystery
drawn to the taste
of the meat of humanity

But strange isn't it
beginning as we do
with the credits already rolling
and the audience applauding

Chapter 25

The Black Stallion

Marcus led the black stallion out into the round yard. The old horseman lent over the rails, his hat drawn over his brow and his weathered face offered only a dead pan expression. He wasn't going to give anything away.

The older man had done it all in the horse world. A pioneer of Arabian horse breeding and the first breeder from Australia to win a world championship, he was the owner of over twenty Quilty buckles, the one-hundred-and-sixty-kilometer endurance race that took place each year through rugged bushland trails where one earned a buckle simply by completing the ride with a sound horse.

These days grotesquely rich Arab sheiks and princes would send their buyers to the Quilty and write cheques of anything from fifty to two hundred and fifty-thousand dollars on the spot for well performed horses. Marcus had recently sold a grey gelding, one of the first he had broken in himself, to a woman who was training him up for the Quilty and he would go on to finish in third place overall. A strong and compact young horse of mixed Crabbet and Egyptian breeding, the Arabs had paid a fortune for him but Marcus hadn't felt good about it.

He preferred his horses to go to good homes.

Like the part Friesian he had sold to a woman in the Northern Territory who had later sent him a photo and article of the horse from the local newspaper.

"Prisoners all vie for their favorite horse," the heading had read in bold capitals alongside a photo at a riding ranch where the local prison population rode once a week as part of their rehabilitation program.

Selling his stallion, however, was very hard for Marcus. He was the horse he had ridden more than any other in his life and although he was going to keep a few horses for himself when they moved to the smaller farm, he had decided to give up his breeding program. The choice had been to geld the stallion or sell him so he could continue doing what was in his nature to do – to mount mares.

But in the end, he had decided to sell, keeping the price very reasonable so he could choose the buyer and there were fifteen buyers interested with two having offered him his asking price.

And it was time to sell the farm too with most of the children grown and off into the world.

Marcus let his horse out into the yard, clicking his fingers and the stallion followed him. He raised his hand to signal him to stop. He stopped. Moving to the horse's flank, he suddenly flicked both hands open towards him and the horse started trotting around the yard. He used no lunging rope.

From his position in the center of the yard Marcus slowed the horse to a walk by moving ever so slightly in front of him and motioning downwards with his hands. After calmly walking him for two circuits he picked up his energy and moved his hands sharply outward towards the horse who immediately went from a walk into a canter. He controlled the canter by positioning his body and eye contact either in front of or behind the stallion depending on whether he wanted him to slow or pick up pace. Next, he slowed him to a trot and then to a perfect halt.

Marcus clicked his fingers and turned his shoulder to the horse and he came walking quietly up to him and stood there while Marcus caressed him, the horse returning the affection by rubbing his nose on Marcus' neck.

Sliding underneath the horse and crawling from between his front legs to come out between his back legs, keeping constant hand contact along the horses' belly as he did so, he emerged to hug the horse from the rear but looking over to the fence he noticed the old horseman had neither moved nor changed his dead pan expression.

"So can you saddle him up and show me how he goes?"

"Sure," replied Marcus, "but he hasn't been ridden in a year - I've been too busy breaking in and training young ones so I'm not sure if you will see the greatest forward movement."

"Understood - no worries - it will give me an even better idea if he is what I want."

"And what would that be for," asked Marcus, as he stroked the horse's flanks.

The question was important to him.

"I've been hired by a French billionaire who has a horse stud in Noumea - he's sent me on a mission to find a quality black stallion but it also has to be quiet enough - he wants it as a gift for his granddaughter - she's only eleven - they love their horses and take good care of them," he added.

Marcus imagined the young girl galloping him along the beach in Noumea living out her dream of the story of the black stallion.

"You see any likely ones yet?"

"Some rubbish, some good ones but not with the right temperament."

Marcus nodded. He signaled to his horse to stay where he was in the middle of the yard while he went to fetch the saddle and the tack.

When he came back and threw the rug and saddle lightly on his back, the horse turned to Marcus and nudged him gently. It almost broke his heart. His horse was showing his pleasure that Marcus was riding him again.

Marcus eased himself into the saddle and walked on a loose rein to the training paddock at the front of the farm, the old horseman strolling slightly bow legged alongside him.

Walking one circle on a loose rein, picking up contact with the bit and, given that the horse had been out of work for a year, he didn't ask for too much collection as he gently pushed him into a trot with the slightest pressure from his lower leg. Once left, changing through the middle, once right and halt. Stand, and then pushing him into a canter from the standing position the stallion moved out immediately on the correct lead.

"The next change was going to be the tricky one," thought Marcus as his horse had failed him more than once doing work outs at shows leading right but he need not have worried. He was, while a little short paced due to his lack of conditioning, working beautifully.

As Marcus slid to a halt after a final hand gallop the old horseman said in his dead pan manner,

"He's quiet enough."

And thanked Marcus for his time before climbing into his Toyota Landcruiser and heading out the gate.

Two days later, just when Marcus thought he may have to consider some other suitors the old horseman called him on the phone.

"No-one else buy that horse of yours yet?"

"No, to tell you the truth I was waiting to see if you were going to call again before I called anyone else back."

"Well, if it is alright with you, we will take him."

There was a pause before the gnarly old horseman said,

"By the way Marcus - in all my years I never saw a better job done with a stallion before - it's a credit to you."

Marcus put down the phone and closed another chapter in his life. How many horses had carried him to pleasure, to love, to death in his recent and scarcely remembered past?

He strolled over to the front of the house, called his horse, Dayaajin, over to him and the two walked slowly together to the mounting yard where he saddled him up, almost tearily. The last ride was a wild gallop across the rolling hills, down the tree lined pathways where a koala lazily chewed a few leaves, casually observing them as they rushed on by.

A black horse
a white horse
a spirit horse of hail and lightning
and a painted pony

To the four directions
they had carried him
to where east met west
and south was but a mirror
of the north wind's coldest breath

Chapter 26

The Sacrament

The canoe's outboard motor was straining at full throttle, driving its much more ancient vehicle upstream as it weaved between shallow sand banks and floating tree trunks and branches. On either side of the river, small farms or roças hugged the banks for a short while before another patch of forest relieved the river of its denuded banks. Modest houses appeared in places with children playing on the shore while their mothers washed clothes in the river.

Crops of newly sown beans and manioc sprouted on narrow flats recently surfacing from the spring floods, but eventually the forest took over almost entirely as they motored noisily beneath its overhang.

The first sign of the village were children along the sand bank, dressed in traditional Ashaninka brown cotton tunics all raising their eyes as one to gaze upon the foreigners drifting into shore.

⌁

The first taste of the muddy brew was foul, but Marcus, shuddering from the experience, returned to his place next to Luciana, sat down and closed his eyes. A woman from the Santa Dime church, a semi-Christian church founded in the jungles of the Amazon that used ayahuasca as its sacrament, began to sing. It was Marcus' first journey into the world of Ayahuasca.

The Ashaninka are one of South America's largest tribes. Their homeland covers a vast region, from the Upper Juruá River in Brazil to the watersheds of the Peruvian Andes.

Marcus, Bia and Niko had arrived from Rio in the village on the Rio Amônia, a tributary of the Juruá via three commercial flights before hiring a light twin engine plane that touched down in a remote grass strip in the jungle. From there it had been another four hours by canoe to the village.

Accompanied by André, a photographer, and his wife, Luciana, they carried with them the recommendation from João, an old friend of Bia's who worked on projects with the Acre tribes.

Walking into the chief's house, by far the largest in the village and the house that served as the communal meeting place and center of festivities, Marcus and Bia had met the Chief's wife, a tall bespectacled woman with a broad smile and dressed simply in conventional clothes.

Donna Marta was the daughter of an immigrant subsistence farmer whose family had eked out a living on the edge of the jungle downstream from the village. She had educated her five boys herself and they had been at the forefront of the indigenous land rights movement that saw them eventually victorious in reclaiming their land from corrupt logging companies. The stakes had been high and the risk of assassination all too real in the then almost lawless state.

～∽

This night, Marcus, Bia, André and Luciana would take ayahuasca with them.

The five of them had been in the village for several days now and had begun to break the social ice.

Bia's friend and contact with the tribe, João arrived later that day with Benke, the most charming and outgoing of the chief's sons and shortly after them and unbeknown to Marcus beforehand, Gilberto Gil arrived with his entourage of six - plus two huge black security guards.

Gil was arguably, along with Caetano Veloso and Carlinhos Brown, Brazil's most loved musician of the time and because of his well-known political and social conscience had been appointed Minister of Culture by the incoming Partido dos Trabalhadores, or Workers party.

Visiting in this official capacity for the gathering of the tribes in the remote corner of Acre he would tonight participate in a ceremony before the big meeting on the morrow.

When Gil saw Bia, he stopped, surprised, and said,

"Why not? first Sydney, now here," before embracing her, referring to the fact that he had last seen her in Sydney at the State function held in his honor two years ago, and Gil, of course, had been a close friend of Juliana.

He turned to greet Marcus who he would hardly have remembered, seeing they had only met once when he was with Juliana.

"O Australiano, não?"

Of course, he knew that Bia's husband was Australian, had been surprised to meet her there, but Marcus looked the part.

Generally, it was not Marcus' thing to take substances, he being of the philosophy that whatever the moment gave you was all you needed to address and that nirvana was never more than a thought away from the present moment.

⌒⌒⌒

The ceremony began with Benke and his older, mystical brother Moisés holding the energy of the circle with their knowledge and attuned sensibility to the needs of silence, the elevating effect of music, or the chanting and sacred smoke as needed for each moment, a circle that had to be doubled to fit within even the large space of the chief's verandah.

Marcus felt exalted by the Dimé woman's voice, beautiful, enchanting. The first thing he noticed changing was when he looked own at his hands and legs and they began to fractal. Looking around him he saw that the whole scene was now shattered by fractals, including Luciana to his side. Luciana then completely disappeared and turning to look at his own body he observed that it, too, had disappeared.

Closing his eyes, he saw psychedelic streams of molten silver flowing through rivers of iridescent green with the threads of insect like antennae spreading through the silver fluid. It was intense so he opened his eyes again but his body and the bodies of all the people there had either disappeared or were ghost like fractals.

"Did I really want to feel like this?" he asked himself, "do I really want to be stuck inside a 'seventies psychedelic art exhibition?"

By this time Gilberto Gil, though not having partaken of the sacrament, took up his guitar and began to play.

Marcus' doubtful thoughts however had by this time changed his experience with his negativity manifested in the form of serpents, throwing his fears directly in his face.

He felt humbled at this point. He had taken magic mushrooms in Australia that had been confronting and intense too but then his ability to be still and observe had carried him though to a blissful experience. This was stronger, by degrees more intense, more confronting.

Gil started making bird calls to complement his guitar but the sounds began to irritate Marcus and a wave of nausea hit him. He had been warned that he would probably throw up but where?

Looking ahead of him the steps to the verandah seemed a mile away and he knew there were many bodies, some now lying down, between him and the steps. He remembered that behind him there was a narrow plank that descended steeply to the ground.

"Will I be able to walk down it? will I be able to walk? I can't even see my feet."

He did get to his feet and, turning in the direction of the plank, he noticed that the seat that lined the back of the verandah was occupied by the Ashaninka women and children. Many had taken the sacrament as well. One face smiled at him and motioned to another woman sitting on the floor to make space for Marcus to pass.

His feet did work after all. He made it down the plank with ease. He walked outside and saw the two big ministerial security guards standing erect in the semi darkness and thought how absurd the whole scene was and how this would never happen in Australia.

He moved out onto the grass of the soccer field that sat in the center of the village and walking to the edge of the jungle, knelt over and was about to vomit when he saw that what he thought had been grass was, in fact, a beautifully fabricated Persian carpet. Fascinated he stayed there staring, thinking this to be too beautiful, too sacred, to vomit on. He threw up nevertheless.

His body and mind somewhat put at ease after vomiting, he walked back to the verandah and decided he would sit next to Niko asleep in a hammock at the back near the women. Benke and Moisés were chanting and blowing smoke over people laying on the ground and by now Gil had stopped playing and the traditional drumming and incantations of the Indians had taken over. He fell into meditation.

For the next days, Marcus felt his mind to be stiller, more connected to the earth. Just a subtle difference but it was there.

Bia, keen to know her story asked Donna Marta during a lazy day on their verandah as a bright blue magnificent Araraca sat on Marcus' shoulder – she was happy to tell it,

"My husband's father was the chief and shaman of the tribe and I lived down river from their village with my parents and my sisters - I was the eldest daughter - the chief had a vision that his son had to marry me to ensure his peoples survival so the tribe dressed in their finest robes and came down river to visit us and he asked my father for my hand in marriage - although my father was friendly with the tribe, he could not bring himself to agree but I was listening in my room so I came out and said, 'no father, I will marry him', though my father argued against it but I stood firm and so we were married and I have lived here with them ever since."

They all saw in Donna Marta that mix of rock like strength and limitless compassion but the woman had lost none of her simplicity and humility. She adopted the entire tribe as her family and had faced many a life-threatening moment in the defense of their rights.

The Ashaninka had since restored those devastated areas raped by the loggers into a blend of food forest and jungle regrowth. Concerned with the depletion of fish in the rivers they had built dams on streams feeding into the river and bred their own fish and turtles.

Walking through the village, Marcus and Niko saw stacks of freshly cut arrows drying throughout and cotton laid out on blankets in the sun to be spun to make their traditional brown, knee length ponchos patterned with black dye. They painted their faces decoratively with the red juice of the urucum fruit and adorned their necks and wrists with intricate and colorful bead work and Niko too was soon running around with a painted face.

Beautifully kept, with cut grass in between wood and thatch houses most of which were a single room in a corner with the remainder of the house a roofed verandah with flooring made from flattened palm trunks, the village hummed with life and industry.

Surrounded on three sides by the jungle and the other by the river below, in that rainy time of the year mist hung constantly over the lives of the Indians known as the bird people.

And there were two great skills attributed to them aside from their ferocity in battle. They would practice catching an enemy arrow in midflight and they could astral travel using ayahuasca to find either prey or enemy as required.

Returning to Australia, Marcus fell sick, very sick with pneumonia and his coughing became acute to the point where he moved into the spare bedroom to not disturb Bia. For almost two months he lay ill and nothing would seem to cure him so Bia called a friend who was an acupuncturist and healer, Amba, and as Amba sat meditating on the bed while Marcus lay with the needles doing their work on his meridians, she turned to him and asked,

"When you were in Brazil, did you take ayahuasca?"

He hadn't talked to her about it, nor had Bia.

"Yes, I did, why?

"It just came to me that this is what is happening for you – that you are undergoing a major healing process from taking the ayahuasca."

"You did it for me again then, Amba - you tuned into me," said Marcus with a smile.

Amba had told Marcus in the past that she could not 'read' everyone with her abilities but Marcus was like an open book to her.

Not long after he finally recovered, Marcus, Bia and Niko traveled to their little house at the holy mountain of Arunachala in South India where they had passed every Australian summer for the past five years and it was there that Marcus felt the culmination of the ayahuasca experience as if it were the brew that became baked to perfection in Holy Arunachala's' fire.

It was after Bia went back to Australia with Niko. Rosa had come to join them with her boyfriend from Brazil and like Marcus she had decided to stay on in the house a few more weeks and he was loving her company. She was diving in, so to speak, to Arunachala's cauldron.

Arunachala is a place of deep transformations, if you willingly surrender.

One of the five most important places of the God Siva in India, Arunachala was Siva in his element of fire, the purifier of egoistic tendencies.

Marcus' immersion was getting to the point where his energy wouldn't allow him to sleep at night. He just wasn't tired, sleep had no interest him.

Rosa would often come home late. She was young after all and had been meeting new friends every day or two and staying out.

"Rosa, there is no way I can sleep, come and talk to me," he would say.

"Sure," she replied laughingly.

They would chat for a couple of hours before Rosa would drift off to bed. He was close to her then, there being something very especially beautiful about her and their friendship grew beyond their previous relationship of father and step daughter.

Internally, however, a process was underway in Marcus' body and mind of which he had no control.

Marcus hit the wall one day when he called his trusted friend Ganga in Portugal who had become the friend with whom he would bounce off his insights and revelations. She likewise enjoyed his company and years later they told each other of their dream visions that had occurred on the same morning during the break of dawn,

"We have some strange connection, you and I," she would say - and clearly to Marcus, not giving all away.

"Ha," laughed Marcus, "I think I know who you were – I think you were my mother-in-law in the past – you are looking more like an old native American medicine woman as you age," he answered to her laughter, before adding, "that mother-im-law, I liked and respected greatly also."

Missing her presence in Arunachala that year he called her in the middle of a sleepless night. He wanted to tell her of his latest insight, and insight and understanding Marcus had by now understood, never ceases.

Marcus had called Ganga but she had replied,

"Marcus that sounds to me like mind," meaning she felt his revelation was a product of mind rather than a deep insight of direct experience.

Marcus felt it had not been so, but the fact he was now shattered by what she had told him, whatever it was or was not, triggered a darkness that enveloped his being and drew it into its most turbulent depths.

He felt that all of his past understanding and enlightenment was worthless, nothing, mere egoistic futility.

He was about to enter Ramana Ashram for the evening pujah and singing when Bia called from Australia.

They talked regularly when apart and normally he loved to chat with her but now all he could say was,

"Sorry Bia, I can't talk to you now - I'm in a bit of a dark space."

"Ok, Marcus, take care of yourself. I love you."

"I love you too."

Ramana Ashram was a collection of buildings, temples and shrines where people who wished to bathe in its peace could come and stay for one or two weeks at a time. Set in amongst its banyan trees and coconut palms and neatly swept avenues it housed a bookshop, a library, accommodation and even a herd of immaculately cared for cows. Peacocks cried out from the roof tops and fluttered to the ground amongst the devotees while we'll behaved monkeys waited to be fed by the kitchen cooks.

At the back of the ashram there were three shrines to honor the enlightened cow, the enlightened dog and the enlightened peacock. Directly behind the ashram, loomed the holy hill that Ramana had always referred to as his living master.

Marcus sat in the temple of the mother that had two doors opening into the newer hall where sat Ramana's' shrine. He preferred to sit there on the old granite in the candle lit semi darkness than in the marble, brightly lit hall where the singing took place. He had been sitting there more than an hour with his head back on the cold wall, knees drawn up to his body, his arms resting on them, when the pujah began inside the inner shrine of the old temple.

His despair had reached breaking point. The temple bells began to crash violently in his ears. The chanting droned from the inner sanctum of the temple as the priests warmed to their incantations.

Devotees and pilgrims from all parts of India and from all parts of the world filed past him as they walked clockwise around the temple, some in devoted reverence, some in curiosity, and others in deep meditative enquiry.

The bells clanged louder and louder. He looked at all the people in their earnestness and wondered what they were doing. He wondered what he was doing there. It was all so futile - lifetimes of futility, of war and love and hope. Marcus' embraced his despair and accepted it. He gave up. The despair evaporated into nothingness. That is all that was required. He gave it all up, again.

Freedom, as always was but a moments surrender, a moments total surrender to the abyss.

He remained where he was until the chanting and singing in the main hall, drifting into the old temple, finally ceased. It was good to be nobody who had achieved nothing at all.

Life was perfectly simple like that.

"Who am I? I am nobody."

"What are you doing now? I am walking along the Pradakshina Road past the temples and the sadhus and there are monkeys in the trees. And I wish for nothing more."

From the fading morning star
to the barking dog moon
love lies in waiting
in her transparent dress

As always
for her lover's death

Chapter 27

Bia Needs Change

"Marcus, how would you feel about moving to Brazil?"

Marcus' answer surprised her.

"I'm open to it Bia - I don't mind change - you should know that - and besides, you've lived in my country now for thirteen years, so maybe it's my turn to live in yours - but why the sudden need for change?

Bia pondered a few moments. Marcus had not been wholly unaware of the shift in her.

She had told him more than once in the past that she just couldn't feel the pull for transformation to the same degree that others in their circle of friends talked about but Marcus had said that maybe she didn't need to, that because she grew up with a mother who always talked about the mind being illusory, she didn't have the same entrenched belief systems as most people.

"Our trips to the Amazon and especially the last journey I made by myself to the Santo Daime community seems to have awoken in me a need to re find my connection with the sacred feminine, to learn more about the healing plants of the Indians."

She searched Marcus' eyes for his reaction and in that moment her face seemed to Marcus to change as he caught a glimpse of Bia from a different time. Like most Brazilians she had indigenous blood in her veins, being a descendent of the sailor Diogo Alvares, known as

Caramuru who had married the Tupinambá princess Paraguaçú and presided over a village of a thousand warriors in Bahia. That was on her father's side but on Juliana's side her great grandmother had been a full blood Indian from Mato Grosso.

"And your children and grandchildren, you want to be closer to them, don't you?" he answered.

"That too, and my father - after his heart scare, I realized I don't want to be so far away."

"And are you sure you want me to come with you?"

Marcus surprised himself with that question because he had always felt very confident in Bia's love and her dependency on him. A dependency he both loved and disliked in that he wanted her to reach out for her own freedom yet at the same time he knew he didn't want to lose her and, in that moment, he wondered if she would have to let him go in order to find it for herself. He didn't know the answer to any of those questions back then.

But Bia only hesitated to ask Marcus again if he really wanted to make the change.

"Would you go without me if I said no," he asked.

"I thought about that," she said while looking searchingly into her beloved's eyes, "and I couldn't find the answer to it but sure, I was hoping you would say yes."

"Yes, I will," he answered.

"Australia has been great for me, Marcus, and it has been great for Rosa too but it is time for me to go back."

~⁓~⁓~

But Bia was worried about Marcus' relationship with her family.

Things between Marcus and them had been developing well enough. Her father always very welcoming in his own stifled manner and miraculously Marcus had maintained good relations with her step mother, Dona Vera, a relationship that Bia herself had had to work hard on improving after it being her worst nightmare at the beginning of her father's new marriage.

And her grandmother, the Matriarch of eight children, twenty-seven grandchildren and over thirty great grandchildren had since died years ago had been much loved by Bia but a thorn in Marcus' relationships with the rest of her family.

He had hated to have been unable to go anywhere where the grandmother was likely to be and he complained somewhat bitterly to Bia that this would never happen in his much more warm and welcoming family in Australia.

"I will live with you in Brazil, Bia, on one condition - that we don't live in Rio," he told her.

Bia thought about what Marcus had said and replied,

"Maybe that's possible - the difficult part is to find a school for Niko that's a good school - I t's not like here in Australia, Marcus, where you can find great schools outside of the big cities - Brazil in the country side is more like the third world."

But thinking about it, Bia realized it would be better for Marcus not to have to live in too close a proximity to her family.

"Parati," said Marcus, "I love Parati."

Parati was an historic seaside town four hours south of Rio. A beautiful little place that had been the port in centuries gone by for the gold and precious stones hewn from the rocks of Minas Gerais and destined for the Kingdom of Portugal. Named after a local brand of rum the port had stood for almost four hundred and fifty years but abandoned to pirates during its infancy where time had since passed it by unchanged for centuries.

Until tourism had turned on its rough cobbled streets and old colonial houses and Inns and dragged its lost three hundred years into the twentieth century.

"Itaipava is another possibility," said Bia.

"We could live in your house in the valley, or maybe stay there in weekends and rent a house in Itaipava if it is too far for Niko to go to school each day," added Marcus.

"You know I went to see a psychic about this, Marcus," Bia had told him.

"You did? who, my best friend Rhonda?"

Rhonda was a psychic who Bia had visited but whom Marcus had never actually met but when Bia had gone to see her, Rhonda had talked about how wonderful Bia's husband was. So, for Marcus she became, 'my best friend, Rhonda'.

"No," laughed Bia, "it was this man in Ballina who Christiana recommended."

Christiana, Bia's Chilean friend who rented Marcus' house. She was keen on visiting psychics and singing bhajans, but mostly singing bhajans and sometimes she and Bia would form a Latin singing group and sing Bossanova together at events and parties.

"And, what did he say?"

"I asked him how it would be for you and for Niko and he said for Niko it would be great and for you? he said you would be fine too."

"Bia, if we find somewhere nice and I can have a little farm I am going to be happy - let's do it," said Marcus quickly enthusing about the change - actually, you know what?"

"What?"

"I am over Australia, and anyway, we can come back to visit my children every year and they can come visit us too."

So, they travelled together to Brazil once more, spending time with Bia's family in Rio, and taking time out relaxing in her house in the valley at the foot of Maria Comprida, but mostly, they explored places to live.

"Come to Trancoso, Bia," Carlinhos had said, "you're going to love it there and I know people who are starting up a new school in Trancoso next year."

Marcus and Bia flew to Porto Seguro twice that visit but found the school for Niko in Arraial D'Ajuda.

Up until the eighties, Arraial, as it was generally shortened to, was, like Trancoso, just a small fishing village centered around a church in a single rectangle of simple cottages,

But Arraial was also a pilgrimage place where abided the Lady of Help and Succor and the Lady had her sacred spring that pilgrims came to bathe in.

Over the last thirty years, the two towns had boomed, first with the influx of hippies and then the full-scale tourism invasion as Europe, Argentina and São Paulo simultaneously discovered the allures of Bahia's south coast.

And the coast was beautiful. Beach after tropical beach stretched out from Arraial all the way to Trancoso some twenty kilometers to the South with a backdrop of pink, white and red cliffs and the occasional small river mouth that meandered out of the forests. Forests where the odd jaguar, puma or ocelots would still appear from time to time.

Club Med was already there, however, up there behind the cliffs, and other mansions and condominiums had encroached into the forest above but even so, it had lost little of its natural beauty.

Along the beaches that fronted the town, busy beach cafes and bars, competed with each other with their offerings of loud music and Bahiana food such as fried cod cakes, steaming pots of moqueca, char grilled beef and chicken, picanha and baked whole fish plates of dourado and robalo.

To get from Porto Seguro to Arraial, you had to take a ferry and there was something about that ferry from Porto to Arraial that just, well, slowed everybody down as you passed the time meditating on the waters, or for the locals to exchange a bit of gossip during the half hour or so it took for the ferry to first embark and then cross the Rio Buranhém.

Marcus loved the river crossing and the difference it made to the atmosphere of the arrival.

Porto, as the locals called Porto Seguro, had been the first landing place in Brazil of the Portuguese and the fact was celebrated everywhere as you entered or left the small city.

'Bem-vindo, Brasil Nasce Aqui' - 'Welcome, Brasil had its birth place here!'

The old port was a bustling fishing port with fabulously colorful wooden boats and preserved historic streets of what had once been fisherman's and poor people's cottages now brightly painted with the buildings, fronting the sea and the river, housing souvenir shops and cafés, each one a contrasting color.

Across the Rio Buranhém, Arraial had grown into an eclectic mix of races and religions.

From the original Indian tribe, the Pataxós who had survived with their culture more or less re-invented in a kind of postmodern indigenous form, to a mix race of Caboclos of primarily Indigenous and African blood, to the older Brazilian locals to the influxes of Paulistas, Argentinos and Italianos the latter of whom ran yachts from Arraial to Ibiza on an annual basis - their holds stacked with cocaine to rival the ancient Spanish gold trade.

A wave of immigration had soon followed the tourists from the collapse of the cacao plantations further north as former plantation workers surged into the towns looking for employment in the now booming tourism industry.

Hastily erected poor suburbs had literally appeared overnight on the outskirts of Arraial and Trancoso and they became both the source of cheap labor and the theaters of quickly forgotten tragedies as crack, drug dealing and the occasional murder vied with evangelism on the muddy and garbage strewn streets.

In the better parts of town, there were offerings of Buddhism, Spiritualism, Candomblé, Yoga and Capoeira while the Ayahuasca based church of União do Vegetal thrived in inland Eunápolis, 'a burning hell inhabited by angels', as Marcus described it.

At the heart of Arraial stood the simple church of Our Lady of Help as she gazed out onto the ocean in compassion for all. Once a year the Lady was taken on a walk around the town to restore the faith of the waverers and fill the little church's alcove with yet more stories of miracles. The crippled would walk again, the blind would see, the deaf would hear while the politicos would keep on keeping on, stealing from the schools and hospitals.

∿∿

Bia and Marcus happily booked Niko into the school before heading back to Rio where Bia's stepmother, Donna Vera had been spending enormous amounts of money on a lavish beach side retreat two hours south.

Donna Vera had spent twenty-thousand dollars on a landscape plan she decided she didn't like so she had called Marcus and Bia over to her roomy sea front apartment on the Avenida Viera Souto overlooking Ipanema beach to the front and the country club from the windows to the South.

Donna Vera was deemed eccentric but not mad due to the benefits of wealth, was re-stitched on an annual basis and, Marcus had to admit, re-stitched pretty well.

He had seen far worse cases. Especially in Rio where botox and plastic reigned supreme and the best of the plastic surgeons took on heroic and God like status amongst the rich while the poor could only turn to their Orixás and saints to beautify their souls if not their haggard faces.

Dona Vera said she was running out of the money she had budgeted for on the project. She said she was undergoing a life change and that she realized family was more important than keeping all of her money in a bank. Carlinhos told Bia she wasn't spending any of her money and told Bia that she never spent any of her considerable wealth, that she always spent their father's money.

"Hello Marcus," greeted the step mother, turning her white cheeks for Marcus to peck. She stayed away from the sun, religiously. She stayed away from the streets too, religiously. Everything frightened her.

Born in São Paulo of Austrian-Jewish descent she had married her second wealthy husband when Bia was a teenager.

But Marcus felt a soft spot for her. He often did for eccentric and mad people, the ones left of center, that didn't fit the mold. Up until now they had had a carefully managed relationship of warm civility. She took care to flatter him sufficiently.

"You are looking good, Marcus," she said in greeting.

He took care to treat her kindly. He well knew the precarious relationship that she had with Bia, everything being a political game, each move crafted with strategy.

"So, Vera, what's the problem with your landscape plan? can I see it?"

She snapped her fingers at her man servant.

"Mauricio, get the folder from my desk, and my glasses, where are my glasses?"

After ordering Mauricio to bring mineral water for Bia and coffee for Marcus they sat down on the couch with the plans spread before them, Donna Vera's latest dog jumped on his lap and began to slobber affectionately over his clothes. She went through a dog or two every few months on average, each one expensively imported from America from the best of kennels and treated like royalty until she found some reason to disapprove of it, farm the animal off to someone in her family or circle of friends and then import another one.

"I heard you make wonderful gardens, Marcus," said Donna Vera.

Marcus shrugged.

"I love making gardens, yes, but I kind of do them gradually, waiting for plants and trees to grow before adding more complementary plants."

Marcus left assuring Donna Vera that he would do an alternative plan - simpler and in keeping with the original landscape using a mix of exotics and natives.

"I will do it for free, Vera," he told her while glancing down at the twenty-thousand-dollar plan still spread out on the coffee table, and adding,

"I'm not going to charge for doing something for the family."

Marcus realized that after fourteen years of marriage to Bia he was finally beginning to feel at home and at ease with her family, and to feel accepted by them what's more. He said as much to Bia in the car on the way home.

Bia cautioned him, saying,

"Be careful of Vera, Marcus - you may end up being burned."

A house with too many rooms
and too many secrets
and high conceits
but far away to the North
deep in the great forest
a bird song
an ancient incantation
and insects humming
and a beast stalking
your buried fear
but are you still listening?

Chapter 28

Bia's Wavering Heart

The Agent called early around the time Bia had come back from dropping Niko at school.

"I think I found a place you are going to like."

She sounded excited.

The twenty-hectare roça, or subsistence farm, sat half way between Arraial and Trancoso on the asphalt road that ran inland from the coast and less than ten minutes from Carlinhos' timber plantation. A line of coconut palms had been planted along the road in front of the property and a sandy track led to a small two room house set in a neatly swept area surrounded by an assortment of fruit trees and palms. Mangos, soursop, guava, urucum, jack fruit and everywhere, growing naturally along the front of the land were mangabas. Small plots of pineapples and cassava grew in the cleared areas near the house but most of what had once been pasture for long gone cattle was now overgrown in varying stages of weed infestation, long grass or young tree growth.

"Ok," said Marcus after being introduced to the family of roçeiros, "show me the water."

Water was the first thing that Marcus looked for before buying property, always the water. With good water you could do anything but without it, life on the land was always a struggle.

He noted the sandy soil but that didn't bother him that much, making a nice feel to the place and where they wanted to grow things,

218

like an organic vegetable garden which was always a standard feature of any property Marcus owned, the soil could be improved.

"Not ideal, but manageable," he considered.

The farmer led them down through the forest to the water.

"Around half the land is forested?" enquired Marcus of the man.

He was probably no older than Marcus but years of a hard life on the land had etched his face and bowed his legs and now his wife was too ill to stay living on the farm.

He loved his land, however, and Marcus could see the care he had taken to clear parts of the forest undergrowth and thin the trees to create food forests of cacao and cupauçu with carefully placed bromeliads he had taken from inside the forest to decorate the surrounds. This was the traditional native way, to make small clearings for manioca and beans, corn too maybe, and then clear out the undergrowth of the forest, cut some trees for extra light and plant the food trees.

The man nodded.

"Exactly half," he replied.

When they arrived at the water, Marcus was sold. The forest, a remnant of the Mata Atlântica, was luxurious and welcoming and while he saw they had harvested the bigger trees from time to time, the ecosystem was abundantly healthy with a great variety of tall trees and a forest floor full of green leaved plants, bromeliads, heliconia, philodendrons and thick vines winding their way to the canopy. But the water, the water was a pure azure.

Fascinated, Marcus noted the construction of the small dam they had built to contain the spring which flowed out from the ground about sixty meters upstream. The farmer and his sons had carved out one of the banks by hand with their shovels to form an earthen dam, selecting a place of pure white clay while reinforcing the clay with thick hand cut wooden stakes the size of fence posts. Due to the white clay, the water was as blue as the sky and because it sprang from the forest floor, as pure as the waters of Eden.

The next thing Marcus wanted to know about was trails, were there good trails for horse riding?

"Yes," the farmer replied,

The neighbor, the owner of a media empire had bought a huge tract of land to preserve the forest and there were many trails on it.

"But would we be able to use them?" asked Marcus.

"No problem," replied the farmer.

"He is Carlinhos' partner in the timber plantations," added Bia.

"Let's find out - make sure we can use them and if all's good we can buy the property."

Marcus was rapt to hear from Carlinhos that all would be fine and the sale was quickly finalized.

What Marcus had not fully understood was that a Brazilian promise or assurance can be a fluid thing – that and the fact that the wealthy of Brazil consider themselves a class above which is what irritated Marcus the most about them and this is what subsequently ensued;

～ᵔᵕᵔ⌒

"Come on Bia, I asked Carlinhos if he had spoken to Roberto and he said he had – he has either just out and out lied to me or else he totally forgot and didn't want to admit it, and this is the third time something like this has happened with Carlinhos – how can I trust him anymore and that comment of his that I am being gross by contacting Roberto directly just leaves me stunned - what's he thinking? that we live in the colonial past still?"

Marcus waited for Carlinhos' next visit but it never came and Carlinhos was clearly avoiding them. Marcus wrote him an e-mail venting his anger.

He shouldn't have.

"Gross," Marcus wrote, "is not anything to do with having the inclination to speak to a powerful person directly, no that isn't gross - but what is gross is the way people like you, Carlinhos, believe that some people are a class above others..." it began.

～ᵔᵕᵔ⌒

The e-mail that sealed their fates continued in that vein and some of Marcus' words were too harsh. He could be harsh when angered but in Marcus' world he would always be there to discuss and resolve things later and he believed that Carlinhos had enough intelligence and maturity to be able to sit down and discuss it. Marcus was just trying to force his hand, to bring the misunderstandings to the fore, to throw a small incendiary device into Carlinhos' carefully guarded world so he would come to treaty and resolve things. They would finish off by making peace and hugging. That was Marcus' way. He had thought that is what would happen.

But it was not Carlinhos' world and not Carlinhos' way.

⌒⌣⌣⌒

The fated E-mail became completely lost in translation as the misunderstandings led to shocked anger, bursting out like acacia seeds in a bushfire to land, seed and fester in the collective minds of the family.

For fifteen years Marcus had diplomatically trodden carefully around Bia's family and the results of all that patience were now a smoldering ruin. If he tried to explain things honestly to her father and step mother it would only implicate Carlinhos even more so he could say nothing in his defense. The worst part was that he knew who would suffer most and that was Bia.

He walked up to her as she sat in their bungalow near the beach feeling about as bad as it can get.

"She didn't deserve this," he thought while taking her shoulders in his hands and kissing her lightly on the top of her head.

"Bia, I have done something that may mean you may not want to stay with me anymore," he told her.

"Yes, Marcus, what's going on? I saw all those e-mails from Carlinhos but I haven't opened them yet - what's happening?"

"I stuffed up with Carlinhos, that's what happened."

Bia tried to bring Carlinhos to talk to them but he would not. Not this family where nothing was ever properly resolved. There were thick expensive carpets to sweep that shit under.

"I pleaded with you not to get too involved," said Bia.

"What can I do now, Bia? I would gladly sit down and talk with all of them to try and make things better but what can I say now? everything I said to Carlinhos was directed at him and what he always says about his own family but he has either totally misunderstood what I said or else he has twisted it around to make it look like it was my opinion."

"You should not have, Marcus,"

"How would I know about these things? all the information I have of your family, all the talk about Vera abusing your father's accounts, about the way the wives treat their servants - all comes from Carlinhos and you - all I've done is feed it back to him to try and show him he has no notion of what the meaning of gross really is - he really pissed me off, him saying that."

In Marcus' mind, he knew Carlinhos well enough, thought him open enough to be able to resolve things. Carlinhos was not a bad person at all, a good person even, but he was arrogant, not in the way he treated people so much as the way he couldn't accept criticism and Marcus had misjudged both the depth of offense he had caused and Carlinhos' inability to face it. It was also a cultural thing as well – Brazilians, he would learn, would prefer to be nice than to be too real.

Sitting on the beach a week later he began to feel the futility of it all. He was troubled. Bia was not in a good space either, understandably so. She was going through many changes and was now in the middle of the full hormonal fluctuations of menopause, but powering ahead with her own projects in her own land and making many new friends. Stepping out from Marcus' shadow.

"Bia, I don't know if we can go on together - what do you think?" he asked after returning from the beach.

If truth be told he wasn't sure if he really meant that or if he was just seeking reassurance from his companion of fifteen years and lifetimes more.

When she answered him, he knew he was really seeking assurance. Her answer was completely unexpected and shattering.

"I don't know either, Marcus," she said, staring vacantly beyond him, "I think maybe it is time for me to be alone in this world."

Coming from the woman who had begged him so many times to tell her that he would stay with her forever, he found it hard to believe at first.

"I feel like something has just broken between us," he said.

"Yes, Marcus, maybe it has."

Niko was alongside them and his innocent little face took on a look of terror as he realized they were talking about separating. He began to cry and clutch desperately to Marcus while Bia looked ahead vacantly. Marcus' mind was in turmoil.

Seeing Niko like that broke his heart.

The following morning Bia changed her mind.

Marcus and Niko were hurting and on the ferry a few days later Marcus prepared Niko for the possibility of separation, but on the Sunday, something shifted in him and he felt he just had to forget about what could happen in the future and hold the space, to be there for them both in a positive frame of mind.

～✫～

In the summer they were back in Australia and then they journeyed on to Arunachala and after Bia left for Brazil with Niko, Marcus stayed on alone at the sacred mountain he loved.

He thought about not returning to Brazil. In Arunachala he was surrounded by friends, his tribe if you will.

"Bia, I am here in Arunachala and feeling free of all that's happened between us - I'm good here, but I will come back if you feel certain in your heart that you want me with you."

He wrote that to her when the time approached to return.

"I guess that is just what is happening," she replied, sounding to Marcus almost disinterested.

"If you are that unenthusiastic, Bia, I can stay here."

"No, Marcus, that isn't what I meant - we want you back, of course we do."

But back in Brazil a few months later, the day of Marcus' birthday it changed again. They made love in the morning but Marcus felt Bia not really present, the absence of that mutual satiated pleasure they would share as they languished together afterwards, so he asked her what was happening and then she told him.

She was wanting to separate again.

"Marcus, I have been in relationship all my life. I have never lived alone, I have never explored what it is to be an independent woman, to do the things that I want to do and not have to worry about what my partner wants."

"Bia," replied Marcus, "I have always allowed you to do whatever you want. You wanted to study - I did everything to give you the space for that - you wanted to travel to visit your family when I couldn't go, I gave you the space - you wanted to go out to parties or music shows when I didn't want to and I never stood in your way or objected and I trusted you wholly, and now whenever you want to go to Rio to visit your family you go and when you wanted, to spend time in the Amazon, I let you go while I took care of Niko - how much more space can I give you? you're doing things now that you want to do that don't involve me, what is it then?"

Bia had a look of helplessness as she tried to find an answer.

"Marcus I'm changing inside and I don't altogether understand everything that's happening to me, and…and there are things about you I find difficult - what happened with my family and yourself has made life hard for me, and now I feel I need the space from you to go through these changes."

She looked at him imploringly, as though trying to make herself understand as much as he.

"You changed my life, Marcus, and showed me things I would never have otherwise seen and learned things I would never have learned without you, but now I have to do it on my own."

The sadness that Marcus felt was palpable as he pleaded with her,

"Bia, we are a family - there's no need to throw all that away for you to go through the changes you feel you need to - I can give you the space for that too within the marriage - I am not stopping you from changing inside."

And so, once again the following day Bia told Marcus that he was right. She could do what she needed to do, undertake the transformations that were happening within her alongside him. Once again, they would walk on together.

That year they busied themselves with building the new house. It seemed a bit surreal for them to be laying down new roots in new land while the turmoil between them lay brewing beneath the surface but it wasn't to say that happy days were not plenty or that the affection between them had ceased. And Marcus was immersing himself in the creativity of transforming yet another piece of run-down land into a beautiful paradise although Bia, to Marcus' perception, fluctuated between her normal self and being what he could only describe as not being present with him, distant.

In August of that year, however, on a sunny day, Bia asked to walk along the beach with Marcus after dropping Niko at school and Marcus was at first happy to hear that. It was becoming rarer for her to want to do things with him but his happiness changed to frustration and anger when she began to speak. It was a beautiful day and the beach near their house in Arraial curved around from the mouth of the Buranhém to the point past the painted fishing boats, the 'Praia dos Pescadores'. It was in the direction of the fishing boats they walked as Bia began to speak,

"Marcus, everything is not Ok with me, with us - I need things to change still."

"Ah, Bia, enough then!" snapped Marcus, "sorry but I can't take any more of your doubts about me and us - chega!"

"It's not you, Marcus, it's me - I don't feel good - I don't even feel sane and I don't know what to do - of course I have doubts about us, and all sorts of things are going through my mind all the time - I feel like I am going crazy but I am not saying I want you to leave."

"Then what are you saying?" asked Marcus irritably.

"I don't know, I just don't feel good."

"Ahh, enough, I am out of here," said Marcus as he stopped to turn around

"Please Marcus, don't walk away."

"Then explain yourself better," he demanded.

"Ok then, I went to see a counsellor, a woman," she began, knowing well that Marcus didn't have such a high opinion of psychologists or counsellors.

Marcus nodded and kept walking, saying,

"Go on, I'm listening."

"She suggested to me to do an ayahuasca ceremony that she does with a group in Santa André - I want to do it."

"Bia, when have I ever stopped you from exploring yourself in whatever way you want?"

Marcus stopped, and turning to Bia asked her,

"Bia, how then would you feel about me doing the ceremony with you? I think if you head off on this journey alone, we might just drift apart, but maybe if we do it together it might be good - what do you think?"

Bia paused, but not for long, before asking,

"Would you really?"

"Yes, sure - I would like that."

Beyond the shore
the children of the darkness
navigate the stars
and to the serpent prow
with wiccan eyes
surrendered hope
and all of hope's lust
to the heaving mist
of the serpent's lingering kiss

Chapter 29

Sacred Love

What Marcus and Bia didn't realize as they found the place on the beach north of Santa André was that the ceremony was going to be a large one. A kind of inauguration of the new ceremonial lodge. A high conical building made of bamboo and coconut palm thatch set back from the beach. The visiting shaman was a woman from Alto Paraíso in inland Goiás, a center for all things alternative and a town built on a bedrock of amethyst crystal where many shamans of Brazilian rather than indigenous origin plied their trade.

⌇⌇⌇

This one had brought with her a following of at least fifty people including a few shaven headed acolytes. The altar displayed a dogs' breakfast of deities, Iemanjá, the goddess of the ocean, the Madonna, the Christ, the Buddha, Krishna, Siva, Durga and Ganesha. They were all present. In the center of the sandy floor was a fire pit.

Aside from the Shaman's followers from Alto Paraíso there were a sprinkling of locals from Santa André and people from Arraial, a few of whom Marcus recognized and vaguely knew. To complete the mix, some dentists and lawyers from inland Eunapolis.

Dividing the circle, men on one side, women on the other they formed a line to take the sacred tea. Marcus noticed that most people took about a half a cup but when he arrived and they saw his size they gave him a whole one.

"Ah well, whatever is given," he thought, and as in the Ashaninka village four years before, the medicine worked quickly for him.

The shaman began to preach but what she was saying didn't impress him much at all, but what made a worse impression on him was the electronic music that followed. It grated his now acute senses. People began dancing around the fire and he knew none of them, unfamiliar people, bad music, low grade teachings. His mind was judging and the judging mind with Ayahuasca brings on negativity and negativity becomes very confronting within. He decided to leave the circle and walk to the beach but on the way there, was stopped by one of the shaven headed acolytes.

"Sorry, but no-one is allowed on to the beach."

"Really? don't worry, I will be fine, I'm not going to go into the water."

"No, you're not allowed on the beach - it's the rule."

"Really? but the beach is calling me," said Marcus as he continued past the earnest spiritual policeman.

Marcus sat on the beach and looked up at the stars that were multiplied a thousand-fold and he began to relax into the effects but his tranquility was interrupted by the owner of the property, a psychologist who had been cured of cancer by Ayahuasca he claimed, who now sat down next to him.

"Look, Marcus, I know that you come from a history of much spiritual work and you may be fine here alone but we have to obey the rules here - we can do this because under the law we are a church so everyone who comes here has to obey the rules."

"Well," replied Marcus, "this mind is way beyond any capacity to argue, so as much as I find it funny, I'll head back to the circle, ok."

Back in the circle, however, it was worse than before. The music was worse anyway and made him feel violently ill. Recalling how vomiting had made him feel so much better the time before in the jungle, he went outside but this time he couldn't manage to bring anything up.

"Damn," he thought, "I shouldn't have fasted beforehand, now I have nothing in my stomach to throw this stuff up."

"Interestingly he was experiencing the exact same internal vision as before when with the Ashaninka Indians, the insect like threads reaching through molten silver streams that coursed in turn through a back drop of fluid iridescent green, and he didn't want to deal with that vision as well as deal with his physical wretchedness but his resistance only agitated the intensity of it.

His discomfort was acute. He placed almost his entire hand down his throat and felt as if he could have reached all the way to his stomach if he had wanted to, but still, he could not vomit.

"Marcus is that you?"

It was Bia just off to his right in the darkness, also vomiting.

"Argh, I feel better now," she said.

"I feel terrible. I can't throw up," he replied.

"What's happening," she asked.

"I was given a huge dose - my body is too sensitive for that much - I feel like shit."

He realized he was shaking.

"I'm cold, Bia, terribly cold - and that music is crap."

Bia laughed at that.

"Argh, for me too - I couldn't stand it in there."

"I'm going to get you an apple and your blanket - wait here."

Munching the apple was very strange in the state he was in but with each bite he began to feel a little better. More strangely still, he began to feel the spirit of the apple as a live entity entering and soothing his body and he didn't know if it took him two minutes or two hours there kneeling in the grass slowly eating the apple.

"Marcus, I have your blanket, come here and lie with me."

Marcus and Bia lay down together wrapped themselves in two, ultra-soft synthetic and fake tiger and leopard skin blankets that Marcus couldn't resist buying from a sidewalk sale in Eunápolis a while back.

"You're shaking Marcus - here, come closer."

Bia wrapped her body around him.

The insect like tentacles were reaching for Marcus' solar plexus as the molten silver and iridescent green show continued in his mind's eye. Without thinking, he moved both hands on top of his hara just below his belly button. He realized these fine tentacles were in fact, healing his subconscious hurts and surrendered to them in one simple act of letting go.

"Do with me as you will," he surrendered.

Everything changed and became beautiful, even while he felt the terror of things from the past exiting his being through the healing threads of whatever entity it was that worked within him. It was all beautiful and perfect in the way it was meant to be, the pain, the bliss, the tears and the laughter.

He began to laugh, saying to Bia,

"You know, my mind is really, really, really insane."

Bia laughed in return.

"I know, I know."

"You know what else Bia?"

Bia giggled.

"What?"

"All these years I thought it was me teaching you and leading you to higher teachings, and I was, but you know what?"

Bia remained silent, her arms around him.

"You have been teaching me all the time about life and about love - you are my Durga to whom I devoted my past life so now I have to touch your feet and thank you for all that you have taught me - it has been good for me that you put me through all this - I needed it."

Bia hugged him.

They both lay on their backs in silence and gazed at the stupendously radiant stars, the dancing and music interrupted every now and again by the monotone of the shaman's boring preaching another world away. That world was fine too. They were just other forms moving through the universe, doing what they were doing.

The love lapped upon the shore in waves
and she moved my heart
To her sacred keep
Through the currents and the eddies
of the wide river's course
nothing could disturb
This sacred love
of waters deep

Chapter 30

Mae Divina

While in Brazil, Marcus had bought three horses for the farm and chose a white horse for himself that he found in a small town in the interior of Bahia. He wrote to his friends about his horse.

I bought a white horse some weeks ago from a little town in the interior of Bahia - he has no name and he is still a little bit lame and is very frightened but what a beautiful ride. So, we are working together, my patience, my impatience, his fear and his courage, my rage and my freedom to do senseless things. We are working quietly, tentatively brushing him and talking to him and in the end, I don't know whether he will kill me or kill me with love.

His next stay in Arunachala was a blessing after blessing for Marcus that year. He had many friends there but that South Indian winter exceeded itself with the quality and depth of friendship and play and the sweet joy he found in silent moments in the ashram, or walking the mountain or sitting in the caves. His heart was filled with love and he wrote this poem to Bia, to Durga, to the Goddess.

You think I need your love
I don't need your love

My heart already overflows with love
Love has no need, it overflows onto my sheets, onto the earth upon which I walk
and it surrounds and spills out from everywhere I look
and in every sound I hear
and every smell and taste
No, I don't need your love
I need your touch and your caress
I need your passion and grand appreciation
I need your breasts to lay down my head
your hands where it feels so good
your mouth on mine and your sweet intelligence, your worldly dance
No, I do not need your love
And if it be so that I have no need
then I sleep and you cease to be
And then you must dance upon my sleeping form again
That I may awaken to your need

Bia and Niko were there waiting for him at the airport. Niko with his long hair that he refused to let anyone cut. Always eager to tell Marcus about something that had happened or about his latest obsession or fantasy story.

They crossed the ferry to Arraial, the Buranhém was in high tide and the water a beautiful blue, Niko demanding his attention while Bia held his arm. Her favorite, or maybe second favorite, part of his body.

The garden he had planted just before he left had grown unbelievably fast. He would always walk around his gardens first thing after coming home. Checking each plant like old friends, noting what had been neglected and what needed to be done. He walked out into the pasture and called the horses, coaxing his white horse whom he had named 'Karkara',which translated as 'hawk', into the yard. He passed his hands over his neck. Shy at first, the nervous horse recognized him and began to relax to Marcus' touch.

"Come, Niko, come for a walk to the spring," he called as he passed the house, seeing Niko bouncing around in the garden inside his imagination.

They were joined by Dendê, the even bouncier and huge but still growing ten-month-old Rhodesian ridge back. Together they wound their way down through one of the new paths that Marcus had built with the farm's two workers. Down to the new stone dam that was twice the size of the previous one where it now held back a fifty-meter stretch of blue water.

They took off their clothes and plunged in naked, swimming the length of the pool, bordered on each side by dense forest and creepers and Açai palms that Marcus had planted before he left. He loved this land. Loved the forest and it was here he would come when wanting time alone to rejuvenate and fall into silent communion with the trees. The Jaguar watched, always watching, unmoving, from the undergrowth, and later he wrote,

"This morning a wave of large monkeys passed by overhead and as I walked back along the forest trail my jaguar was watching from the shelter of the undergrowth. Dendê was by my side and she sniffed the air suspiciously,"

"Marcus I am going to a ceremony this weekend with a guy called Leonardo from the Chapada Diamantina - I did one with him while you were away and I'm sure you're going to like him more than that other shaman."

Bia was still enthused about continuing her journey with Ayahuasca while Marcus, in that moment, was feeling peacefully content from his time at Arunachala and felt no need for anything outside of what was - outside of whatever presented itself to him in life. But he felt that Bia wanted him to join her and he had given that commitment to her six months before. And besides, it was what was being presented now.

"Ok, I will join you," he replied, "why not? I only hope my body can handle it."

There were only around twenty people at this gathering and besides Leonardo, all of them from Arraial. A few faces were familiar, but Marcus didn't know any of them well. After two years in Arraial he was beginning to meet more people but mainly through Bia. Most of his time he spent at the farm. At least his Portuguese, by now, had improved to a conversational level.

The first phase of his ayahuasca experience followed a familiar pattern. He soon felt sick and left the circle to try and vomit. But once again it didn't come easily and as soon as his mind felt negative about having succumbed to the invitation to take the medicine his experience became confronting. Huge snakes writhed above him, beautiful snakes, colorful snakes. He recognized them simply as manifestations of his negative mind but he wished they would leave him alone anyway. A black cat appeared out of the bushes in front of him and crawled into his lap, purring. The cat was real.

Leonardo came out with Bia to check on him. He felt warmed by their kindness.

"I'm ok, not great, but ok - the cat is keeping me company."

Shortly after he did manage to throw up, got up and walked back to the circle, taking a sip of water as he went. He lay down in the circle and immediately felt the energy of the circle very loving and different to the madness of the last experience. He placed his hands on his hara and surrendered to the circle, and surrendered to Leonardo's music as he sang the anthem,

"Mãe Divina,
Vem surgindo um novo tempo,
Traz glórias do divino
Mais puros e atentos
Nos tornamos canais do infinito
Mãe divina eu quero ser
Um filho realizado

E é perante o seu poder
Que me entrego pra se libertado
Estou morrendo para o passedo
E nem anseio pelo o futuro
Minha coroa tem brilho dourado
Provo o néctar do amor maduro"

Marcus was elevated into an extraordinarily divine and ecstatic space. He saw the spirit of the ayahuasca plant herself hovering and dancing with her butterfly like wings above him and blessing him with the most indescribable beauty he had ever experienced in his entire life.

If beauty could be drawn with ultimate perfection, she was that. If beauty could be felt in its entirety and ultimate purity, she was that.

Leonardos' compassionate and gentle voice floated around her, and alongside to him, a woman he would later get to know well was adding to the joy with her poetic interjections and giggles, a huge smile across her angular face, her long red hair cascading over her shoulders as she danced her hands along with the music. Next to her Bia was laying down.

Marcus sat up and moved into the half lotus position. Everyone else was laying down except the red-haired woman, Antonia, and a young man to his right, while Leonardo continued to sing. Marcus sat with his eyes open and his heart blissful. Bia sat up again after a while and began looking at Marcus and after observing him keenly, she reached out in front of Antonia and took Marcus' hand and held it tightly.

"I love you - you look so beautiful."

"I love you too."

Antonia, with a huge smile, folded her hands across her heart as the two lovers shared theirs on either side of her. Being with Bia was beautiful.

If I were to see
your kaleidoscope wings
again
I should want you
and this blessed night
But to lose this gift of divinity
this radiant smile to infinity
I might
as well die to me
where upon these black raven's wings
I be borne
to dark eternity

Chapter 31

Filling the Void with Dreams

Marcus passed the following months feeling that things were back on an even keel with Bia. He still spent much of his time tending to the farm and garden and working with his white horse, improving and expanding his treasured walking trails in their forest and exploring new horse-riding trails into the vast and mostly forested lands across the road.

That was until around August when he began to inexplicably feel a torment brewing within him. It didn't worry him unduly at first, just something moving through the stars that he would accept and surrender to and soon pass.

But it didn't pass and it was at this time he began to feel that Bia was once more not so keen about riding with him, or spending time at the beach with him or enthusiastically sharing her thoughts.

When they started planning their next trip to India, Bia became irritated. She wanted to spend more time by herself while Marcus wanted them to spend some time together, visiting Varanasi which he hadn't seen in eighteen years, and once again, he felt he had to fight to find time together with her - both now and in their future plans.

***

Marcus' veterinary surgeon was a young and pretty woman of thirty-three. Her angular profile reminded him of an ancient Indian miniature, with her hair tied tightly back from her handsome face. Having known her now for the best part of two and half years they had steadily become firmer friends,

Marcus would drive her some days to Eunápolis to find vet supplies for himself and for her clinic. It was a friendship that had begun cautiously but of late had quickly blossomed and for Marcus it was really the only friendship he had with someone who was not first and foremost Bia's friend.

After a while she began to ride with him since Bia was rarely inclined and Marcus searching, as he often was, for riding partners just like he had done in Australia.

The fact that Ana Maria was young and beautiful was also not that unusual as far as choice of company went for Marcus. He had younger, beautiful female friends in Australia, and in India too, an issue for Bia in the past but something she was much more accepting of now, understanding that Marcus was really very faithful to her.

Bia had placed much emphasis during the last year or more that she no longer felt any jealousy, so for Marcus his friendship with Ana Maria was ideal even though in his heart he was more content than ever with Bia.

Until she showed signs of becoming distant again that was.

Even still, sex with Ana Maria didn't even cross his mind, after all she was far too young for him. Of course, he thought her beautiful and she was but Marcus loved all things beautiful, be it flowers and gardens, blue water or elegant trees, tasteful houses or clothes. His eye was born to appreciate it. When he went with Bia to shop for clothes, he would judge her choice by the arousal he felt in his sex.

"He likes that one - no, he loves that one," he would laugh as he drew her to him in the change room.

"Not here, Marcus," she would object, but Marcus knew she loved his desire for her in those moments and it was all she could do to stop him from making love to her in the change rooms sometimes.

So, on that score there was nothing unusual about his friendship with Ana Maria.

That was until one day they were out riding together, a fifteen-kilometer round trip through the forest where they stopped and rested their horses at a primitive house of roçeiros who worked a clearing of land deep in the forest.

Here they grew cassava and bananas, bred donkeys and a collection of mangy dogs that fought over scraps of food in the dust. Marcus and Ana Maria hitched their horses and sat down with them to drink thick black sweet coffee from recycled jam jars as shirtless men sat around the table playing dominoes. A middle-aged woman who had seen too many hard years crease her rugged cabocla face and sag her large breasts and belly, served them all the coffee along with battered aluminum plates of beans and farina.

Marcus joined in the game. He had quickly become adept at dominos while playing during the lunch breaks with the workers building their house the year before and Bia would sometimes comment that Marcus liked to 'fica com um pé na sujeira', 'to stay with one foot in the dirt'.

She was right, he did. It was the other side of him. She could never sit down, for example, on the floor of the house Marcus had bought for three fatherless children in the slum of Tiruvannamalai back in India and eat chicken curry with them like he did.

And while Marcus played and won at dominoes, Ana Maria went about vaccinating their dogs. She was a compulsive when it came to caring for animals, couldn't help herself and one of the nice things about her was that she healed animals more often than not without getting paid for her work.

Marcus loved riding through the countryside calling in on poor farmers and their families and sharing coffee and stories. He was beginning to really enjoy his life in the South of Bahia.

Riding home they galloped the first few kilometers through the tail trees of the Mata Atlantica, the track soft and sandy, occasional pools of water from the recent rains forming puddles on the trail and they drove their horses through them sending water and mud over their clothes.

Marcus was in love with his white horse, Karkara, his white horse loved him back in spades, but slowing to a walk, Ana Maria turned to Marcus and said something to him that made him wonder, made him rethink what was really happening between them,

"Oh Marcus, riding alongside you I am getting too hot," she said in Portuguese, a language that has two different words for hot and several different implications as well.

What she said was slightly ambiguous. But he could feel a charge in her energy, a sharpness in her eyes as she uttered those words to him.

He didn't respond directly, saying,

"Hey, when we get back to the farm, come down to the spring in the forest and we can cool off."

Lunch was on the table when they got back to the house and Bia asked Ana Maria about the ride and then commented,

"Those men at the roça, I bet they never saw anyone as beautiful as you out there in their lives before."

Ana Maria walked to the natural pool at the edge of the verandah and dived in clothes and all and when she emerged her white cotton shirt and riding jodhpurs clung to her skin showing her flesh and her curves for all to see. She had it all in all of the right places, but the Cabocla cook didn't miss it either and narrowed her eyes visibly at Ana Maria as she placed the last plate of grilled farm chicken on the table.

⌒‿‿⌒

Marcus drove his friend back to her clinic in Arraial. He went to say goodbye. She stared at him plaintively with her big eyes, saying,

"Marcus, I can't not say anything anymore - I'm in love with you."

Her eyes misted over as she reached for Marcus' hand, "and I don't know what to do about it - today I just wanted to make love to you right there in the forest, but I love Bia and I really don't know what to do - my body wants you so badly."

Marcus smiled at her while holding her hand and replied tenderly,

"There is nothing wrong with loving someone - we can all love different people so just stay with the love and maybe it will turn into something else - here, come here."

He drew her to him and gave her a hug and she rested her head on his chest. He kissed her forehead but easing out of the embrace he turned away giving her his shy smile as he did so.

Driving home Marcus felt both excited at the unexpected declaration of love and at the same time a sense of foreboding troubled his soul. Marcus was getting older. Yes, many people reminded him that he was still good for his age but nevertheless he had thought the days when young women would fall in love with him were past. It was flattering, it was insane, but where was Bia?

He was feeling her lack of presence again and all he wanted from Bia was more presence, more appreciation of his company but it was less and less forthcoming these days. He had often wondered if he could resist a beautiful woman whom he liked if she threw herself at him, and yes, he had resisted that in the past, but then in the past he felt Bia's love and loyalty to be solid and pure and he could never betray that strength of loyalty she gave. But now? A year ago, Bia had woken up telling him that she had dreamed he was with another woman and in the dream, she had felt fine with it.

⌒⌣⌒

"Bia, can I ask you to do my chart - to see what's happening for me now?"

"Ahh, Marcus, what for?"

"I feel really troubled by something."

"Ahhh, Marcus, don't be so indulgent - I'm busy with other people's charts at the moment and in the next few days I have too much to do - when I find the time, I will have a look."

But she never did. Marcus started to rethink his life, to question his destiny and he recalled how he had often told Bia that they could not commit to forever. He remembered how he had sometimes wondered to himself if maybe their destiny was to finish this story between them, to cut the strings that brought them back to each other lifetime after lifetime.

Was Ana Maria a player in this path? Had she arrived here to help him make the move? Part of him felt negative towards Bia for wielding power over his emotions the past two years. Yes, it was a lower emotion and he recognized it as that but it whispered to him nevertheless.

The day he seriously thought he might leave her, he felt a well of love rise up from his heart and he found himself offering to cook Niko's dinner when he saw how tired she looked, he spoke sweetly to her and massaged her neck and head. It was not unusual for him to help and be caring but now he exceeded himself in his attention and love and she began to respond, saying to him,

"When I was in Caraiva yesterday at the seminar I looked at all these other women my age who didn't have partners and listening to them talk about searching for men and love I felt so lucky I have you."

They made love that night and afterwards they looked at each other saying,

"Was that the best ever?"

"Yes, it was, it was the best ever."

But Marcus and Ana Maria were still seeing each other, not making love, not yet committed, but the attraction between them wasn't going away. More than that, it was steamily brewing and there was little chance of sobriety reclaiming either of them.

The day Ana Maria met with Bia to discuss the chart Bia had drawn for her, Marcus was in Eunápolis shopping for farm supplies but he knew they were meeting and he knew that Ana Maria would tell Bia about her feelings for him. Now he felt annoyed that two women were probably deciding his fate in his absence.

He had to leave his car in Eunápolis to be fixed and wait for Bia to pick him up from the bus at the crossroads between Arraial and Trancoso much later.

He did what he always did when he had to kill time in the middle of the day during the two hours of siesta and went to the cathedral to sit in silence. Sitting in churches was a strange habit of Marcus' when he had nothing else to do in a town and if the priest came in and began to preach, he would leave, but an empty place of worship was one of his loves.

"My fate is out of my hands," he acknowledged while surrendering to his foreboding.

And meeting Bia at the crossroads, she seemed quite normal and didn't mention the meeting and later in the evening he asked her how the meeting went with Ana Maria, curious, probing.

"She cried a lot - she has some serious problems but I can't tell you about it because it's confidential between us."

Now Marcus felt really annoyed. She was his friend and confidant, not hers.

Bia left the next day for Rio for three days and driving her to the airport Marcus asked,

"Bia you know you never got round to doing my chart when I asked you to do it - I only wanted to know what was going on for me then."

"Oh, I didn't have time - anyway I don't think too much is going on for you right now but I didn't really look."

"Nothing affecting our relationship?" he asked.

"Oh, in a couple of years I have something passing through my seventh house and I might want to leave you then," she replied casually.

That was it. Marcus decided what he was going to do.

⌒〰〰⌒

Niko was still at school after he dropped Bia at the airport so he went straight to see Ana Maria in her clinic.

She was tense when she greeted him. He knew that look, the watery eyes, the hard-set mouth. She led him into her office and locked the doors.

"So how was your discussion with Bia?" he asked.

"She was very beautiful - I really love her," she said holding herself straight in her chair the way she would when dealing with a client she hadn't met before, or one she had to tell that their life long pet friend had died.

"So, I gather you didn't tell her that I knew about your feelings for me?"

"No of course not, Marcus - that is for you to tell her isn't it, but you don't need to because I have decided I have to be strong and not show my feelings for you anymore," she said softly as tears came to her eyes and her bottom lip lost its rigidity and began to ever so slightly tremble.

"She said she still wants to stay with you."

"It's too late," said Marcus.

Ana Maria stared straight at him her eyes widening, questioning.

"I decided I want to be with you - she's been pushing me away on and off for too long now and I feel that deep down she wants the change - anyway, I have fallen in love with you and I can't go back."

"You mean that?"

"Yes, I mean that - I want you."

"To be with me forever?"

"If you can handle that," he laughed.

"Of course, I can!" she cried as she threw her arms around him saying,

"I'm so happy."

"Me too," he smiled

⌒ᵕᵔ⌒

Marcus waited until the last day that Bia was in Rio before he sent her the message and then he took Niko for a walk into the forest to tell him what was about to happen. A plaintive look of despair and panic came over his face so Marcus explained the best he could that he wasn't going away this time but would live close by, that he was going to live with Ana Maria.

Still, it was very hard for both of them but in Marcus' mind, by being with Ana Maria he could stay around Niko, give Bia the chance to be alone yet still be her best friend. It was her friendship he was most afraid of losing and her reply to his message was heartening. She was in shock she wrote back, but yes, of course she would always be his friend.

Changes and tidings
that darken the uncertain hour

The sea runs cold
and its swirling currents
coursed through their drowned hair
while out upon the waves of the Aegir
jealous sirens rejoiced

Beneath the waves of the Aegir
her tearful dreadful eyes
had already turned away

Chapter 32

Grasping for Love

Marcus had picked up his cousin, Amrita and her boyfriend that same weekend. He felt bad about what they were walking into as Amrita had been so much looking forward to her visit. She had lived with them for two years at the farm in Australia and during that time Marcus and Bia had helped her through many difficulties so, no, he thought,

"Actually, this is perfect - she owes us this and Bia will have her in the house while the worst part is happening for her."

Amrita was his fourth cousin and originally it was her mother who was Marcus' friend from his childhood in Tasmania, having grown up as neighbors on the farm next door, and Marcus had spent many afternoons playing with her mother in the gardens of the old and elegant farmhouse and later, in their early teenage years, her best friend had been Marcus' first girlfriend.

⌒〰⌒

"Amrita I need to talk to you."

"Sure Marcus."

Amrita always had her playful smile. Marcus adored her and over the past ten years Amrita had come and gone from their lives on a regular basis, meeting them in India more than once or returning to stay with them in Mullumbimby. Four years before she and a popular female singer songwriter friend of hers had travelled with them to the

Ashaninka village in the amazon a year after Marcus' first visit.

That time they hadn't participated in an Ayahuasca ceremony but a three-day nonstop party when the Ashaninka drank a brew called cauim. The cauim was made by the young women of the village by chewing cassava and spitting it into pots, heated and finally left to ferment in a huge wooden trough resembling a dugout canoe. It was only young women who could do this work and it was the young women and girls who served them the drink as well.

"How long does the party go for?" Marcus had asked.

The Indian looked at him quizzically as though it were a stupid question.

"When the cauim is finished," he replied, shaking his head.

"How long does it usually last?"

"We don't know."

They had a completely different relationship to time, catching but an hour or two of rest when they felt tired, and no matter whether it was day or night there were always people awake in the village and time, was only the hours or days that passed to complete something. It was very simple.

The first person who had dragged Marcus in to the dance had been an old toothless grandmother, the next, a twelve-year-old girl and then finally the chief's son, Benke had handed his wife to Marcus as a straight swap for Misty, the singer.

Later in their trip around Brazil with Bia and Marcus, Amrita and Misty had been taken to Salvador and then to Rio, searching out street parties and samba houses in both cities. It had been a time of much laughter and play back then but now, as Marcus was about to give her the news, he felt a bit bad about how different this trip to Brazil was about to be for her.

Amrita was an artist and sometimes art teacher. A free spirit who for most of her life had chosen to travel the world in the pursuit of art, music festivals and romance but for the first time in her life she was beginning to settle into a more stable relationship. Marcus guessed that she was eager to show off her new 'husband' so he knew it was going to be a shock to her to discover that the ideal couple in her life were about to separate just at the point where she had taken their cue.

And Amrita and Marcus, it seemed had history.

There was a time a few years back in the middle of one of their many conversations over chai on the farm in Mullumbimby when she had asked,

"Marcus, did you ever know anyone who drowned while on acid?"

Marcus had been jolted by her question. Of course, he did, but instead of immediately saying yes, he asked her,

"Why do you ask that?"

"Because I had this vision once that in my past life I drowned on acid."

Marcus had smiled at Amrita when he told her,

"Yes, you did and you were a young American and you died in the Ganges and your last words were, 'nothing matters, nothing matters', and then you disappeared smiling beneath the waters."

Amrita had stared at Marcus with her mouth open and her eyes bulging for a full half minute before he spoke again.

"But that wasn't the worse thing."

Amrita had paled.

"The worst thing is that your name was Harvey."

<hr>

Marcus had waited until Amrita was comfortably settled with a cup of tea.

"Amrita, you know that we have been there for you many times before," he began.

"Sure, Marcus and I thank you and Bia for that from the bottom of my heart."

"Well, now I am going to ask you to return the favor big time."

"What's happening, Marcus?"

Amrita's face was suddenly grave as she realized that her anticipated holiday with her second family might be about to turn out very differently.

"I'm leaving Bia and am going to be with someone else."

Shock passed over Amrita's face.

"No Marcus, don't do it, I love you guys, please don't do this."

"It's too late - I've already made up my mind, Amrita and I need you to be here for Bia after I pick her up tomorrow."

"No Marcus, don't do it, just don't," she repeated.

But Marcus was not about to change his mind. Inside his thoughts he saw this as a way out, being certain he didn't want to lose his connection with Bia and Niko. They had been too close for too long and he never wanted that. In his dreams he would be with Anna Maria living close by and he and Bia would remain friends. In fact, this very scenario had at first been Bia's vision and was about to come back and test her to the limit.

Marcus saw the pain on Bia's face as she made her way out of the baggage security. She walked up to him and embraced him, her body feeling tense, her face drained by emotion.

It was around nine in the evening and the ferry to Arraial was almost empty, the waters of the Buranhém dark beneath the stars as they sat close to each other holding hands and talking. The ferry ran aground on a sand bar and they waited there, both of them in a way happy to be able to pass more time with each other until another tug made its way slowly through the night to dislodge them.

Bia was sweet but she confessed that she never expected it, not even after Ana Maria had told her that she was in love with Marcus. She never thought Marcus would leave her but now she had to accept the path that she herself had in part chosen.

"Marcus I even went to talk with an old friend of mine when I was in Rio who I knew had carried on a three-way relationship with a man for many years - I went to ask her how it was for her, thinking that I might have to face that myself after the conversation I had with Ana Maria."

"You should know by now Bia that I am a one-person guy – to do otherwise would be just too scattered for me," Marcus replied.

She wanted to make love to him that night but he wouldn't.

"Now I've made my choice Bia, I cannot."

"Have you made love with her already?"

"I wouldn't do that behind your back, Bia."

Bia was angry at that point and she was angry with him the next day when they walked to the spring and swam in the pool but after a while her anger subsided and she asked him to sit beside her, once again holding each other tightly, her eyes watery. Marcus left the house with some of his belongings in the afternoon.

If Marcus thought that all would work out as he planned, or rather as he hoped, he was not counting on how his own soul would react even if Ana Maria and Bia had played their parts like he hoped they would. He had promised Niko that he would have lunch with them as often as possible so they could all be like a family sometimes. Niko had begged him for that and Marcus readily agreed - if Bia could handle it.

As it was, she tried and mostly succeeded over the next weeks but sometimes she broke and it disturbed Marcus to see her hurting so much. She wasn't sleeping nights and the pain on her face began to be too much for Marcus to bear.

That first week with Ana Maria was all that it promised to be, a new love, two people in love, enjoying each other's company in all its excitement, its thrill and its freshness, but the cracks started to appear after only ten days, just after Marcus left his holiday apartment and moved in with her.

There were things she did and words she spoke that unnerved him and he realized how fragile he was at that point and he didn't enjoy his fragility, not a bit, not then - not now that he had taken such a reckless step into the unknown.

They made love. But it felt strange and somehow disconnected and while Marcus was impassioned by her beautiful body, seduced by her watery eyes and her willingness to give of herself, something didn't feel right.

But that was the risk of the unknown. You can never really prepare yourself for it because even if you think you have been there before, you haven't, not really.

And Bia was hurting. Each time Marcus saw her it stabbed at his heart to see her like that. In his mind he had decided she was ready for this but she was suffering more than he anticipated she would, and, much more than she had thought she would too, he guessed.

Three weeks after he had left, Marcus knew he had made a mistake. Could he call it a mistake, however? For whatever reason it simply had to happen, each of them for too long having lived with the uncertainty of what they wanted. Now Marcus fell into a downward spiral realizing that it was never going to work with Ana Maria and realizing it was probably too late to restore his marriage with Bia - but he was decided to see what was still possible.

Leonardo had arrived from the Chappada to hold a ceremony at their house. He was there when Marcus turned up to take Amrita and her friend for a horse ride but when her boyfriend declined the ride, Bia asked if she could come and Marcus was very happy that she did.

They rode out on a march at first, on through the papaya plantation across the road and then descended into the forest and across the Rio Da Barra before pushing their horses into a long gallop up the other side and into a broad expanse of overgrown pasture. Here Marcus let go of his reins and spread his arms urging Karkara ever faster. He trusted this horse wholly now. The three of them were letting go of the weeks of pain and hardship and laughed and whooped as they rode.

Slowing to a walk as they entered the forest and then looping round to follow a trail crossed with fallen logs that ran back through the trees to the pasture, Marcus took off at a gallop again thrilling how Karkara took to the jumps.

Easing back into a walk again, Bia pulled up alongside Marcus, saying,

"So, Marcus, tell me I am a better rider than Ana Maria."

He looked at her smilingly, replying,

"You are a better rider than Ana Maria – although I wished you would have ridden with me more often," he added, and he wanted to say more to her at that moment. He wanted to tell her he was coming home the next day. The only reason he didn't was because she was going to take Ayahuasca that night and he didn't want to add any more turmoil to her mind for the journey she would be making.

Amrita too was going to partake that night and for her it was a challenge. The only time she had taken it, in Australia, had been a traumatic experience and had left her scared and in doubt of her own wisdom. There was a danger in taking such powerful medicine with the wrong people but both Marcus and Bia were sure her experience would be better this time, for Leonardo had the shaman's gift of creating what Marcus could only describe as a cosmic womb where a man or woman could unleash all of their fears or their ecstasy in a protective field of safety and he did it through his music and his simple caring attentiveness. But while the shaman was like the conductor, the plant itself was the orchestra and the divine experience.

Marcus walked back into the house mid-morning of the next day, finding Bia and Amrita sitting in the corner of the large verandah. It was a clear morning after a rainy night and the sunlight danced off the water of the pool that was by now covered in water plants of many varieties. Colorful fish darted between the stems of the plants and beyond the house and garden and across the pasture, wisps of mist rose through the canopy of the forest.

He walked over to them knowing that Bia knew. He had sent her a message that morning.

They hugged, Bia saying,

"Well, what a crazy journey you have been on."

"Yes, I know - I have - how was the ceremony last night?'

He looked down at Amrita who was lying across the cushions with a smile and guessed it had been a good experience for her this time.

Bia answered.

"I spent half the time howling like a wolf, Marcus," her eyes meeting his with an intensity demanding his full attention, "I was the mother wolf crying for the loss of her mate and I just howled for ages and eventually, after some time, I became peaceful and I saw that you are also my teacher - yes, I saw that too, but knew I had to let go of you."

Marcus nodded. He was not surprised by any of this.

He looked down at Amrita saying,

"It looks like you had a better time than before."

"Yes, I did," she giggled, "I spent the second part of the night with my head on Bia's lap and I had all these humming birds, buzzing around me and it was beautiful - I had such a good time with Bia there - she was amazing."

That too didn't surprise Marcus as Amrita had long held an affinity and love for the delicate little birds. He had even bought her a crystal humming bird once.

They chatted there for a little while until Amrita went to make some tea for them.

Bia stared fixedly at Marcus, asking,

"Did you want to stay here?"

"Yes," he replied, "but I am happy to stay in the little room in the guest house."

"That's alright, you are welcome to stay there," and then, pausing before continuing, "Marcus don't expect you can just walk back into my life like this - too much has happened for me to assimilate."

"I understand, but I would like to find ways we can be together again - not necessarily like it was but in a way that we can give each other more space yet be together with more presence when we meet - I have been thinking about this."

"Not yet Marcus, maybe, when I am ready for that - If I ever am – but not now."

"I understand Bia - I understand and that's OK."

Marcus stayed for two days before Bia came to his room on the second morning.

"I can't do it Marcus - I need to go through with this wish I have had to learn to be alone - I saw that during the ceremony, that I chose this path - I have to do it."

Marcus sat on his bed observing Bia. Seeing her beauty and her pain and fragility and her strength all at once. In her late forties she was still an extraordinarily beautiful woman.

"Make love to me."

"No, Marcus"

"Make love to me before I go - please."

"Don't make me do this."

"I just look at you and see the woman I love, Bia - you are so beautiful."

She looked at him with a helpless and plaintive face. After all, she found him beautiful too and that hadn't changed.

"Oh God," she let slip as she moved over to him and kissed him fully on the lips.

He unbuttoned her shirt and began to move his hands over her. The touch of familiarity as he ran his fingers along the curves of her breasts brought about an immediate response from his sex and with his free hand, he removed the sarong he wore and drew her hand to fill it with his hardening flesh. Bia's touch felt exquisite. She knew him and he knew her so well and as he reached for her soft wetness they kissed deeply and feverishly.

His body now shuddered with passion and moving her over on top of him and guiding his sex slowly into hers with her legs straddling his waist and, her arms around his neck, they entwined and writhed, lips on lips, breast on breast, the flowering lotus, lost in pleasure, drowning in sorrow, the tears streaming down their cheeks.

He took her hand
beneath the silver moon
and they shed their tears
into the Buranhém

But even the ferry had no wish
to cross that river
nor the heart
to break
their love upon the shore

Chapter 33

Take These Golden Spheres

Marcus awoke feeling like a decision had been made for him sometime in the night. He would go to the next ceremony at their farm but not knowing if Bia would want that or not, he decided to turn up unannounced. The decision surprised him because he had more or less decided it was not really his thing to keep taking Ayahuasca. The aftereffects had been quite hard on his body the last two times he had done so.

He and Bia had exchanged messages more than once in the past week since he moved out and their exchanges had been very loving and all about their insights into what was happening for them on their inner journeys. There was no animosity whatsoever but still, he was not sure how she would react if he turned up at the farm.

As it was, he left it until the very last minute and it was dark and the circle already forming around the stone sacred fire that he had himself built in the middle of the lawn. Dendê was overjoyed to see him and insisted on lying and flopping all over him as he found a place in the circle. And when Bia called Dendê to put her outside the huge dog wouldn't leave him yet still, in the darkness, Bia hadn't noticed that Marcus was there. She did when he appeared out of the line to take the cup from her hand and drink it.

This time Marcus didn't feel sick. As usual he was the first to feel the effects and lay down to surrender and the cat came to lie over his solar plexus as he stretched out. This time he just gave himself to the great whatever. He had arrived in humility and with no expectations and this time the journey was an inspirational one.

It wasn't long before he was sitting erect again and as he did so he noticed that many people in the circle of more than twenty women and just four men were laying down and some, by the sounds of it, were passing through difficulties. The plant was pushing them beyond their boundaries

He glanced over to Bia and she seemed at that moment to be uncomfortable and had gotten to her feet and begun to walk around. He started to wonder perhaps if she was not feeling good about him being there. He stopped that train of thought and cast it aside,

"No, I have nothing to do with anyone else here - I am in this circle but I am also alone, completely alone and concern myself with no-one - I am in the forest and the jaguar is watching me - why am I not afraid?

Now I am the jaguar and the jaguar has nothing to fear but himself
He walks alone
Now I see myself. A long time ago.
The medicine man with the jaguar scalp adorning his head.
For a while I am him again. Power, presence, intimidating.
It felt good and I wake up.
With no need to roar."

Marcus opened his eyes to see that Bia had moved to sit close by the fire. She was just a short space in front of him but her eyes were lifted upwards to the gathering clouds in the night sky as raindrops spat from the heavens.

"You have taken my power away for too long, Bia, and now I begin to take it back," said a voice, "I know now, the source of my strength again and although I may yet weaken at times, I know who I am," it affirmed.

The rain began to fall and Bia urged everyone to get up and take their cushions and blankets to the verandah. They all left except for Marcus. He was a rock in his place and he was feeling ecstatic and the rain bothered him not a bit as he sat erect in his fake leopard skin blanket poking more sticks into the fire.

⌒〜⌣〜⌒

"I need nothing more than this, the fire, the rain, the sky and the earth on which I sit. I need no-one but my very own self."

He fully sensed that he had met the Ayahuasca spirit in another light and felt that he knew her now. He reflected on the relationship between the ego, power and the infinite self and he loved that illusory yet existent ego as a vital and important part of existence, the vehicle through which a person is to fulfill themselves.

But knowing that ego itself as just the woven fabric of the illusion was the secret that directed this ego to serve his true self rather than the false one.

Marcus sat there alone and then he saw someone coming towards him carrying another blanket. It was Rosa. He hadn't even known she was here. She laid the blanket around him and sat for a little while silently by the fire with him but when the rain came down again, she moved off back to the house.

"Beautiful girl," he thought.

When people began to leave in the middle of the night, Marcus quietly made his way to the gate.

"Marcus, is that you?"

"Yeah, it's me."

"Come and give,me a hug."

He hugged Bia at the gate.

"You know you went into a trance?"

"I didn't know but I was far away - I was not in this time."

"Yes, several people went over to you to see if you were OK but you were completely gone - Leonardo told everyone not to worry, that you were fine."

"I was fine, totally fine - Leonardo was in the circle with me but a long time ago and we both looked very different then - your spirit was there too, but not your body," he added before asking, "did you mind that I came?"

"No, not at all, Marcus, I was happy to see you in the circle."

Marcus searched the net the next day to discover the Indigenous Indians spirit connection with the Jaguar.

"The Jaguar, for many Amazonian tribes, is the spirit that is the beginning of all things - the Jaguar spirit seeks out the man to call him home to his Jaguar."

Marcus and Bia saw each other several times over the next two weeks and once again Marcus talked about the way he saw them being able to be together and for some days, Bia was willing. She visited his little apartment near the beach one day and they made love again. Passionately and hungrily but the next time she came it was to tell him that she had to end it forever. She had to be alone.

He left the next day for the Chapada Diamantina a shattered man. The first four hours of that drive were perhaps the loneliest and most desolate hours of his life and as he was driving through Vitória da Conquista, an ugly city in the inland of Bahia he broke down into tears. Nearing the Chapada he felt his strength returning as if those flat-topped mountains looming in the distance lent him their power bit by bit, but an empty hole gnawed away at the pit of his stomach as he drove through the Caatinga and wouldn't leave him.

After finding a pousada, a bed and breakfast, in Capão he visited Leonardo and his family and they arranged to do a ceremony on the Sunday. For the rest of that day and all-day Saturday, Marcus sat in silence in the forest and walked trails and let go and let go until by late Saturday night he was in a state of bliss that stayed with him all night, not allowing sleep to visit him for a moment. His was a state where pain could not touch for so long as it lasted. It was a welcome shift in consciousness.

Capão was a valley in the southwest corner of the Chapada, an area of table top mountains intersected by steep sided and forested valleys where some of the countries' highest waterfalls cascaded into deep forested ravines.

Capão itself had become a hub of both tribal lifestyles and adventure tourism but it still had a village atmosphere that brought together the culture of old Bahia with a level of funkiness and new age mysticism.

Through ancient paths in these valleys countless slaves had been driven in columns to work the gold and diamond mines that gave rise to the name and then to the wealth of towns like Lencois. Mucugê and Palmeiras that even now retain much of the colonial majesty of its former golden age.

It was to the Cachoeira of Conceicao dos Gatos that Marcus was taken by Leonardo around nine in the morning. They made their way beyond the top of the waterfall and found a quiet place up stream to take their sacrament. Each of them chose their spot, Marcus beneath a rock outcrop just five meters from the stream and Leonardo on a large rock in the middle of the stream itself. And each drank a large dose.

Marcus lay down and asked to die.

Initially Marcus experienced strong, very strong psychedelic images that filled his vision. He sang the Siva mantra, for the God of dissolution, and for a while his journey was mystic, intense and still beautiful but the intensity quickly increased to the point where he momentarily resisted and sat up. He quickly realized that that was not what he had asked for and so lay down and surrendered.

Leonardo had been chanting and singing after Marcus stopped but now Marcus could hear nothing but the roaring of his descent into oblivion. He no longer had any sense of the existence of his body, just the sensation of himself plunging inwards, far, far away to the accompaniment of myriads of images, surreal, psychedelic, beautiful, confronting, frightening, magical.

It was a long journey inward but, in the end, he arrived at a cluster of golden spheres from where all of his pain was emanating. Pain from ages past and present and all contained within these brilliant spheres that he felt to be inside his solar plexus within his physical body.

A beautiful deity appeared before him, her head adorned with a crown of thick colored strands of rope like hair, her garments, multi colored and radiant, as if they were extensions of her ethereal form, that waved and held up in the air as though she were dancing beneath the water with the currents of molten, iridescent green rivers running through them - floating about her as she moved. Her eyes were shining, large, almond shaped green and turquoise orbs and her long and lithe fingers fell like tentacles across Marcus' center of pain.

He knew her so well. She had been accompanying him all of his life. She would be waiting for him at the end too.

"Take it," he said to her, "it is all yours."

"If I take it," she answered, "you will die - this is not only your center of pain but also your center of power and your life force itself," she told him while her eyes bored into his.

"Your anger and pain and your power are of the same source - you have come a long way but now you are getting weak and you will have to use all of your will to return - you must try."

And he had to use all of his will.

His journey took him to realm after world after universe.

He experienced the realm of old age and he felt and saw himself old and frail and this realm was filled with other aging bodies like his. He surrendered to it, experienced it fully and then had to summon his will to keep moving on and not stay there.

Next, he came to a realm of sickness and dying where he and everyone in it were sickly and near death. Again, he surrendered to it accepted it and moved on.

He experienced himself as dead, his body buried in the ground and being eaten by worms and ants, yet consciousness remained with him as he passed through each of these realms, observing, witnessing and moving on. There was nothing pleasant about each experience. On the contrary he felt fully the pain and horror of each but he remained as the witness within the seat of consciousness that still flickered weakly within.

He passed through many more worlds. Some beautiful at first like the seductive snake women with whom he danced ecstatically before realizing that if he stayed there too long, he would remain there, unable to find his way back.

The place that really disgusted Marcus was the hell realm of saccharine love, full of teflon and pink and fakeness, lies and deceit. He refused to even enter it and passed on by. There were places that appeared to be other planets and worlds, with strange creatures who challenged his presence there and other realms where all was in semi darkness and filled with a smokey haze, and eternal sorrow. Each time he thought that joy and lightness was returning to his experience it would vanish in despair and gloom again. It was a massive trial he was having to pass through to not lose himself in the despair of hopelessness of one hell after another.

As he gradually came back to being conscious of his body and surrounds, he met Niko and he almost broke to realize he would be leaving him so he spoke to him about growing up and how Niko had to understand their souls were not going to part. He understood their link with each other and how they were almost one and the same. But it was heartbreaking in that moment. He loved him like no-one else and wanted to stay and protect him but this idea too, he had to let go. Trust, only trust, he told himself.

Finally, he was back, exhausted and drained but he pulled himself up and walked upstream, noticing as he passed, that Leonardo was lying down on his rock. He had never seen Leonardo laying down like that during a journey.

He bathed in the cold rushing waters and chose a shady tree with a rock that happened to be sculptured comfortably enough to sit and watch the water pass by. He looked at his cell phone and saw that seven hours had passed. He had been gone for more than six of them. Marcus' mind stilled itself, his emotions emptied. He became a hollow man as if the storm that had swept through his subconscious had blown everything away within.

A nothing man
with nobody around him
but the careless whispering trees
and a gurgling
disinterested stream.
and the jaded watcher
padding through the shadows
of a wasted past

Chapter 34

Forever is Who We Are

Marcus stayed in the valley of Capão for another two weeks spending most of his time sitting by waterfalls and exploring some of the more remote corners of the Chapada. He was by one of those waterfalls when he saw some people approaching. What he had thought was one group of people turned out to be two and the second was a woman and her small child who came over to where Marcus was commandeering the best and shadiest spot and she asked if she could sit there with him.

It was like one of those ultimate lonely man dreams. You are sitting alone in a beautiful place and for a moment, you allow yourself to imagine the perfect woman appearing out of nowhere also alone and sit down beside you. She must have been no more than thirty, maybe less but she was the epitome of the Brazilian beauty. Perfect body and dark olive skinned with almond eyes, high cheekbones, full sensuous lips and long black hair. The ultimate blend of coffee, part Indian, part African, part white and probably an even mix of the three. Manicured lime green nails on hands and feet with tasteful jewelry around her neck and wrists, she said she had recently left her husband and was staying with friends in Capão. Marcus played with her son, chatted about nothing in particular and then asked her if she was the goddess herself come to him in human form to test him. She didn't understand. And then he said goodbye.

He laughed to himself as he walked back up the stony path and looked down to the most beautiful woman he had probably ever seen in the flesh, wondering what if.

"Too many what ifs to fit into one lifetime," he thought to himself.

Arriving back in Arraial he was just a bit surprised to hear from Bia and to hear that she wanted to see him before she left for India in three days.

Marcus drove into the farm, noticed how the bougainvilleas that he had been propagating and planting over the past two years had grown. They were blooming along the front of the farm, red, pink, apricot, yellow and white. He saw himself in every corner of the garden he had planted, the house he had designed, the colors he had chosen and finally in the wife whom he had loved for so long and who stood before him.

"How many lives and worlds must we create and watch wither and die," he wondered as Bia came and hugged him and then it felt just like it always had. She slipped into his arms and felt so right, so natural, so desirable, every sinew of bone and soft flesh and supple muscle talked to his skin of their sensuality and they walked hand in hand in conversation until eventually he turned to her, saying,

"I can't look at you this way and hold you without wanting to make love to you - I have never felt so turned on in my life as I feel in this moment."

"No Marcus, I can't do this anymore."

But on the third and last day before she left for India, he said it again and once again she answered,

"No Marcus, please don't do this to me."

"I want you, I want to make love to you, you're just so beautiful, Bia, what can I say? every part of me wants you."

"No Marcus, please."

But Bia looked into Marcus' eyes which focused only on her lips as she spoke.

"I want to kiss those beautiful lips, I want to hold your breasts - Bia, I want you now, at least just this one more time."

She looked back at him with a look of helplessness,

"Oh Marcus!"

They took each other's hand, walked to the bedroom and made love for the last time. Now there were no tears, just joy and immeasurable pleasure and for the last time they lay in each other's arms, searched the other's eyes and said,

"Was that the best time ever?"

"Easily the best ever."

"I love you Marcus, I always will."

'And I love you too and I always will - no doubt."

Marcus wanted Bia to stay open to the future and while she didn't negate what may be possible, she told him that she must let go completely and that is all she knew. But on the day that she left, she said to Marcus,

"I felt really good after we made love yesterday - and last night, I slept well for the first time - don't worry, Marcus, I think we may get back together one day."

He felt elated by that and kissed her goodbye at the airport with a glow in his heart. Lack of love was not their issue, not at all.

〜〜〜

Niko traveled with her to Rio to spend Christmas with her family and grandchildren so Marcus turned back home to the farm alone but decided to stop and visit the art gallery of Antonia's partner, Rafael.

Rafael was an artist, impromptu musician and part Ninja. Born Filipino and raised in the US, he wore his long black hair in either a pony tail or a Samurai top knot and had a disarmingly outrageous ego laced with Buddhist wisdom and Chicago Street humor. Marcus had grown to like him. He liked them both, this unusual and devotedly mystical couple.

He visited them more than once over the next few weeks at the gallery, the artist and the writer, the couple who themselves insisted on being the major work of art and expression within their own gallery, the headline act upon their own stage. She was taller than him, red haired of part German, part Brazilian descent, he shorter, Asiatic, she elegant, fiery, he relentlessly creative with a bravado and aggression born of the streets of an immigrant community in Chicago, they fought and loved each other with a passion.

Felipa, a handsomely beautiful woman from Columbia around thirty years of age was there too. Dark, olive skinned, with a natural and disarming friendliness that quickly won and charmed you. She had lived with a local Bahiano in the forest for seven years while traveling with her homemade jewelry to sell at the beach every day. Her current partner was away in Ibiza.

Marcus knew her but not that well. Her lover had been Marcus' neighbor when they lived in town. Felipa asked if she could come and visit for a horse ride.

"Please do, anytime," he had said immediately.

The next time Marcus called in at the gallery Rafael was there alone, working on a painting that made Marcus suddenly catch his breath. There before him, depicted in Rafael's painting was his vision of the Jaguar Shaman. Rafael looked up from his painting.

"So, you been a bad boy, Marcus?"

Marcus smiled and shook his head, saying,

"It's a long story."

But his attention was on the painting.

"Well, she has great tits - who wouldn't want to put their face in those?" referring explicitly to Ana Maria's stand out assets.

Marcus winced but Rafael, looking for the buttons, searching for the story in his own charming way and not letting up, continued,

"Well, man, Bia is probably getting her pussy slammed right back over there in India as we speak - how does that make you feel?"

"Actually, I am looking at your painting – your painting is who I am and I am kind of stunned by it - but, no, I wouldn't blame her, but I don't think that's where she is at right now, Rafael, but yeah, it might happen - it makes me feel like shit if that is what you want to hear," he laughed.

Marcus was reminded of himself when Rafael said that. It could just as easily have been him probing the depths of base feelings from someone in his predicament. He remembered what he had said to a friend a few years back at the farm in Australia after the friend's woman had gone back to her old lover,

'Well, Nick, there are two ways of looking at it - one is that you just lost the love of your life - the other is that you just had a great time screwing someone else's woman - you choose.'

Not that it had any parallels with Marcus and Bia but it did with the way Rafael went about bringing it all down to an animalistic level. In a perverse way it made Marcus feel better. Sometimes you can only laugh at the drama of our lives rather than bleed.

Meanwhile the half jaguar man continued to stare out from the painting – demanding of Marcus to remember himself.

It was that time of year, approaching Christmas and new year and Arraial was now filling with tourists and festivity but it was right on Christmas Day when Marcus received the message from Bia,

"Yes Marcus, I am distant, very distant - when I arrived in our house in Arunachala, I saw many things that reminded me of our past and I cried, but now I am doing better but I know we have to separate and I have to be strong in taking this path I have chosen - that is what is happening for me, and by the way, Happy Christmas."

Marcus was saddened. He arrived back home and opened the fridge door, took out the bottle of Ayahuasca from inside and drank. He lay down.

"Do with me what you will - if there be any pain inside, any more hurt, I invite it all."

He took it on his own - every weekend until he left for India, each time inviting the pain to ride its course, to open the pathways for the ancient karmas to be absolved upon the altar of naked knowing.

On one of those weekends Felipa shared it with him. He had met her on the beach in Arraial on New Year's Eve. He had met Ana Maria there too and they had sat together a little while and hugged. Anna Maria had been a bit drunk and they took a photo of themselves in the firelight and waved good bye and that was the last time he saw her.

Days later Felipa visited Marcus with another friend, Camila, and the three of them made a ceremony together. Niko was in the house, back from Rio but he was by now well accustomed to the ceremonies and left them in peace by the fire.

Without Leonardo's presence, Marcus took it upon himself to chant whenever he felt the energy in their small circle of three required it.

Once more the cat sat on his lap, this journey, though, was different for Marcus as he accepted the care of the other two's well-being. Both he and Felipa drank a second dose half way through the night but Camila declined. He returned to chanting,

Ya devi sarva bhutesu, shanti rupena sansitha
Ya devi sarva bhutesu, shakti rupena sansthita
Ya devi sarva bhutesu, matra rupena sansthita
Namastasyai, namastasyai, namastasyai, namo namaha!

He was not the singer that Leonardo was but he could chant and his chanting rolled out from his deep voice, holding the energy of the circle.

Hours later he left the other two by the fire to put Niko to bed and he couldn't not smile out loud at his funny little boy, how he loved him. He told him a funny story.

"Oh, Papai, I just had a love attack for you."

"And me for you too," he laughed, hugging him strongly good night, and then, "aren't you going to say it?" asked Niko.

"Sweet dreams, Niko. Sleep with angels," before adding, "with tight little butts."

Marcus walked across the verandah to the kitchen and cooked some soup which he brought down to the women by the fire. Camila was pretty much back to post Ayahuasca normality which under most circumstances is a very clear and calm state of mind. She was clear and calm.

Felipa was still absorbed by the sacrament but slowly coming back. She sat up and looked up at the stars. She had taken it many times before but now she looked over at Marcus saying,

"That was the strongest journey for me ever - you started chanting each time in the perfect moment."

"It was the chant of Durga, the mother Goddess, Felipa."

"It was perfect," she said.

They slept overnight and the following day Marcus took Felipa on a horse ride through the forest pathways. She had been thrown from a horse when eighteen years old and hadn't found the courage to mount again since, so she watched apprehensively as Marcus trimmed the hooves of her horse, his muscular, wiry body arched beneath the mare's head, shaving away at the hard overgrown feet.

Finishing the job, he stood erect and sweaty and smiled at Felipa. She was truly beautiful he thought.

Long dark hair, arms adorned with jewelry that she made herself from woven vines and grasses and studded with large stones, bright intelligent eyes. He could easily have listed more but she was gorgeous. And close to half his age.

He allowed no time for her fear to set in before helping her on to the back of the horse, gave her some basic instructions and then, bare foot and stripped to his waist for the hot January day, swung his legs over the waiting Karkara and set off for the forest.

Within twenty minutes he had Felipa galloping, her eyes wide with delight, he riding no hands, teaching Karkara to respond to his legs. His beloved horse was beginning to learn and understand.

On the way back home, Marcus pulled up by the river, swung the lead rope over a branch and dived in, jeans and all. Felipa, did the same, but stripped to her panties before plunging. Marcus stood up on a sand bar in the middle of the river, waist deep in water. It felt so good. It was a wonderful day.

Felipa swam a little way past him and then stood up, saying,

"I think I have a thorn in my foot can you try and get it out for me?"

"Sure, if my eyes can find it."

She swam over to where Marcus stood and getting to her feet, she put her arm around his shoulder while standing on one foot, her naked breast nestling deliciously into Marcus' chest while lifting the other foot for Marcus to take a look. He strained his eyes, holding her delicate foot.

"I think it's too small for me to find," he laughed, "my eyes aren't that great."

She put her foot down but didn't remove her arm from around his shoulder but now leant her head on to his chest saying,

"Marcus, you are my ideal sort of man - what can I do?"

Marcus was surprised, very surprised, he had fallen somewhat in love with her and loved her company but again he had not been expecting this, not at all.

For a few long moments he didn't reply but then a smile broke his lips and slowly, he turned to her, saying,

"Felipa, you are so beautiful and in any other circumstances I would just say yes, yes, yes, but I like your boyfriend very much and so long as you are still with him, I just can't do this – hey, I adore you but until you find out what you really want for yourself, I can't do it," and with his smile breaking into a grin, added, "and now I must love you no matter whether we are together or not, because in this moment you have loved me for who I am – the rest? that's for you to decide."

Felipa lingered by his side, her head still resting on his chest, saying,

"I can understand why Ana Marie fell in love with you."

He inclined his head to hers and hugged her to him momentarily yet wondering if he should make love to her there and then and be damned with the consequences. He didn't, he may later regret it even. We always regret the choices we didn't take if we allow ourselves to pause for a moment.

As he remounted Karkara, Marcus asked himself the question.

"Is it that I really miss Bia's love and company or is it just that I enjoy life better with a companion whoever that may be?"

But of course, he knew the answer to that.

"It is the companionship that I love and enjoy but what is so rare, is to find the woman that you can share your journey with on every level and the one who can accept you for who you are and whom you, in turn, are able to accept equally for who they are."

Marcus wondered if that sense of them belonging one to another would ever change, after all, nothing is forever, but it would move on, forever onwards.

But Bia was gone and for her it was important to step back from what bound her and for her to know that she could be happy as an independent woman.

"There are times we have to face what stands in our way before we can shed our garments of illusion and this is what she had seen she must do," he thought.

"To untie the knots," she had actually said.

And Marcus recalled how often he had said to her,

"We never know, Bia, how long we are meant to stay together - forever is who we are, not what we do in this world."

He hoped she would be able to return to the fire one day and allow the flames to scorch her soul again, unafraid.

Perhaps she would have no desire to. Anyway, her fate was hers now.

They had been lovers for a long time down through the ages and the love between them was only changing like the sands of the Ganges shifting beneath their footsteps, their story but another falling star burning its way through the stratosphere of the infinite stories, tragedies and wonders of existence, the timeless dance of the mother within the spinning wheel of life.

And echoing within that dance, Marcus recalled once again the names of Naitara, Komeha'e and there came to him a vision of a handsome woman with a shock of jet-black hair and wondered, and wondered again, what rich and colorful yarns had already woven themselves into the fabric of his life's destiny that might still await him.

But there is no end to these threads of karma that sustain the worlds.

There is only an end to ownership of them and those threads are but the melody that freedom sings to us if we are willing to listen with an open heart.

In the meantime, the dream still beckoned, the dream of the sleeping Vishnu. And as Vishnu, you are the final dreamer itself and all belongs to you. And darkness and light are one and the same. And you love, you love it all and none of it in particular.

Marcus pressed the flanks of his white horse and leaning over his neck motioned him into a steady canter. He began to sing to himself in a barely audible voice that only the watching Jaguar could hear, a song of Leonard Cohen's,

You can add up the parts
but you won't have the sum
You can strike up the march,
there is no drum
Every heart, every heart
to love will come
but like a refugee.
Ring the bells that still can ring
Forget your perfect offering
There is a crack, a crack in everything
That's how the light gets in.

Marcus left for India soon after. Back to the sacred mountain, his heart of hearts. He travelled north with a young friend from Brazil but left her at the side of the Ganges after she fell in love with the river and after she started asking too much of him and there, she gave herself the name of Deveshi.

Departing for the mountains on his Enfield he visited the holy lake of Renuka, the birthplace of Parashurama of the Axe, and sat where Karna had once cradled his Guru's sleeping head in his lap but only to be cursed for his great endurance of pain.

He rode across the fields of Kurukshetra and paused there for a short time. At first only the cawing of ravens could be heard but their cries eventually turned to voices and raised shouts and trumpets and the plaintive moaning of dying men.

He turned north again into the mountains crossing high passes full of snow melt until, riding alone, he reached an ancient Krishna temple that was said to have been built by the Pandavas themselves. That is where he stayed for a while.

In the spring he received a message from Bia. At the end of it she wrote this,

"So, beloved Marcus,
I thank you for finding me and bringing me home.
I thank you for loving me so well and allowing me to experience love in highs never known before.
I thank you for India and the Master and the wonderment that that is.
I thank you for planting in my body this dream child of ours.
I thank you for Leonard Cohen and for the cracks, both yours and mine, that could only be revealed in the meeting of our souls.
I thank you for the vast Australian skies and although there is not such thing as "me," let alone a "you"
there are many thanks that want to be thrown on to the blue,
Much love from the heart of hearts"

Marcus felt she had gone. Her message was like a yellow rose left upon the pillow. He could have felt sad, should have, even did a bit, but who he truly was, was not that, nor this, nor anything of this world, nor anything that comes and goes. In time to come he would hear her sing again and he was amazed at her voice. It was strong and beautiful and could not be denied, by either heaven or earth and nor by him, for to deny her, her song of freedom, would be to deny his own.

THE END

The Jaguar

Meeting the Spirit Man

The following night the Jaguar went again to dream with the half jaguar man and he saw the same spirit man as before but more mature, in the prime of his life, and he was mating with his partner in a clearing in the forest. The big cat watched fascinated this time, almost lovingly, to see the spirit man entwined with his mate in their complete and natural state and they were making delicious sounds as they writhed in turn, one on top and then the other. They reminded him of two snakes he had seen mating once back in his own forest.

For three nights he slept soundly and didn't dream of the half jaguar man at all but on the fourth night he dreamed once more that he was being beckoned to the fire of the half jaguar man with great urgency. This time he was very curious and he felt that this was his final journey with his dreaming partner, so he willingly dreamed himself padding up to the fire and laying down quietly on the opposite side of the half jaguar man but without any need to assert his superiority.

On this occasion, however, the spirit man came to him and it startled him at first to know that the man had learnt how to find him. He saw the spirit man sitting around the same fire and it was raining in the spirit man's dream but it was nothing to him that he was being soaked. He was even more surprised to see that this spirit man was now seeing through his own eyes and feeling the strength of his jaguar heart and suddenly he understood that he, the jaguar, was the very strength that the spirit man was searching for as though he, the jaguar, had been temporarily lost to him. Now there was no difference between them at all and there were no boundaries between man and beast and each was rejoicing the fact. The spirit man had tears streaming down his face, tears of gratitude while the jaguar felt a true contentment of being that resulted in a low, almost imperceptible growl of pleasure at being exactly who he was.

As time went by, he sensed the spirit man visit him whenever he felt he needed his jaguar strength and each time he came he came with wonderful visions just like the visions the jaguar himself had when he ate the fungus he so liked. This fungus wasn't easy to find in the forest but when he scented it, he would never miss the opportunity to eat it. It gave him beautiful dreams and, in these dreams, he found he could also visit his other half, the spirit man. His spirit man was very much like him. He was wild at his core and he even roared when he wanted to.

About the Author

Mac Nicolson was born and raised on a farm in the middle of Tasmania, was gratefully expelled from boarding school at fourteen and after a series of childhood mystical experiences and with the impending possibility of having to go into the army and kill people for whom he harbored no ill will, left for India when only nineteen.

He passed the next five years travelling the long since separated lands of ancient Gondwana – India and South America – searching for answers to the mysteries of existence before returning to Australia to start a community.

Mac's time in Australia included a stint as a City Councilor and political activist, a columnist for a local news journal, a snake catcher, a horse breeder and tamer and a forest regenerator but after fifteen years or more and after raising a few children he began to venture back to India and Brazil, until settling in Brazil with his then Brazilian wife.

Mac never planned to be a novelist and claims no great ability – he simply had a desire to share the stories that flowed out from a past that had both inspired and haunted him, each of which had first appeared to him in dreams and visions to be then confirmed by chance meetings with shamans, witches, and random fellow travelers.

In all of his writings, the author strives to adhere to historical authenticity and many of the characters in his books are based on real people and events, as in The King of The Lochlains and The Sun Dancer, and in the case of his first book, The Asva Sani of Khasi, based on the story of that great Indian epic, The Mahabharata.

His fourth book, The Road to Ndawo, recounts a series of stories from the current dream that we call real life and includes the culmination of his inner search along with the karmic tale of his love of a woman.

The 'Road to Ndawo, at times, touches subtly upon his past life memories as they are told within the first three books.

His fifth book, Henne's List, is pure fiction that explores in-depth, Mac's life experiences and musings on the mysteries of existence, quantum physics and parallel universes - a rambling tale that crosses continents and time and where characters jump out from the pages of his previous books.

Mac currently resides in Portugal with his Argentinian partner of five years, Claudia Escobar, a textile artist, and is beginning work on his next book, 'The Secrets of Dona Eiliva', inspired by the story of Claudia's grandmother, a rural town doctor and healer and ardent Peronist who married five times.